First World War
and Army of Occupation
War Diary
France, Belgium and Germany

7 DIVISION
Divisional Troops
Divisional Signal Company
4 October 1914 - 30 November 1917

WO95/1646/1

The Naval & Military Press Ltd
www.nmarchive.com
Published in association with The National Archives

Published by

The Naval & Military Press Ltd

Unit 10 Ridgewood Industrial Park,

Uckfield, East Sussex,

TN22 5QE England

Tel: +44 (0) 1825 749494

www.naval-military-press.com

www.nmarchive.com

This diary has been reprinted in facsimile from the original. Any imperfections are inevitably reproduced and the quality may fall short of modern type and cartographic standards.

© Crown Copyright
Images reproduced by permission of The National Archives, London, England, 2015.

Contents

Document type	Place/Title	Date From	Date To
Heading	WO95/1646/1 7 Division		
Heading	7 Division Troops Divisional Signal Coy 1914 Oct-1917 Nov To Italy		
Heading	7th Divisional Signal Company October To December 1914		
War Diary	Lyndhurst	04/10/1914	06/10/1914
War Diary	Zeebrugge	07/10/1914	06/11/1914
War Diary	Bailleul	07/11/1914	26/12/1914
Heading	7th Divisional Signal Company R.E. December 20th 1914 To 31st March 1915		
War Diary		20/12/1914	26/02/1915
War Diary			
War Diary		27/02/1915	23/03/1915
Map	Communications 7th Bde 10th-12th March 1915		
Miscellaneous	Report On Signal Work During Operations VII Area 11.3.15 To 14.3.15		
Heading	7th Signal Co. R.E. Nov. Dec. Vol II		
War Diary		01/11/1915	31/12/1915
Map	Communications 7th Div 10th-12th March 1915		
Map	Communications 7th Division		
Diagram etc	Circuit Diagram 21-12-15		
Map	22nd Infantry Brigade Offensive Arrangements (Signals)		
Heading	7 Signals Jan Vol III		
War Diary		02/01/1916	29/02/1916
Diagram etc	Circuit Diagram 7th Division		
Diagram etc	Circuit Diagram 7th Division.		
Diagram etc	Existing Communications VII Div Div H. R. To BN. HQ. 24.2.16 Circisit Diagram		
Diagram etc	Becordel - Becourt		
Diagram etc	Cable Trenches 7th Division R.A. and Infantry		
Diagram etc	Advanced Brigade Signal Dugout		
Miscellaneous	20th Infantry Brigade Offensive Arrangements (Signals)		
War Diary		01/03/1916	31/03/1916
Operation(al) Order(s)	Signal Coy R.E. Vol VI		
War Diary		01/04/1916	30/04/1916
Diagram etc	Diagram Of 7th Division Communications		
War Diary		01/05/1916	31/05/1916
Map			
Diagram etc	R Circuit Diagram 7th Division Signals		
War Diary		01/06/1916	30/06/1916
Diagram etc	Circuit Diagram VII Division		
War Diary		01/07/1916	31/07/1916
Diagram etc	Circuit Diagram 7th Division		
Diagram etc	7th Division. Circuit Diagram		
Diagram etc	Circuit Diagram 7th Division		
Heading	7th Divisional Signal Company R.E. August 1916		
War Diary		01/08/1916	31/08/1916
Diagram etc	Circuit Diagram 7th Division		
War Diary		01/09/1916	30/09/1916

Diagram etc	Circuit Diagram 7th Division		
Diagram etc			
Diagram etc	Lines In No. 5 Area (H.Q. Hallencourt)		
Diagram etc	Circuit Diagram 7th Division		
Diagram etc	Circuit Diagram 7th D.A.		
Diagram etc	Circuit Diagram 7th Div. Arty.		
War Diary		01/10/1916	31/12/1916
Miscellaneous	Circuit Diagram 7th Division		
Diagram etc	Circuit Diagram 7th Division		
Miscellaneous	Circuit Diagram 7th Division		
Diagram etc	Circuit Diagram 7th Div.		
Diagram etc			
Heading	7th Divisional Signal Company. January 1917.		
Miscellaneous	9 Bridge 7th Coy		
War Diary		01/01/1917	31/01/1917
Diagram etc	Communications 7th Division		
Diagram etc	Circuit Diagram 7th Div		
Miscellaneous	Circuit Diagram 7th Division		
Diagram etc	Circuit Diagram 7th Division		
Diagram etc			
Diagram etc	Communications 7th Division		
War Diary	In The Field (Maveuse)	01/02/1917	16/02/1917
War Diary	In The Field	17/02/1917	28/02/1917
Diagram etc	Telephone Circuits From Bde H.Q Batn H.Q.		
Diagram etc	Communications-7th Division		
War Diary	In The Field	01/03/1917	30/04/1917
Diagram etc	Circuit Diagram 7th Division		
Diagram etc	7th Division Communications Working Circuits		
Diagram etc	7th Divisional Signal Coy Line Diagram Of Routes		
Diagram etc	Table Of Traffic deals With By Signal Office 7th Div April 1917		
Heading	7th Division. 7th Divisional Signal Company. May 1917		
War Diary		01/05/1917	31/05/1917
Diagram etc	7th Div Special Battle Communications		
Diagram etc	7th Division Communications From Y.G.R.		
Diagram etc	7th Division Battle Communications		
Diagram etc			
Heading	7th Division. 7th Divisional Signal Company June 1917		
War Diary		01/06/1917	30/06/1917
Diagram etc			
Heading	7th Division. 7th Divisional Signal Company. July 1917		
War Diary		01/07/1917	31/07/1917
Diagram etc	To Div.on Left		
Diagram etc			
Heading	7th Division. 7th Divisional Signal Company August 1917		
War Diary		01/08/1917	31/08/1917
Diagram etc	Diagram Of Construction 7th Div Area.		
Diagram etc			
Diagram etc	Bretencourt Area Proposed Circuit Diagram 7th Div Signals		
Diagram etc			
Heading	7th Divisional Signal Company. September 1917		
War Diary		01/09/1917	30/09/1917
Diagram etc	Coy Moved From Reninghelst To Hazebrouck		

Heading	7th Division. 7th Divisional Signal Company. October 1917		
War Diary		01/10/1917	31/10/1917
Diagram etc			
Diagram etc	7th Divisional Signal Coy. R.E.		
Diagram etc			
Diagram etc	7th Divisional Signal Coy R.E.		
Diagram etc	Communications At HS and MS With One Brigade In The Line		
Diagram etc			
Diagram etc	7th Divisional Signal Coy. R.E.		
Heading	7th Divisional Signal Company November 1917		
Miscellaneous	7th Div A.Q.		
War Diary		01/11/1917	30/11/1917

WO 95/1646/1   7 Division

① Divisional Signal Company
   Oct 1914 - Nov 1917.

7 DIVISION TROOPS

DIVISIONAL SIGNAL COY

1914 OCT – 1917 NOV

To ITALY

7th Divisional Engineers

7th DIVISIONAL SIGNAL COMPANY

OCTOBER to DECEMBER 1914.

Army Form C. 2118

7th Signal Company R.E.

WAR DIARY
or
INTELLIGENCE SUMMARY.
(Erase heading not required.)

Instructions regarding War Diaries and Intelligence Summaries are contained in F. S. Regs., Part II. and the Staff Manual respectively. Title pages will be prepared in manuscript.

Hour, Date, Place	Summary of Events and Information	Remarks and References to Appendices
Lyndhurst. Oct 4th 1914.	At 5 p.m. orders were received to march to Southampton. H.Q. and No 1 Section marched off at 6.50 p.m. Arrived at the Docks at 11 p.m. and marched alongside the Transport "Winifredian".	
At Sea. Oct 5th 1914	The whole company were entrained by 1 a.m. Lt Col A.T. Moore C.R.E. commanding the troops. Off Beachy Head about 4.30 p.m. Dungeness 7.30 p.m. At 8 p.m. were informed we were not likely to disembark until tomorrow. About 9 p.m. passed Dover.	
At Sea. Oct 6th 1914.	When approaching the Belgian Coast, wireless instructions were received to return to Dover at full speed, on account of submarines being seen. Steamed off Zeebrugge. At daybreak off Dover and asked the Harbour to refuse at 9 a.m. Remained all day. Left at 9.30 p.m. with another transport and escort of destroyers.	

Army Form C. 2118

WAR DIARY
or
INTELLIGENCE SUMMARY.
(Erase heading not required.)

Instructions regarding War Diaries and Intelligence Summaries are contained in F. S. Regs., Part II. and the Staff Manual respectively. Title pages will be prepared in manuscript.

Hour, Date, Place	Summary of Events and Information	Remarks and References to Appendices
Zeebrugge 7th October	At anchor off ZEEBRUGGE. Went to War Transports. At 7. a.m. weighed anchor and steamed into the harbour and brought up alongside the wharf. Much delay in disembarkation, but all the men and horses were landed by 1 p.m. Coy I was to stand wit vehicles. Was marched to BRUGES, the last part of the march by moonlight. Arrived about 8 p.m. H.Q. in a hotel, the Trsp. to being billeted in the cavalry barracks about 1½ miles away. About 2.30 a.m. orders were received to move at 7 a.m. They were distributed to billets with great difficulty. Marched to G'tend. Arrived about 2.p.m. but the Convoys were kept waiting about near the Railway Station and did not fill it billets till dark. H.Q. in a hotel on the sea front. About 11.p.m. orders were	
8th October	issued for Two brigades to proceed to GHENT.	

Form/C. 2118/11.

Army Form C. 2118

WAR DIARY
or
INTELLIGENCE SUMMARY.
(Erase heading not required.)

Instructions regarding War Diaries and Intelligence Summaries are contained in F. S. Regs., Part II. and the Staff Manual respectively. Title pages will be prepared in manuscript.

Hour, Date, Place	Summary of Events and Information	Remarks and References to Appendices
	and fatigue. Proceeded to BELLEM, where we expected a lengthy halt. The march was resumed as news came that the enemy had occupied GHENT. We billeted for the night at THIELT, where the rest of the company arrived.	
Tuesday 13th October	The march was resumed through ARDOYE & ROULERS where we halted for the night. The company did not arrive in the town until after dark and were billeted in a convent.	
Wed 14th October	Marched to YPRES in three columns are being French, arrived about 2 p.m. and joined the main body of the Expeditionary Force. The infantry very exhausted.	
Thursday 15th October	Halted at YPRES. The infantry rapidly picking up after a rest. The whole of the Telephone system of the town had been destroyed by the Germans, but we	

Army Form C. 2118

WAR DIARY
or
INTELLIGENCE SUMMARY.
(Erase heading not required.)

Hour, Date, Place	Summary of Events and Information	Remarks and References to Appendices
	were able to telephone to POPERINGHE and DUNKIRK by a wire which had been overlooked. Orders out for a march out tomorrow.	
Friday Oct 16"	The Div. marched at 5 a.m by two routes to a line ZILLEBEKE–HALTE, which were garrisoned by French Territorial troops. Comm was at first maintained by motorcyclists, but in the afternoon H.Q. was advanced to the Château de ZILLEBEKE at Kilo 5" MENIN–YPRES road and then cable lines were laid to communicate with the two flank brigades. The officer at YPRES station was taken over by IV Army tps. who ran a line out to the Château. Sig. G. billeted in the grounds of the Château.	
Sat. Oct 17"	Day on the while uneventful. 2 Brigades cable-communication with H.Q. & future "The Château" refers to the Château Zillebeke at 5" kilo.	

Army Form C. 2118

WAR DIARY
or
INTELLIGENCE SUMMARY.
(Erase heading not required.)

Instructions regarding War Diaries and Intelligence Summaries are contained in F. S. Regs., Part II. and the Staff Manual respectively. Title pages will be prepared in manuscript.

Hour, Date, Place	Summary of Events and Information	Remarks and References to Appendices
Sunday Oct 18th	Forward move imminent. Brigades advanced a short distance towards MENIN, covering under artillery fire. Two cattle detachments sent, one in reserve. H.Q at the Chateau. Men in good spirits and quite recovered from their march from GHENT.	
Monday Oct 19th	The Division advanced to cooperate army's frontier at GHELUVE and KLEYTHOEK. All three brigades employed in attack. Div H.Q in a small inn all day, at the N of POEZELHOEK. Leui-Grave will be cattle ref. with 22nd Inf Bde, which was attacking KLEYTHOEK. As the attack was on the front of succeeding two battalions were taken in flank by enemy's artillery. Gen. Lawford was forced to retire, which he did in good order. Lieut-Grove and his detachment kept up communication, under heavy shell fire. By evening the Div retired to its entrenchment	

WAR DIARY or INTELLIGENCE SUMMARY.

(Erase heading not required.)

Army Form C. 2118

Hour, Date, Place	Summary of Events and Information	Remarks and References to Appendices
Tuesday Oct 20th	position. Bde. H.Q. Winning is the Chateau Dunem the right. The cattle hire were released at 20hrs BEKE. The night with have remaining in original position. Confused dawn; waterprint wire short closed him a sentry of 111 Battn when escaping departure. Orders received for a reconnaissance in force on our right, but the enemy were in such force that it could not be carried out. The Div remained in line offensive all day and night. Considerable shell fire. Communication improved and made more permanent. Sergt Anderson and his sect, at considerable risk, reversed the cattle line laid an enemy to 115th, which was now in front of the entrenched line.	
Wednesday Oct 21st	The enemy made an attack on the position, which were on special strength, on 22nd Bde Bde on the left all 3 cattle wagons were out with Bde H Q. and continually	

WAR DIARY
or
INTELLIGENCE SUMMARY.
(Erase heading not required.)

Army Form C. 2118

Hour, Date, Place	Summary of Events and Information	Remarks and References to Appendices
	under shell fire. Communications were maintained under exceedingly difficult conditions. The cable teams often out by shells, and wireless sets/aerial to repair it under fire. The clerks in we [?] were blown off by a blast of a shell but was unhurt. Enemy's roll also fell near H.Q, but the men and horses sheltering in the wood in the ground were not touched.	
October 22nd	An attack was expected but did not develop till late in the day. It was successfully repulsed, a counterattack of 1/5 W. army troops, advancing at the château was struck by a shell and 15 driver wounded. Communications as per diary, but lines frequently cut from shells. Enemy's artillery fired at irregular intervals. The MENIN-YPRES road.	

WAR DIARY
or
INTELLIGENCE SUMMARY.
(Erase heading not required.)

Army Form C. 2118

Hour, Date, Place	Summary of Events and Information	Remarks and References to Appendices
October 23rd	Fairly quiet morning but the enemy developed in strong attack on the centre. The trenches were heavily shelled with shrapnel and at times were known in several directions. Three cable wagons went to the three brigades. The shells cut the improvised section Telephone cables, and communication between had never ended only be maintained by messengers.	
October 24th	A number of Germans had broken through 21st Bde, and were in a wood. Our last reserve, apparently and Germans were dispatched to endeavour to turn them out. Troops looked so denier that evening things at HQ were looked ready for retirement. This was at 9.30 a.m. At 10.40 a.m. large British reinforcements arrived and the 3rd Brigade relieved the 20th Inf Bde in the Trenches. The Germans attacked at 9 p.m. but were promptly repelled.	

Army Form C. 2118

WAR DIARY
or
INTELLIGENCE SUMMARY.
(Erase heading not required.)

Hour, Date, Place	Summary of Events and Information	Remarks and References to Appendices

25th October

A large number of Spencer prisoners brought in; 7 officers and 192 other ranks. The 7th Div Commander advised by the arrival of reinforcements, who took charge of a part of our line. G.O.C. moved ordered to advance his H.Q.

26th

H.Q. moved out at 6.30 a.m. but could not find the suitable place near GHELUVELT, so occupied a chateau in the woods near VELDHOEK, which had been Gen Watts H.Q. It was only ½ mile from our chateau and not nearly so commodious. Lieut Osborne relaid up the cable but lines that were out and laid new ones. The named gap was disconnected and the G.O.C. went out at night with the 22nd Inf Bde to mark trenches and fill it. He was out all night; with a line to the

27th October

Coty 1 cyclist detachment out, with a line to the 20th Bde, who were entering at the chateau Elkereka. Signal Company also resting but under shell fire

Army Form C. 2118

WAR DIARY
or
INTELLIGENCE SUMMARY.
(Erase heading not required.)

Instructions regarding War Diaries and Intelligence Summaries are contained in F. S. Regs, Part II. and the Staff Manual respectively. Title pages will be prepared in manuscript.

Hour, Date, Place	Summary of Events and Information	Remarks and References to Appendices
	from the enemy (I know you). A complimentary message to the 7th Div. was received from Sir John French, also a message to the Army from Lord Kitchener.	
October 28th	The VELDHOEK Chateau was so much burnt the G.O.C. decided to return to the old Chateau which necessitated a rearrangement of cards. We returned there at 4 p.m. The 7th Div. was attached to the 1st Corps.	
October 29th	The enemy made a strong attack on our entire command at 6 a.m. It was not unexpected and we were prepared for it. At 11.30 the position became critical and the order was issued for a counter attack all along the line. This continued until slow progress might full firing in occupying our old positions except in the immediate vicinity of GHELUVELT. The firing at times was exceedingly heavy and communication with the 21st Inf Bde very difficult. Lieut Gibone and 3 motor cyclists succeeded in running	

WAR DIARY or INTELLIGENCE SUMMARY.

(Erase heading not required.)

Army Form C. 2118

p.12

Hour, Date, Place	Summary of Events and Information	Remarks and References to Appendices
October 30th Friday	The gun. Lt. at 3.30.p.m. the G.O.C. again advanced H.Q. to the VELDHOEK chateau. Saint Colome had made arrangements for communication but after 3 hours the staff returned to the Chateau ZILLEBEKE. The G.O.C. had relieved a point 1 mile East of ZILLEBEKE as his day headquarters, and proceeded there at 1.30.p.m. It was only ½ mile from the trenches and exposed to shell fire. In the morning the enemy captured the village of ZANDVOORDE were our side joined the cavalry on the right. Our line had to be with-drawn and a new one established. Both the 21st & 22nd Brigade Cavalrymen were abandoned with the train wagons as well. Sergt Anderson's detachment were nearly taken prisoner but escaped with the loss of men killed and wounded. The enemy made a fierce attack on all our front but were everywhere repulsed.	

Army Form C. 2118

WAR DIARY
or
INTELLIGENCE SUMMARY.
(Erase heading not required.)

Hour, Date, Place	Summary of Events and Information	Remarks and References to Appendices
	After dark H.Q. returned to the Chateau. Lieut Gibson and 5 men very gallantly seized the opportunity of a counter-attack by the Bedfords, and brought in one of the cable wagons by means of two wounded horses. The whole team was however lost.	
October 31st Saturday	A very fierce attack on the GHELUVELT front of the position. Shell fire exceedingly heavy all day. The G.O.C went early to his wound dressing station, there it was only possible to maintain communication by Despatch Riders. Our part of the line appeared to be holding well, when at 1.30 p.m alarming messages were received from 1st Div. that part of their line to the N. of GHELUVELT was falling back. Div. H.Q. were retired to the level crossing, marked HALTE on the MENIN-YPRES road. The company were collected and spent the night here, but the G.O.C remained at	

Army Form C. 2118
p.14

WAR DIARY
or
INTELLIGENCE SUMMARY.
(Erase heading not required.)

Hour, Date, Place	Summary of Events and Information	Remarks and References to Appendices
	Chateau, and sent for the Staff to join him there. It	
	Osborne remained at the Chateau. It appeared two	
	fresh Corps had been launched against our front, but by	
	evening our troops had almost regained their original	
	positions.	
Sunday 1st November	Most of the company at the Halte, but we returned	
	to the day position 1 m. East of ZILLEBEKE. We	
	remained there all day under heavy shell fire, which	
	however did not reach us. As soon as it was growing	
	dark we returned to the Chateau, under a fire of high	
	explosive shell. It was reported that the German Emperor	
	in person was superintending the attack on YPRES from	
	GHELUWE. The Chateau had been slightly damaged	
	by shells but nothing serious. Two neighbouring chateaux	
	had been struck with very serious results. A quiet	
	night on the whole.	

WAR DIARY or INTELLIGENCE SUMMARY

Army Form C. 2118

p.15

Hour, Date, Place	Summary of Events and Information	Remarks and References to Appendices
Monday Nov. 2nd	Moved early to our dressing station, where we also found the staff of two Cav. Bdes. Much shrapnel about, which however did little harm. About 2 p.m. the G.O.C. decided to return to the chateau. From then on till 6 p.m. it was heavily shelled but not actually hit, most of the shells falling in the main road. There was a keen German attack in the centre at GHELUVE LT, supported by numerous H.E. shells. Supports of British troops and Zouaves were pushed in and the position maintained. The Household Cav. Bde. also galloped across to reinforce the left of the position under shrapnel fire, which emptied several saddles. Capt W.S. Dennison S.I. was severely wounded and the Gn's A.D.C. Captain Butler wounded — the by fire ceased shortly after dark and the night was fairly quiet. Genl. Capper decided to move to a hay at Tomorow, which was much lower down the night in the Fd. Ambn. R.E. We lost 6 horses from shrapnel.	

Army Form C. 2118

p.16

WAR DIARY
or
INTELLIGENCE SUMMARY.
(Erase heading not required.)

Hour, Date, Place	Summary of Events and Information	Remarks and References to Appendices

Tuesday Nov. 3rd

At 6.30 a.m. moved H.Q. and the whole Signal Co. to a position in the woods about half a mile from the chateau. 3 dug outs had been made for the staff, and our own men made some more. Periodical shelling all day, but mostly falling in the road. A message from Sir John French promising speedy relief and asking the army to stand firm. Communication maintained by certain riders. Lt. Osborne carrying a good many himself to the firing line near fire. The 1st Corps endeavoured to connect us by cable, but the enemy were shelling Ypres so heavily that it was of little use being normally down. The Zouaves were in the woods with us. The horses were scattered about the woods and so avoided all harm. The G.O.C. and staff returned to the Chateau at night. Lt. Osborne and myself remaining in the dug out, because of the cables.

Army Form C. 2118.

p. 17

WAR DIARY
or
INTELLIGENCE SUMMARY.
(Erase heading not required.)

Hour, Date, Place	Summary of Events and Information	Remarks and References to Appendices
Wednesday Nov 4th	The Staff returned about 6.30 a.m. Our situation remained much covered by the enemy, so we remained safe during the usual shelling. Major James, Brigade Major 22nd Div. Batt. was killed, a great loss to the Army and the 7th Division. Osborne had run out two cables to the Brigades, but they were often shot due to the shell fire. There was some rain and the roads became very muddy, rendering the use of motorcycles almost impossible. Lieut Osborne took some messages to 22nd Batt. Trenches under fire. A cyclist of the 20th Inf. Batt. was killed by a shrapnel shell on the main road, shortly after leaving Div. H.Q. with a message. An artillery duel in progress all day and some half hearted attacks on our trenches. It rained at night. The staff slept in the Château. Lt Osborne & self sleeping in a new dug out made for us	

Army Form C. 2118.

p. 18

WAR DIARY
or
INTELLIGENCE SUMMARY.
(Erase heading not required.)

Hour, Date, Place	Summary of Events and Information	Remarks and References to Appendices
Thursday Nov. 5	The 15th consecutive day of the battle for the possession of YPRES. A heavy artillery and all day, but distinctly less than usual. A good deal of infantry fire from the trenches and about 4 p.m. very heavy fire to the south. Orders were issued for the 20th & 21st 2nd Bedes to be relieved and withdrawn from the firing line to rest. About noon the weather cleared and it turned out very fine. As soon as it was dark the relieving Bedes arrived and I marched off with the Company leaving Lieut Roberts and two officers behind to maintain communications until the relief could take them over. We arrived at YPRES at 10 p.m. to find it being bombarded by the enemy. The company however found a sheltered position for the night under the lee of the Hotel de Ville. The bombardment increased in violence and soon there were reports of shells everywhere	

Army Form C. 2118.

P. 19.

WAR DIARY
or
INTELLIGENCE SUMMARY.
(Erase heading not required.)

Hour, Date, Place	Summary of Events and Information	Remarks and References to Appendices
	The Staff gave orders for all horses to leave the town at once. So the company hustled in the teeming and manured about 12.30 a.m. As we leaved the Rgt. Italian a heavy shell burst in the road about 20 yds behind the rear of the company.	
Friday 6th Nov	Marched by moonlight and halted at DICKEBUSH at 2 a.m. placing the horses in a field, the men getting shelter in neighbouring buildings. Continued the march at 7 a.m. and arrived at LOCRE at 9 a.m. where we found Divl H.Q at a chateau called "Chateau de la Douve." The men and horses had to bivouac in the grounds as there were no vacant quarters available. The army trip put in a line for us to the Report Centre at BAILLEUL, so we had no lines out; in fact we had no officers or cable available. The roads were muddy and blocked with troops.	

Army Form C. 2118.

p. 20.

WAR DIARY
or
INTELLIGENCE SUMMARY.
(Erase heading not required.)

Hour, Date, Place	Summary of Events and Information	Remarks and References to Appendices
Saturday 7th Nov. BAILLEUL	Lieut Osborne and his party rejoined about 5 a.m. having marched through YPRES by night. About 10 a.m. the Company marched to BAILLEUL and found a good billet in the Rue de Lille, with an adjacent field for the horses. The 7th Div. was scattered in all directions and portions of it attached to other commands, while other units were placed under the orders of Gen Capper making communications exceedingly difficult. Fortunately G.H.Q. have a large experienced and trained office here, formerly adjacent to Divl. H.Q. in the Rue de Lille. The Town still occupied by its inhabitants, being too far out of the shellfire zone. H.Q. and No. 1. section are now 10 men and 29 horses short, and the men have not had an opportunity of taking off their clothes or their boots for the past three weeks, so a rest	

Army Form C. 2118.

p. 2.)

WAR DIARY
or
INTELLIGENCE SUMMARY.
(Erase heading not required.)

Hour, Date, Place	Summary of Events and Information	Remarks and References to Appendices
Bailleul Sunday Nov 8"	is essential. The Company except the N.C.O.'s and men recovery for the signal office had a complete rest, and were busy washing, cleaning and checking equipment. A special report on Trait-Larme, and certain N.C.O.'s and men were sent through the C.R.E. to Headquarters. The chief peculiarities of the recent operations have been the extreme proximity of the Div. H.Q. to the firing line, and the frequency with which they have been subjected to shell fire. The shell fire has destroyed the cable both of No 1 Section and the 3 infantry divisions. The latter have had several men killed and wounded and lost most of their equipment. Many of their N.C.O.'s and men have been recommended for their gallantry by Brigadiers, Lieut Colonels, and what has been	

Army Form C. 2118.

P. 22

WAR DIARY
or
INTELLIGENCE SUMMARY.
(Erase heading not required.)

Instructions regarding War Diaries and Intelligence Summaries are contained in F. S. Regs., Part II. and the Staff Manual respectively. Title pages will be prepared in manuscript.

Hour, Date, Place	Summary of Events and Information	Remarks and References to Appendices
Bulland Monday, Nov. 9th	so conspicuous that the G.O.C. has recommended him for command of the Company, a promotion he has thoroughly earned. Dull and damp. The men employed all day in refitting and overhauling equipment. Genl. Forbes D.A.S. had lunch with the officers and approved of the command of the Company being given to Lt. Osborne. Genl. Lewfred Bale wounded in arm 2/Lt Keker, o/c having been in action continuously for 22 days and with only 4 Officers left. Regt had captured 3 machine guns in a recent counter attack.	

Army Form C. 2118.

WAR DIARY
or
INTELLIGENCE SUMMARY.
(Erase heading not required.)

Hour, Date, Place	Summary of Events and Information	Remarks and References to Appendices
Bailleul Nov 10th	We went out. The Company continued refitting. Communication between Aspin and 20th, 21st & 22nd Brigades at METTEREN, PLOEGSTREET and MORRIS respectively was maintained by orderly.	
do Nov 11th	Third Corps arrived with permanent line and vibrator. Communication was opened with 2nd at MORRIS. An office wagon was put in a B.H.Q. line for 20th at METTEREN. 21st Bde were still under Aspin and messages were sent between at PLOEGSTREET by cable through H.Q. and by orderly.	
do Nov 12th	No change in communications.	

WAR DIARY
INTELLIGENCE SUMMARY.
(Erase heading not required.)

Army Form C. 2118.

Hour, Date, Place	Summary of Events and Information	Remarks and References to Appendices
Nov 13th	Division marched to neighbourhood of Sailly & takes over line from 19th Bde. Connection with Bthn maintained by cable line.	
Nov 18th	Major Garwood left to command 5th Field Coy R.E. 2nd Division, & then came subsequently for 3 Corps & command the company with temporary rank of Captain whilst so employed. From this time the division remained in trenches & the communications were gradually added to by telephones etc. & worked well.	
Nov 29th	H.M. the King George V visited our lines	
Dec 13th		
Dec 21st	Capt James replaced Lt Palmer in command of No 2 Section. The latter appointed Staff Capt. 20th Bde.	

Army Form C. 2118.

WAR DIARY
or
INTELLIGENCE SUMMARY.
(Erase heading not required.)

Instructions regarding War Diaries and Intelligence Summaries are contained in F. S. Regs., Part II. and the Staff Manual respectively. Title pages will be prepared in manuscript.

Hour, Date, Place	Summary of Events and Information	Remarks and References to Appendices

Jan 1st 1915 — In charge. Circuit diagram below.

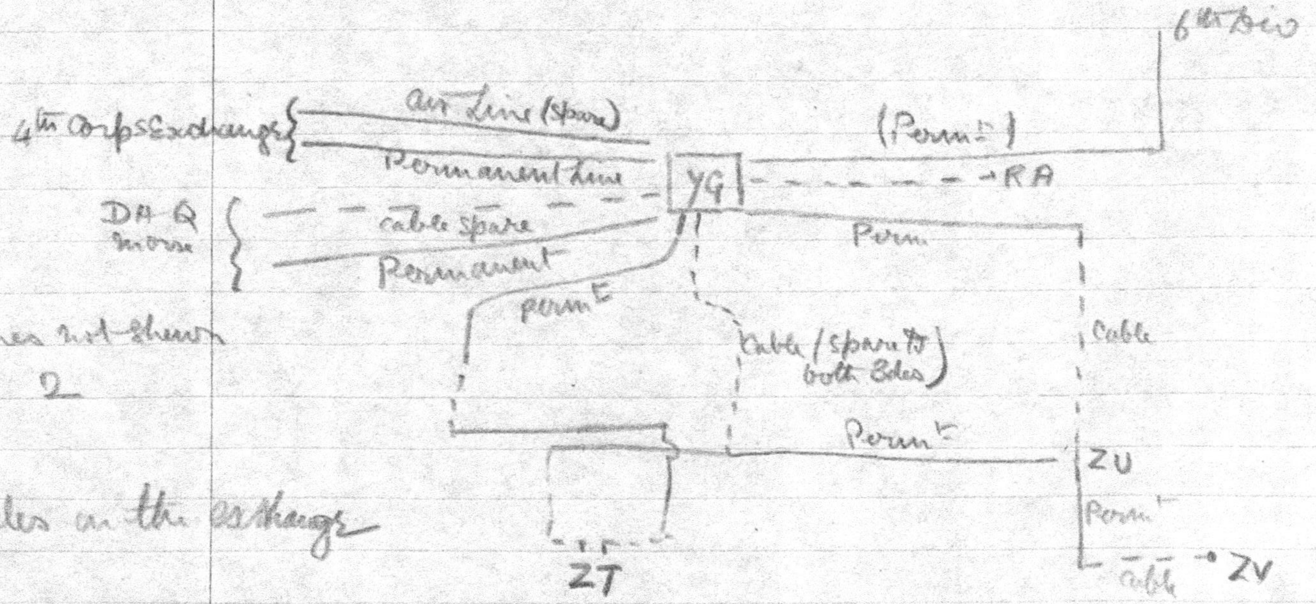

[circuit diagram with labels: 4th Corps exchange, DAQ, Air line (spare), Permanent line, cable spare, Permanent, YG, (Perm?), RA, 6 Batteries, Perm, Cable, Cable (spare to both Bdes), Perm, ZU, Perm, ZT, ZV]

NB Telephones not shown
at Chateau 2
Staff office
B Huts
also all Bdrs on the exchange

Army Form C. 2118.

WAR DIARY
or
INTELLIGENCE SUMMARY.
(Erase heading not required.)

Instructions regarding War Diaries and Intelligence Summaries are contained in F. S. Regs., Part II. and the Staff Manual respectively. Title pages will be prepared in manuscript.

Hour, Date, Place	Summary of Events and Information	Remarks and References to Appendices
4.30 18th 1914	(References in follows map those Reimed sparing 2nd 36 & 36D) On the morning of this day orders were issued for an attack during the evening. A divisional report centre was established at CROIX MARECHALE. Bde HQs as follows:— 20th Bde N 9 B 9 6 21st Bde N 5 a 9 9 22nd Bde H 36 a 11 having the space line to Bdes on extension of 4th Corps Telephone was established at Bde HQ and lines were laid to Bde HQs. The line to 20th Bde had to be laid late in the evening under a good deal of rifle fire. It however did this work well Fighting continued through the night and communication was maintained without interruption. At 8 am report centre closed a little normal state of communication was reported to.	
Dec 19th	Between two dates no action operations took place Officers & most of the NCOs there had short leave	

7th Divisional Engineers

7th DIVISIONAL SIGNAL COMPANY R. E.

DECEMBER 20th 1914 to 31st MARCH 1915.

Army Form C. 2118.

WAR DIARY
or
INTELLIGENCE SUMMARY.
(Erase heading not required.)

Instructions regarding War Diaries and Intelligence Summaries are contained in F. S. Regs., Part II. and the Staff Manual respectively. Title pages will be prepared in manuscript.

Place	Date	Hour	Summary of Events and Information	Remarks and references to Appendices
	December 20th 1914 to February 26th 1915		Between these dates no active operations took place. Officers and most of the N.C.Os and men had short leave.	

WAR DIARY
or
INTELLIGENCE SUMMARY.

(Erase heading not required.)

Army Form C. 2118.

Hour, Date, Place	Summary of Events and Information	Remarks and References to Appendices

From a communication point of view the following work was carried on.

(a) Telephone system. This was extended so that eventually the following was connected to the system. H.Q.Corps (2 lines), 3rd Bde, 6th Bde (2 lines R lines) 25th Bde, Res dires of 90c VII Bn (2 lines) H.Q. office, CRA (two lines) CRE, 55th Co R.E., 20, 21, 22 Bdes, B Mor @ 3 reserve bns B Mor

(b) A great deal of work was carried on by Brigade sections who eventually had a complete system of communication by wire from Bde HQrs to Battalions and thence to Companies in the firing line. All lines in Bde areas were duplicated & most triplicated. A circuit diagram is drawn up after the application of but in this diary. The system in the 22nd Bde (Lt. O'Connor) was especially good.

WAR DIARY
or
INTELLIGENCE SUMMARY.
(Erase heading not required.)

Army Form C. 2118.

Hour, Date, Place	Summary of Events and Information	Remarks and References to Appendices
Feb 27th	The division prepared to hand over to the Canadian division. All lines were to be left standing	
Feb 28th	New division HQ at MAUMERY MONDE G.26.C.6.2 were chosen as a signal office prepared. 22nd Bde handed over to 2/1st Canadian Bde.	
March 1st	They took over E & F lines from 2 Sth Bde lines left standing.	
	4 O'Connor Communicand with an line communications above and improved lines considerably putting about 12 miles of wire into the job	
March 2nd	Capt Rathburn Canadian Signal Company came to take over & 2 NCOs were detached to remain with him for some days & are with each Bde section	
March 4th	The office at SPRIM closed at 11 am & opened 2.30 with Wyldman Captain dentists a diagram of the new system is attached	

Instructions regarding War Diaries and Intelligence Summaries are contained in F. S. Regs., Part II. and the Staff Manual respectively. Title pages will be prepared in manuscript.

WAR DIARY
or
INTELLIGENCE SUMMARY.
(Erase heading not required.)

Army Form C. 2118.

Hour, Date, Place	Summary of Events and Information	Remarks and References to Appendices
	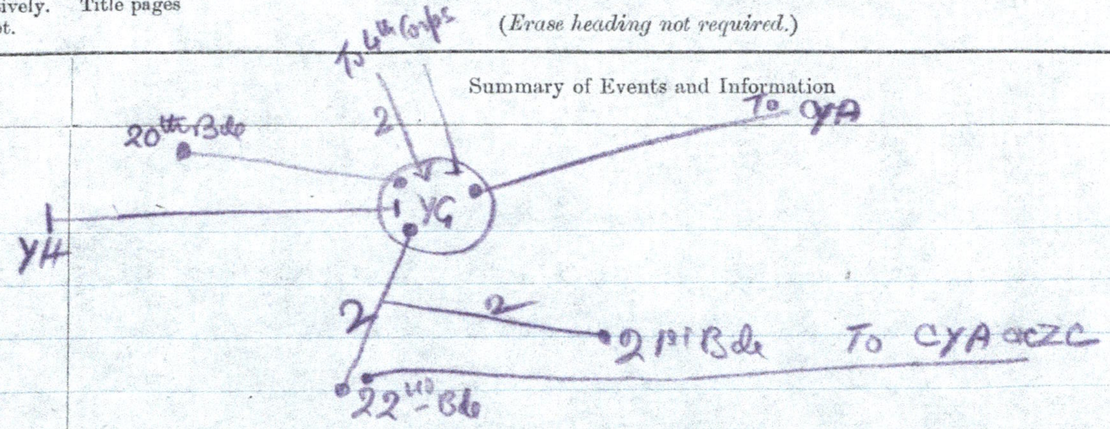To 4th Corps 2 20th Bde To CYA YH 1 YG 2 2 21st Bde To CYA & ZC 22nd Bde	
	Telephone system as shewn connected General staff (2 lines) 4th Corps 2 lines GOC RA (2 lines) Residence of GOC 7th Div (2 lines) B Mess CRE, all three Brigades, A staff.	
March 5th – 9th	Three days spent in consolidating lines and preparing communications for attack.	

(9 29 6) W 2794 100,000 8/14 H W V Forms/C. 2118/11.

Army Form C. 2118.

WAR DIARY
or
INTELLIGENCE SUMMARY.
(Erase heading not required.)

Instructions regarding War Diaries and Intelligence Summaries are contained in F. S. Regs., Part II. and the Staff Manual respectively. Title pages will be prepared in manuscript.

Hour, Date, Place	Summary of Events and Information	Remarks and References to Appendices
10th – 14th	The work was entirely electrical as the weather was unsuitable for visual. A visual station was maintained eventually at H.Q. in case air wires for J.E. we should cease. The attached diagrams show the lines laid & maintained except that Y.G.A. was not established until 9 am on the 12th. The G.O.C. remained at Y.G. during the 10th & 11th. Telephone system Headquarters is that shown on + was maintained. The diagram showing 22nd R.d. duis is also attached. 10th & 11th. The Q line to 2nd 24 Z.T. was dis for 2 hours in the night of 11th & 11th. Owing to many wires & the darkness the line men had a hard job to find it. The remainder of the 2 days communication was as guaranteed without	

WAR DIARY or INTELLIGENCE SUMMARY.

(Erase heading not required.)

Army Form C. 2118.

Hour, Date, Place	Summary of Events and Information	Remarks and References to Appendices
	intestation.	
12th	at 9am YGR was established. About 12 noon E line was broken by shell fire but communication was kept up to ZV on D line. About 3.30pm shell fire broke all three G lines an communication was interrupted for 12 minutes.	
13th 14th 15th	Communication was continuous	
15th	at 2am the heading our of lines D,E,F,G,Z,O being complete YGR was closed. The system of a central centre worked well. Lines men were always available to patrol lines. This was always done first thing in the morning & last thing at night. The country between YGR & ZT & ZV was shelled somewhat unmercifully. Leaving breaks, but the arrangement of three lines & Bridges over two yds prevented the lines going	

WAR DIARY
or
INTELLIGENCE SUMMARY.
(Erase heading not required.)

Army Form C. 2118.

Hour, Date, Place	Summary of Events and Information	Remarks and References to Appendices

completely &

2 Flashlamps were kept at V.G.A to establish a flash system if the division had a big advance. Brigade sections. No 2 section (20th Bde) was unable to keep telephone connection with its battalions as all lines were broken by shell fire.

No 3 section 21st Bde kept continuous communication with an battalion by telephone & intermittent communication with another battalion

No 4 section 22nd Bde was on the defensive. The battalion commanders were in the trenches & telephones were kept working to battalion commanders & companies almost without another. This was due to carefully thought-out system which the O.C. of the section R.E. O'Carroll had prepared.

WAR DIARY
or
INTELLIGENCE SUMMARY.
(Erase heading not required.)

Army Form C. 2118.

Hour, Date, Place	Summary of Events and Information	Remarks and References to Appendices
March 15th	Signal office transferred to cellar under G.O.C.'s chateau. Thineuren gate detachment formed to to complete entrenchment.	
March 16 to 23rd	Lines consolidated. Two brigades moved into reserve & lines laid accordingly. Artillery lines laid & adjusted. Capⁿ Paen of 4th Corps came over for 3 days to take charge of artillery work	

Communications 7th Div
10th - 12th March 1915

Map 1/40,000

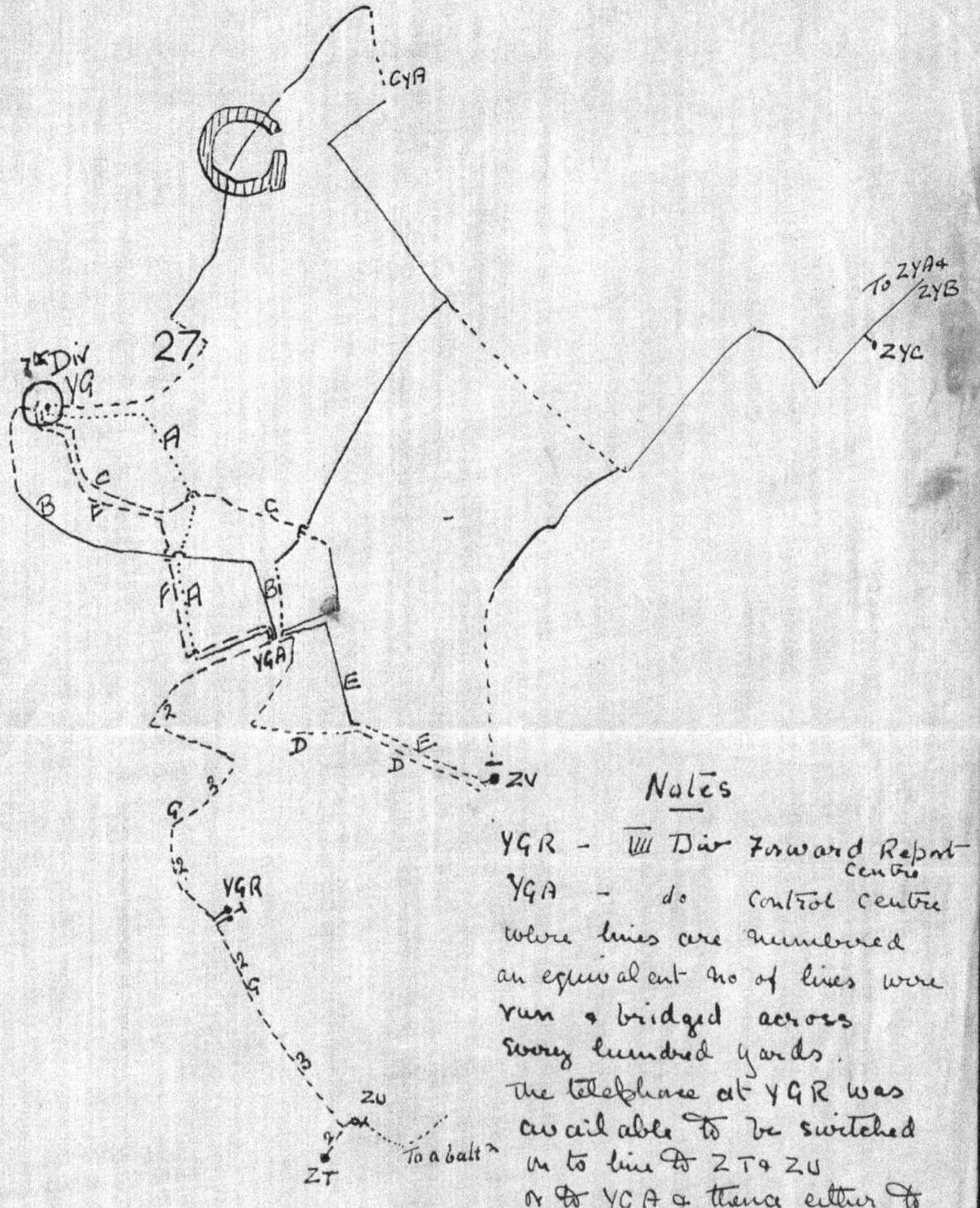

Notes

YGR — VII Div Forward Report Centre
YGA — do Control Centre
where lines are numbered an equivalent no of lines were run & bridged across every hundred yards. The telephone at YGR was available to be switched on to line to ZT & ZU or to YGA & thence either to ZV or back to the exchange at 7th Div. This exchange was connected to 4th Corps, 4th Corps report center, 8th Div, 8th Div report center, residence of GOC 7th Div, Canadian div etc. Telegraph work was sent by vibrator from YGR to YGA & there transferred onto Morse circuit for DCO or DRC.

Report on Signal Work
During Operations VII Div
10.3.15 & 13.3.15

The work was entirely electrical as the
weather was unsuitable for visual
A visual station was maintained constantly
at YGA in case an occasion for its use
should arise.

Diagram The attached diagram shews
the lines laid & maintained except
that YGR was not established until
9am on the 12th. The GOC remained
at YG during the 10th & 11th.

Headquarters & No 1 Section

10th/11th The G line to ZU & ZT was dis
until 2am on 10th. During ~~the remainder~~
~~the~~ remainder of the 2 days ~~all lines~~
communication was maintained without
interruption

12th at 9am YGR was established
About 12 noon E line was broken by
shell fire but communication ~~to~~
ZV was kept up on D line while E was repaired
About 3.30pm shell fire broke all
three G lines & communication was

interrupted for 12 minutes

13th to 14th Communication was continuous

15th At 2 am the handing over of the lines to 8th Div being complete YGR was closed.

Remarks The system of a central exchange worked well. Linemen were always available to patrol lines. This was always done first thing in the morning & last thing at night.

The country between YGR & ZT+ZU was shelled & the linemen were continually mending breaks but the arrangement of 3 lines bridged every 100 yds prevented the line going completely dis.

2 Detachments were kept at YGA to establish a fresh system if the division made a big advance.

Brigade Sections. No 2 Section (20th LdD) was unable to keep telephone connection with its battalions as all lines were broken by shell fire.

No 3 Section 21st Bde kept continuous communication with one battalion by telephone & intermittent communication with another battalion.

No 4 Section 22nd Bde was in the defensive. The battalion commanders were in the trenches & telephones were kept working & battalion commanders & companies almost without cessation. This was due to a carefully thought out system of duplicate wires which the OC of this section Lt O'Connor had prepared.

Shelborne Capt R.E.
OC the Sig

7th Signal Co., AEF

Doc + mon

1915

Army Form C. 2118.

7 Signal Coy R.E.

WAR DIARY
or
INTELLIGENCE SUMMARY.
(Erase heading not required.)

Instructions regarding War Diaries and Intelligence Summaries are contained in F. S. Regs., Part II. and the Staff Manual respectively. Title pages will be prepared in manuscript.

Hour, Date, Place	Summary of Events and Information	Remarks and References to Appendices
Nov 1st – Nov 11th	Nothing of interest to report. Bde. Hd. Qrs. alternating between Waterloo Bridge, F.10.9.8.7, LE QUESNOY Château F.8.t-7.2, HALTE N.29. C.10.3.	Map ref:- Bethune Cambrai 1/40,000
Nov. 4th	7th D.A. Hd. Qrs. moved back from LE QUESNOY to BETHUNE.	
Night Nov 5/6th	Attempt was made to overhear a tapped German wire near Duck's Bill. but no results were obtained	
Nov 10th	Lt. R.P. Hepburn R.E. reported here for duty as supernumerary	
Nov 12th	Commencement of relief of 19th Div. by 22nd Bde. Hd. Qrs. established at CAMBRIN. Lateral cable line laid between CAMBRIN & WATERLOO BRIDGE. Cable line of an hue laid back from CAMBRIN to LE QUESNOY	
Nov 15th	Lt. R.P. Hepburn R.E. left Hd. Qrs. reported for duty at 21st Bde.	
Nov 16th	2nd Lt. J. Walker R.F.A. returned to 22nd Bde. R.F.A.	

Army Form C. 2118.

WAR DIARY
or
INTELLIGENCE SUMMARY.
(Erase heading not required.)

7th Signal Coy: R.E.

Instructions regarding War Diaries and Intelligence Summaries are contained in F.S. Regs., Part II. and the Staff Manual respectively. Title pages will be prepared in manuscript.

Hour, Date, Place	Summary of Events and Information	Remarks and References to Appendices
Nov. 22nd – Nov. 25th	Front extended N. Division moved from 19th Divn. to 20th Inf. Bde. Hd: Qrs. moved to LOISNE. X.29 d 24. Communications used 3 permanent lines along RUE D'ESTAIRES as far as L.E. HAMEL. Thence lead into airlines running from the dwellers at 9. G.C.O.N to LOIS N.E. Sounders installed the circuit telephone. – 22nd (Inf.) Bde. moved Hd. Qrs. to FOUQUIERES F.16 a.10.5. Telephone laid out to them from BETHUNE on 23rd. – G. 25. d. 90.5. Bde. moved VIA HALLIE W. 29. CUR5.	
Nov. 26th – Nov. 30th	Lines in trenches turned out & fitted up generally 15-80 miles D5 cable lifted in case LOISNE area handed over to 1st Corps. Overhauling & labelling of all lines on divnl area carried out. 22nd (Inf.) Bde. moved from HALLE to GONNEHEM V. 18.a.66. 2 Corps lines previously used by 2nd Divn. now out of use utilised for communication to the Bde.	
Dec. 1st	20th Inf. Bde. moved from Loisne to Bethune (Rue de	

BWO'Farrell
Capt: Coy
Condg 7th Signal
Coy 7th Signal Coy. R.E.

(9. 29. 6) W 2794 100,000 8/14 H W V Forms/C. 2118/11.

Army Form C. 2118.

7th Signal Coy R.E.

WAR DIARY
or
INTELLIGENCE SUMMARY
(Erase heading not required.)

Hour, Date, Place	Summary of Events and Information	Remarks and References to Appendices
Dec. 2d	Frederic (George) of Airpola & easlong line was laid to him. 21st moved from Wateles Bridge to Marquillies. O so a 6 6; 2 cavalry lines were used for communication between Divnl. H.d. Brs took over from 33rd Divn. at Bruires & handed over to them at Bethune, the respective offices opening at 12 Noon. From Bruires there were 2 cable lines by the 20th to the 21st Inf. Bdes, no lines being continued across any to the 22nd.	
Dec. 3d	22nd Bde moved to Oeffleure & the 20th to Beuvrshem. The Tracing shows system in use at Bethune during Oct. & Nov.	Appendix 1
Dec 5th - 7th	The Division moved to Cavillon in 13th Corps area. The Int. Bdes moved off before the Hd. Brs Divn. The Artillery liaison from BETHUNE area were taken over by the 19th Divn. on Dec 4th. 7th D.A. moved to LAMPRES but no communication was made to them.	

Forms/C. 2118/11.

Army Form C. 2118.

7th Signal Coy R.E.

WAR DIARY
~~INTELLIGENCE SUMMARY~~
(Erase heading not required.)

Hour, Date, Place	Summary of Events and Information	Remarks and References to Appendices
Dec. 8th	The Signal office closed down at 4.30am on Dec. 6th. The Div. entrained at Lillers & arrived at Cavillon at 1am. on the 7th. An advance party with the lorries opened communication with the 5th Corps hut & a sounder & telephone line laid by the Corps — On the 7th Dec airlines previously laid by the Corps were put through to the 2nd Bde at BELLOY; a Sounder & telephone line being used at OISSY & the 3rd Bde at HOLLIENS-VIDAME, the vibrator being used; & also to the 7th D.A. Billeting at ARTUVIE (Corps) were put through to PICQUIGNY where a Sub-office was opened to deliver to the ADMS, DADOS etc. & also to contain an exchange for the Arty, 20th Bde & the phones. On the 20th Bde were in PICQUIGNY they received their messages through the sub office which worked a sounder to CAVILLON	
Dec. 9th	Lines were put through by a Corps cable section to	

Army Form C. 2118.

7th Signal Coy R.E.

WAR DIARY
or
INTELLIGENCE SUMMARY
(Erase heading not required.)

Hour, Date, Place	Summary of Events and Information	Remarks and References to Appendices
Dec 10th	the Divn. Train, & by our own detachments to the 7th D.S.C. (Belloy) & the local offices in PICQUIGNY. A second line was also laid to the 21st & 925th Bdes. The system was then as follows:-	Appendix No 2

Army Form C. 2118.

7th Signal Coy R.E.

WAR DIARY
or
INTELLIGENCE SUMMARY.
(Erase heading not required.)

Hour, Date, Place	Summary of Events and Information	Remarks and References to Appendices
1915		
Dec 11th	A.L. Cable section reeled up four miles of air-line from Fouendrinoy to Ailly. As all horses are now under cover they are all being clipped.	
Dec 12th-13th	No work on hand, clipping continued.	
Dec 14th	13th Corps Section put up line of poles from CAVILLON to SOUES- PICQUIGNY Road to carry five Corps air-lines.	
Dec 15th	Laid two lines on trees poles- Rifle & Detachment equipment inspection by O.C.	
Dec 16th	Reeled up three miles cable and two miles of 600 irm wire made spare by using two lines laid on 15th. Eight Draft, five riding horses arrived from Remounts, were inspected by the Vet and are in isolation for ten days. Lt: Lee rejoined from England and took over	

WAR DIARY
INTELLIGENCE SUMMARY

Army Form C. 2118.

7th Signal Coy. R.E.

Hour, Date, Place	Summary of Events and Information	Remarks and References to Appendices
Dec 16th cont'd:	No 4 Signal Section relieving No. 1 Smith who returned to No 1 Signal Section.	
Dec 17th	Received twenty miles of 60lb galvd iron wire from Signal Park. Laid remaining three lines to Soues-Picquigny Road, continuing one on permanent poles to Picquigny. Laid two comic airlines to Oissy on poles previously put up by 2/Lt Watson on 12th inst.	
Dec 18th	Court of Enquiry held to investigate cause of Corpl. Huston's death due to injuries in accident on 6th inst: while proceeding from BETHUNE to CAVILLON – Took remaining lines the semi-permanent poles into use – A.L cable section laid two more Comic air-lines to OISSY which were then taken into use.	Singer Car sent to 7th Amm Park in exchange for Sunbeam Car 1A2? Authority D.o.T GHQ 354/2 dated 9/XII/15.
Dec 19th	Reeled up two air-lines from CAVILLON to SOUES–	

Army Form C. 2118.

WAR DIARY
or
INTELLIGENCE SUMMARY.
(Erase heading not required.)

17th Signal Coy R.E.

Hour, Date, Place	Summary of Events and Information	Remarks and References to Appendices
Dec 19th cont'd	P&C QUIGNY road made free by using Cories laid on 17th. All Smoke Helmets Tube Pattern were inspected by M.O. (Capt: Ballingall R.A.M.C.) Two Cories Air-lines to OISSY were lifted by A.L. Cable section - 21st Brigade No. 3 Signal Section moved off today to join 30th Division. Rear Electric Light lorry sent today from G.H.Q.	System of Communication is now as per appendix No. 3.
Dec 20th Dec 21st	Electric light installed in all Headquarters offices etc. A.L. Cable section rebuilt line from OISSY to MOLLIENS VIDAMES. Three officers and thirty N.C.O.s assembled for Divisional Signal School viz: three officers and thirteen N.C.O.s from the Gunners and the remaining N.C.O.s from Battalions of the 20th, 91st and 22nd Infantry Brigades.	
Dec 22nd	Signal training at Divisional School commenced	

Army Form C. 2118.

7th Signal Coy R.E.

WAR DIARY
or
INTELLIGENCE SUMMARY.
(Erase heading not required.)

Instructions regarding War Diaries and Intelligence Summaries are contained in F. S. Regs., Part II. and the Staff Manual respectively. Title pages will be prepared in manuscript.

Hour, Date, Place	Summary of Events and Information	Remarks and References to Appendices
Dec 23rd & 24th	Instruction at Signal School continued	
" 26th to 31st	"	

OC No 7 Signal Coy R.E.
(Capt)

Communications 7th Div
10th – 12th March 1915
Map 1/40,000

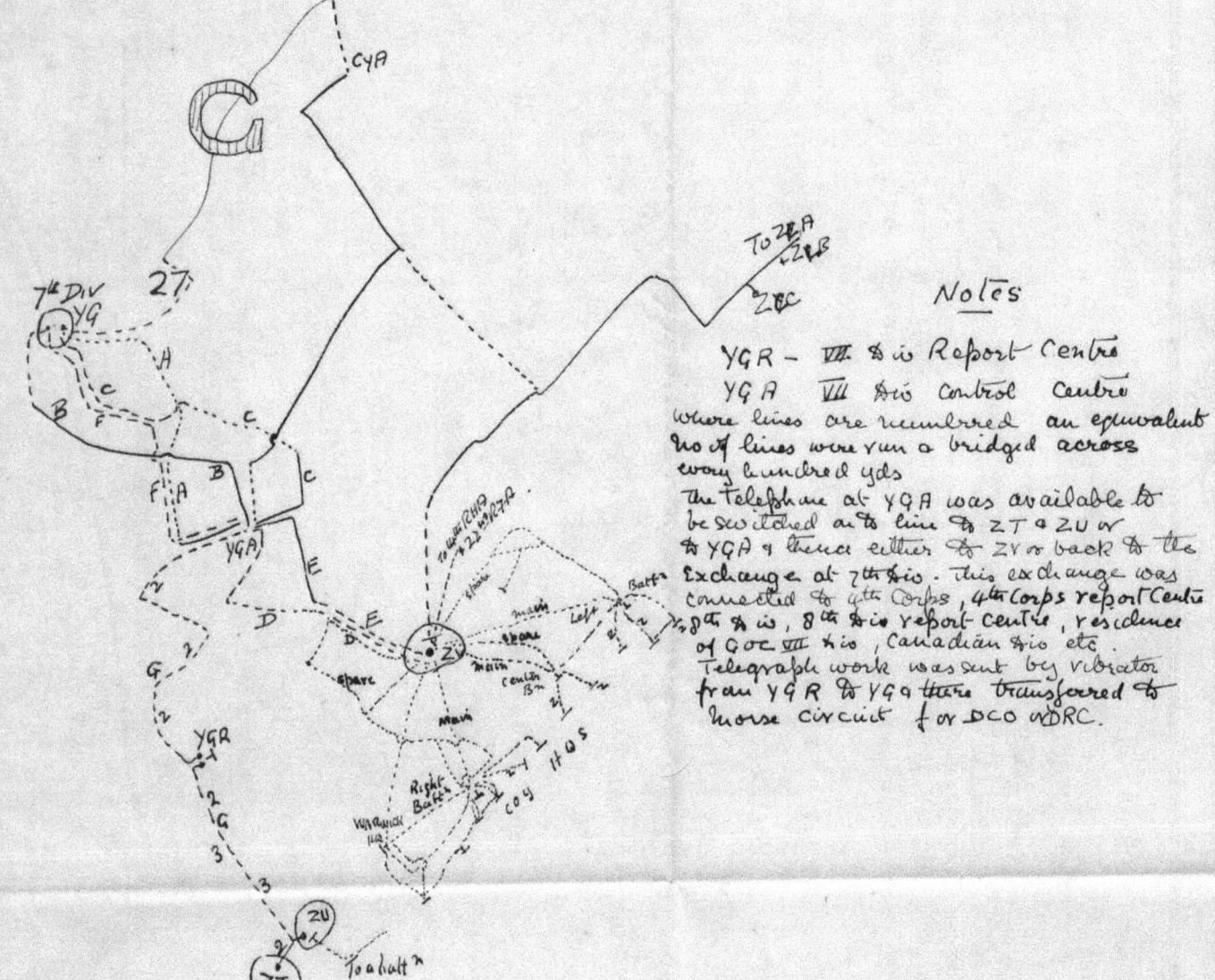

Notes

YGR – VII Div Report Centre
YGA – VII Div Control Centre
Where lines are numbered an equivalent no. of lines were run & bridged across every hundred yds
The Telephone at YGA was available to be switched on to line to ZT & ZU or to YGA & thence either to ZV or back to the Exchange at 7th Div. This exchange was connected to 4th Corps, 4th Corps report centre, 8th Div, 8th Div report centre, residence of GOC VII Div, Canadian Div etc.
Telegraph work was sent by vibrator from YGR to YGA there transferred to Morse circuit for DCO WDRC.

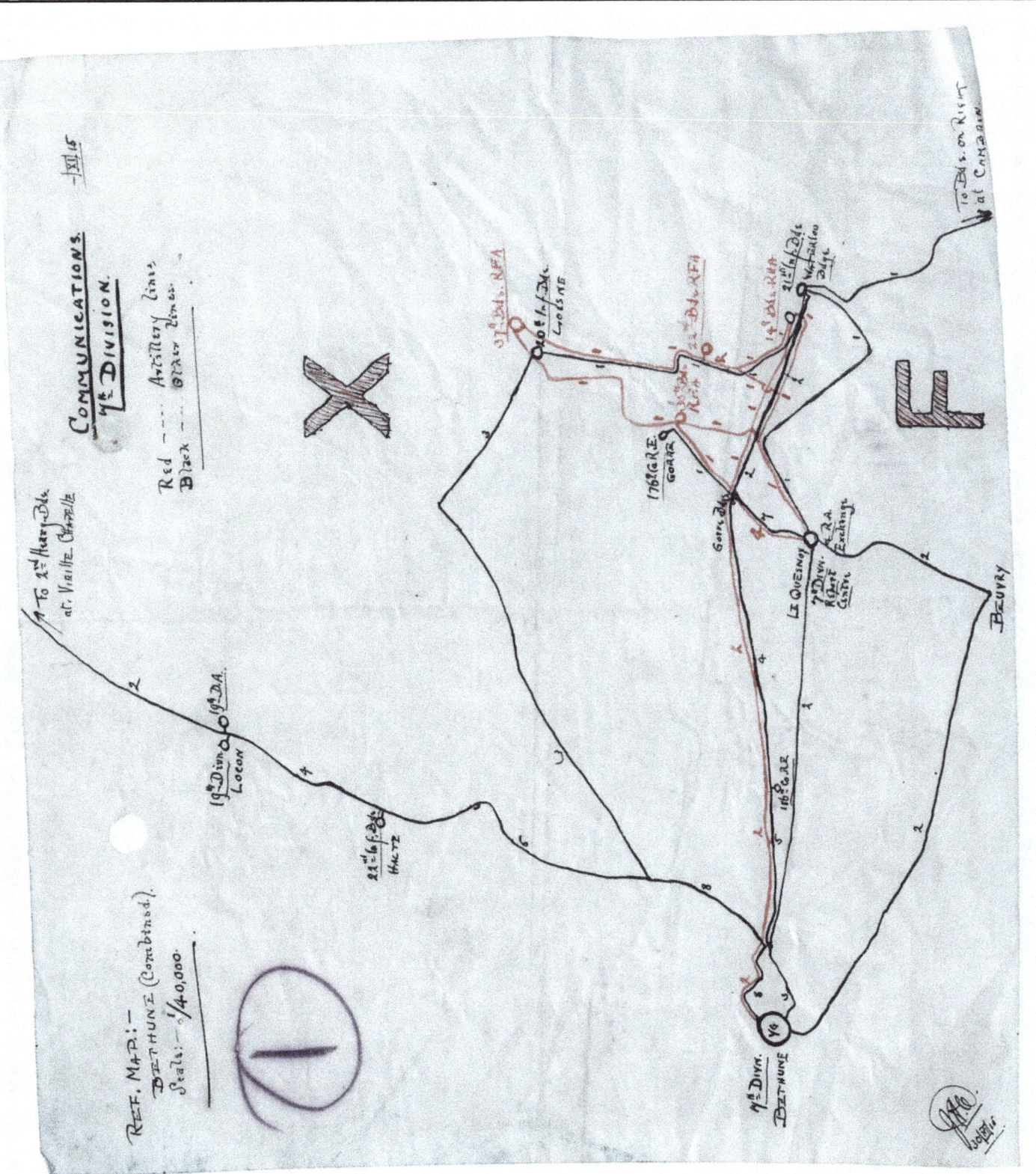

7TH DIV.
CIRCUIT DIAGRAM 21-12-15

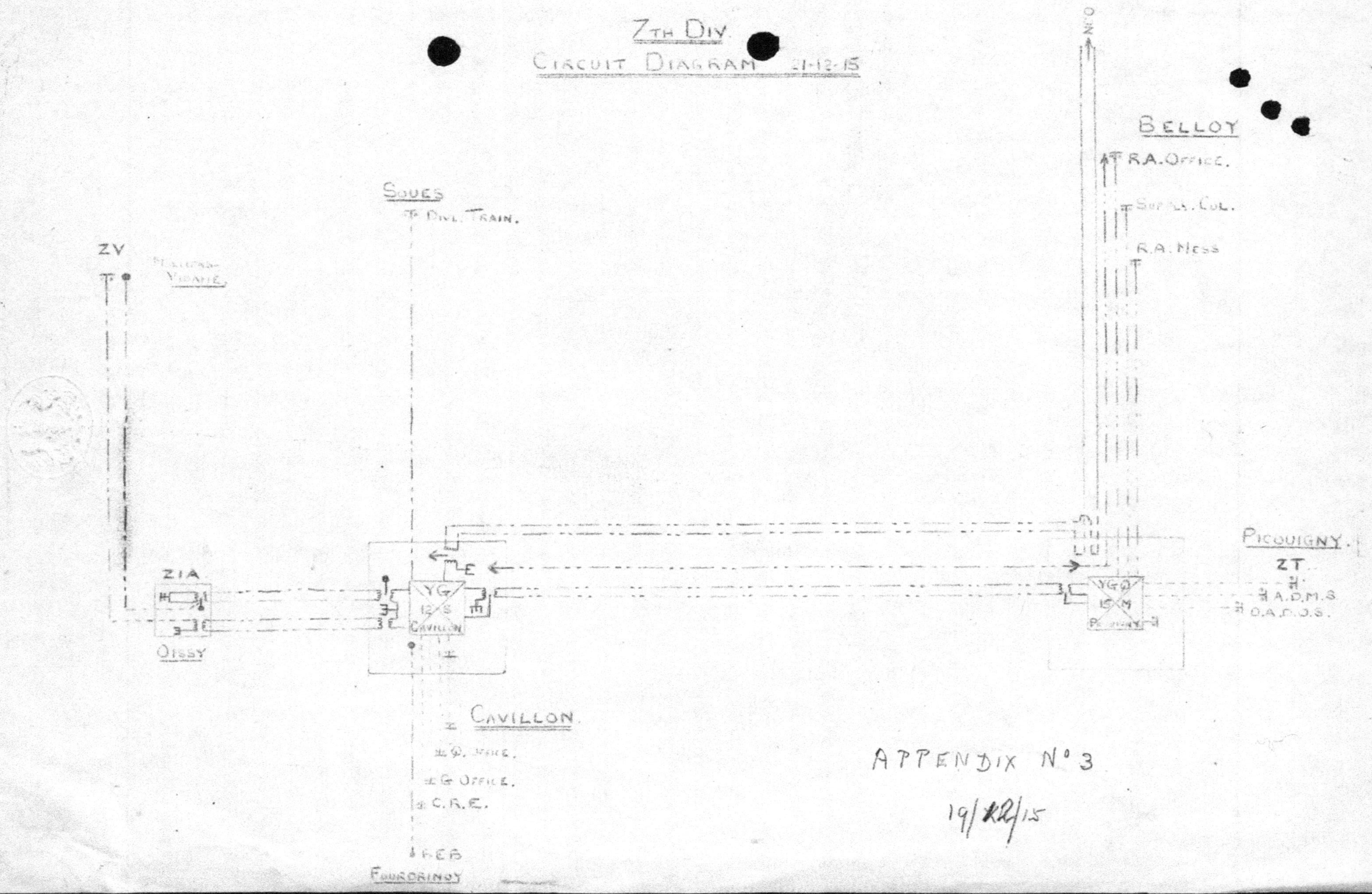

BELLOY
- R.A. Office.
- Sup. L. Col.
- R.A. Ness

SOUES
To Div. Train.

PICQUIGNY
- ZT
- H
- A.D.M.S.
- O.A.D.J.S.

CAVILLON
- H.Q. Mess.
- H.Q. Office.
- C.R.E.

OISSY
- ZIA

ZV

FOURDRINOY

APPENDIX N° 3

19/RQ/15

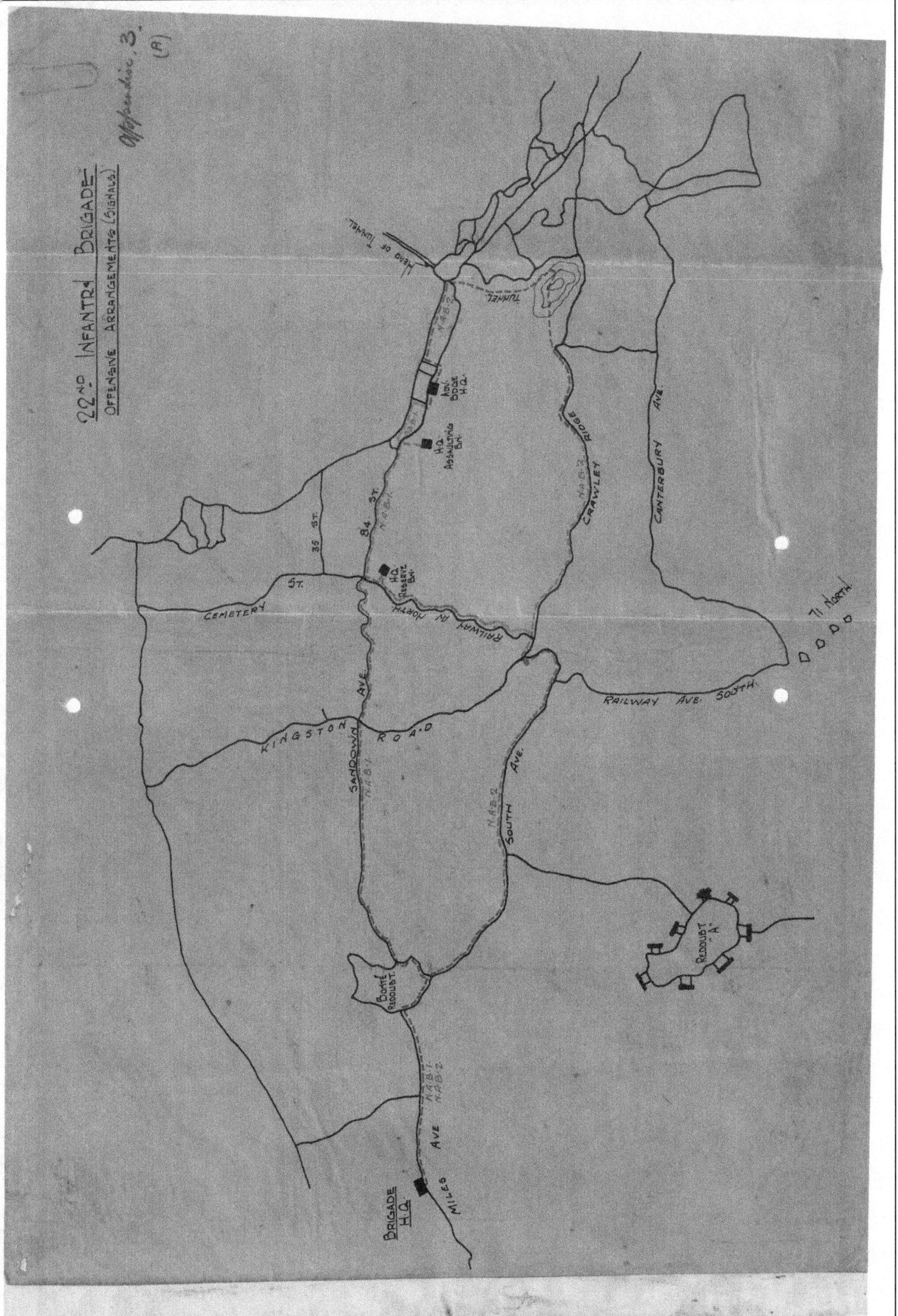

I Siqueiros / Jan / vol III

WAR DIARY
or
INTELLIGENCE SUMMARY.
(Erase heading not required.)

7th Signal Coy R.E.

Army Form C. 2118.

Instructions regarding War Diaries and Intelligence Summaries are contained in F.S. Regs., Part II. and the Staff Manual respectively. Title pages will be prepared in manuscript.

Hour, Date, Place	Summary of Events and Information	Remarks and References to Appendices
1916 Jany 2nd	Instruction at Signal School continued. — Comic Airline from Chateau through the Wood to the Road replaced by G.P. Cable. Airline constantly in contact or breaking through swaying of trees in heavy wind. —	
Jany 3rd	Instruction at Signal School continued. —	
Jany 4th	Signalling scheme carried out efficiently by Officers, N.C.Os and men, (whom) under instruction at Signal School.	
Jany 5th	Instruction at Signal School Continued:—	
Jany 6th	Signalling scheme as in actual operations carried out by Officers and N.C.Os under tuition, together, work on Company Signallers.—	
Jany 7th	Lecture on scheme carried out the day before, — Electrical and General Knowledge examination held.	
Jany 8th	Signalling scheme as on the 6th inst; carried out.	
Jany 9th	First course at the Divisional Signal School completed, Officers and N.C.Os returning to their respective Units.	

Army Form C. 2118.

7th Signal Coy R.E.

WAR DIARY
or
INTELLIGENCE SUMMARY.
(Erase heading not required.)

Hour, Date, Place	Summary of Events and Information	Remarks and References to Appendices
Jany 10th and 11th	Commence polishing up the company at Cable Drill. One detachment of detachment Commanders and N.C.O's out laying cable on the Carillon – Brugnes Meenil road – Linemen out on Flag drill – A series of lectures and practical demonstration in testing commenced for Signal Masters. Lectures on Elementary Electricity for all Linemen.	(Jany 11th Cable detachment Coy Cable on the Carillon – Oisey road)
Jany 12th	Lectures on testing and Elementary Electricity continued. All the Company horses inoculated with MALLEINE.	
Jany 13th	All horses inspected by Veterinary Officer after the inoculation and all pronounced fit – Lectures on Testing and Elementary Electricity carried on with – Flag drill continued – Lecture on Lamps, Electric. Signalling given – An alarm Parade held with everything packed with the exception of instruments etc in office for which the Lorry was left – Company packed and everyone on Parade ready to move in hour and a half after orders were given to pack up – all billets and stables inspected while Coy was on Parade –	

Forms/C.2118/11.

Army Form C. 2118.

1st Signal Coy R.E.

WAR DIARY
or
INTELLIGENCE SUMMARY.
(Erase heading not required.)

Hour, Date, Place	Summary of Events and Information	Remarks and References to Appendices
Jany 14th	Lecture on Elementary Electricity and horses exercised without harness.	
Jany 15th	Testing class for Signal Masters (Practical) - Lecture on lamps. Flag reading and sending for all Linemen etc. N.os 2 & 3 Detachments out on Cable Drill - Remaining horses exercised without harness - Lecture on Elementary Electricity.	
Jany 16th	Practical Testing for Signal Masters - Nos 1 & 2 Detachments out on Cable Drill - Remaining horses exercised without harness. Signal linemen out on Flag Drill etc. Revision of lectures on Elementary Electricity.	
Jany 17th	Practical Testing for Sig: Masters - Nos 3 and 4 Detachments out on Cable Drill - Signal Linemen out on Lamps and running through old Cable. Riding Class to have been held but cancelled owing to rain, so class for new linemen held on jointing, twisting etc.	

Forms/C. 2118/11.

Army Form C. 2118.

1st Signal Coy. R.E.

WAR DIARY
or
INTELLIGENCE SUMMARY.
(Erase heading not required.)

Hour, Date, Place	Summary of Events and Information	Remarks and References to Appendices
Jany 17th cont'd	Binding in on Comic Air-Line - Written examination held in Elementary Electricity -	
Jany 18th	Practical testing for Signal Masters - Nos 1 & 2 Detachments out on Cable drill - Nos 3 & 4 Detachments lectured on Cable wagon, stores carried & testing the wagon - Smoke helmet practice -	
Jany 19th	Practical testing for Signal Masters - Nos 3 & 4 Cable Detachments out on Cable Drill Nos 1 and 2 lectured on testing a wagon Smoke helmet drill - Elementary Electrical papers gone through with the Class - All horses thoroughly examined by the Farrier Sergeant for Ring-worm several cases and suspects being isolated - Rest of horses exercised without harness - Practical testing for Signal Masters -	
Jany 20th	Flag Drill etc for linemen - Cable Wagon testing for Cable Wagon Drill & testing Wagons & Lecture on Elementary Electricity -	

Army Form C. 2118.

7th Signal Coy R.E.

WAR DIARY

or

INTELLIGENCE SUMMARY.

(Erase heading not required.)

Instructions regarding War Diaries and Intelligence
Summaries are contained in F. S. Regs., Part II.
and the Staff Manual respectively. Title pages
will be prepared in manuscript.

Hour, Date, Place	Summary of Events and Information	Remarks and References to Appendices
Jany 21st	Practical Testing for Signal Masters — Nos 3 and 4 Cable Detachments out on Cable Drill. Testing and running through Wagon Stores for Nos 1 & 2, also smoke helmet Drill. Lecture on Elementary Electricity.	
Jany 22nd	No 2 Cable Detachment out on Cable Drill. Lecture on Wagon Stores & Testing for Nos 1, 3 and 4. Smoke helmet drill. Lecture on Elementary Electricity. Five Officers and twenty four N.C.O's assembled from Artillery & Infantry Units for a course of instruction on Signalling.	
Jany 23rd	Course of Signalling commenced. An address being given by the O.C. 7th Signals on the object of the course when classes arranged for Buzzer, Flags etc. The first of a series of lectures given to the 7th Signal Coy by —	

Army Form C. 2118.

7th Signal Coy R.E.

WAR DIARY
or
INTELLIGENCE SUMMARY
(Erase heading not required.)

Hour, Date, Place	Summary of Events and Information	Remarks and References to Appendices
Jany 23rd Cont'd	by Capt. Ballingall R.A.M.C on general sanitation in billets etc -	
Jan. 24th	No 4 Detachment Cable laying - Practice in air-line joints, jumping holes etc. - Riding Class of 12 mules, Lectures by the C.S.M. - 2nd lecture by Capt. Ballingall R.A.M.C. - Instruction in flag-signalling, buzzer reading, electricity, T.M.S. etc & Lamp-reading continued at Div. Signal School.	
Jan 25th	No 2 Detachment Cable-laying - Horse management & riding class. - Last lecture by Capt. Ballingall R.A.M.C. on Smoke-helmets. - Instruction at Signal School continued; some N.C.O's passed out at 10 words per min. (error 2%).	
Jan. 26th	No 3 Detachment Cable-laying - Horse-management & riding class by C.S.M. - Instruction at Signal School continued	

Army Form C. 2118.

7th Signal Co 122

WAR DIARY
or
INTELLIGENCE SUMMARY.
(Erase heading not required.)

Hour, Date, Place	Summary of Events and Information	Remarks and References to Appendices
Jan. 27th	No 1 Detachment Cable-laying. — Riding class & harness lecture continued by C.S.M. — Wireless operators tested; results fairly satisfactory. — Instruction at Signal School continued.	
Jany 28th	Signal School continued during morning, all officers and N.C.O.s returning to their Units during afternoon owing to the Div.n to move up into the line. — Riding Class and Harness continued.	
Jany 29th	Commencement of packing up for move & collecting stores. Riding Class & Harness lectures continued. — Some Units of 22nd Infantry Brigade move off, also two Units of 91st Bde. Arrangements were made by Division to keep in touch with these Units while detached from their respective Hqrs. — All communications throughout entire move carried out without a hitch	

Army Form C. 2118.

7th Signal Coy R.E.

WAR DIARY
or
~~INTELLIGENCE SUMMARY~~
(Erase heading not required.)

Instructions regarding War Diaries and Intelligence Summaries are contained in F. S. Regs., Part II. and the Staff Manual respectively. Title pages will be prepared in manuscript.

Hour, Date, Place	Summary of Events and Information	Remarks and References to Appendices
Jany 30th	Collection & Packing of Stores etc continued – Headquarters & remaining Units of 22nd and 91st Infantry Brigades move off – Communication kept up by Division.	
Jany 31st	Collection & Packing of Stores, Wagons etc finished – 22nd & 91st Brigades still on the move –	

RNO Carr Capt. R.E.
(Cmdg 7th Signal Coy R.E.)

Army Form C. 2118.

7 KDiv Signal Coy R.E.

WAR DIARY
or
INTELLIGENCE SUMMARY.
(Erase heading not required.)

Place	Date	Hour	Summary of Events and Information	Remarks and references to Appendices
	1916			
	Feby 1st		Detachments 1, 3 & 4 and Headquarters left CAVILLON (SOMME) at 9.30am under command of Lt Smith arriving at Coig COISY at 3.0pm where they were billeted for the night. Horses were picketed in a field and men in two barns.	
	Feby 2nd		Above detachments left COISY at 9am arriving at new Hd Qrs TREUX at 3.15pm command being taken over by Lt Lowson.	
	Feby 3rd		Commenced laying lines to Infantry Brigade Hqrs etc getting Office fixed. Existing lines taken over from 18th Division and diverted to Signal Office. New lines laid as follows:- to 22nd Bde Artillery at BRAY. A.M. Cable section under command of OC Blood put through two lines to BRAY taken over from 18th Division, part being buried. Divl Head Qrs move to AMIENS from CAVILLON. Capt O'Connor two Signal-masters and Despatch Riders proceeded with it. N° 2 Detachment left CAVILLON for TREUX.	
	Feby 4th		Divl Hq opened at TREUX at 4.0pm. Communication was then as per attached diagram.	

Army Form C. 2118.

WAR DIARY
or
INTELLIGENCE SUMMARY.
(Erase heading not required.)

7th Div: Signal Coy RE

Place	Date	Hour	Summary of Events and Information	Remarks and references to Appendices
	Feby 5th		Metallic telephone pairs to 1st and 35th Arty Bdes installed in MEAULTE. R.A. Signal Office fixed up.	
	Feby 6th		R.A. Hdqrs opened at TREUX. Communications as per diagram.	
	Feby 7th		Telephones to Supply Column and Ordnance at MERICOURT installed. Horse standings commenced. No 2 Cable detachment put at disposal of 22nd Inf. Bde. Line laid from 22nd Inf: Bde: Hdqrs to 35th Bde: Artillery and one to MEAULTE — ETTINEHEM road for trenches.	
	Feby 8th		Company Sgt Major Rodwell attached to 91st Inf: Bde to assist officer in command.	
	Feby 9th/12th		Construction of lines from 7th Division to 91st Infantry Brigade Battle Hdqrs.	
	Feby 13th/14th		Construction of lines from 7th Division to 22nd Infantry Bde: Battle Hdqrs.	
	Feby 15th/16th		Prospecting routes for buried lines from Battle Headquarters to 20th, 22nd and 91st Inf: Bde Battle Headquarters.	

Army Form C. 2118.

7th Div. Signal Coy R.E.

WAR DIARY
or
INTELLIGENCE SUMMARY
(Erase heading not required.)

Place	Date	Hour	Summary of Events and Information	Remarks and references to Appendices
	Feby 16th to 17th		2/Lt Watson returns from Wireless Signalling Course at 3rd Army School. Diagram of Communications to date attached.	
	Feby 18th		Commenced building covering for horse standings. Commence digging parties for advanced lines. Digging party supplied by 2nd Btn Royal Warwick's and 24th Manchesters.	
	Feby 19th		Cutting keys for French cable laying.	
	Feby 20th		Comic Airline from 22nd Inf: Bde to 91st Bde at Bray laid. Div cable laid from 7th Div Battle Headquarters to 22nd Brigade (Inf:) Battle Headquarters.	
	Feby 21st		Lee off line from Div:l Battle Hdqrs = 22nd Inf: Bde Battle Hdqs = 20th Inf: Bde Battle Hdqrs line to 35th and 14th Artillery Brigade Hdqrs.	
	Feby 22nd Feby 23rd		Continuing line to 22nd Inf: Bde Hdqrs. Commence laying line in trench from 91st Inf: Bde Battle Hdqrs to 7th Div:l Battle Hdq:s	
	Feby 24th		Communications are now as per attached diagram.	

Army Form C. 2118.

WAR DIARY
or
INTELLIGENCE SUMMARY.   7th Divl Signal Coy R.E.
(Erase heading not required.)

Place	Date	Hour	Summary of Events and Information	Remarks and references to Appendices
	Feby 25th		Completed covering of Horse Standings. Continue laying line from 7th Divl Battle Hdqrs to 91st Infy Bde Battle Hdqrs in French.	
	Feby 26th/27th		All R.A. lines adjusted and put straight. Laid Comic Air-line from 7th Div to 7th Divl Battle Hdqrs	
	Feby 29th		Laid in and joined up 7th Divl Battle Hdqr line to 91st Infy Bde Hdqrs. Replace 22nd Infy Bde line with Comic Airline	
	Feby 19th		Capt O'Connor (O.C.) sent to Isolation Hospital with German Measles. Lt N.C. Fowton took command of the Company. During month digging parties were supplied by Northumberland Hussars & 7th Divl Cyclist Coy for digging Trenches from Battle Headquarters to Brigade Battle Headqs.	

A.N.C (?) Capt
(mdg) 7th Divl Signal Coy R.E.

CIRCUIT DIAGRAM
7th Division
4.2.16

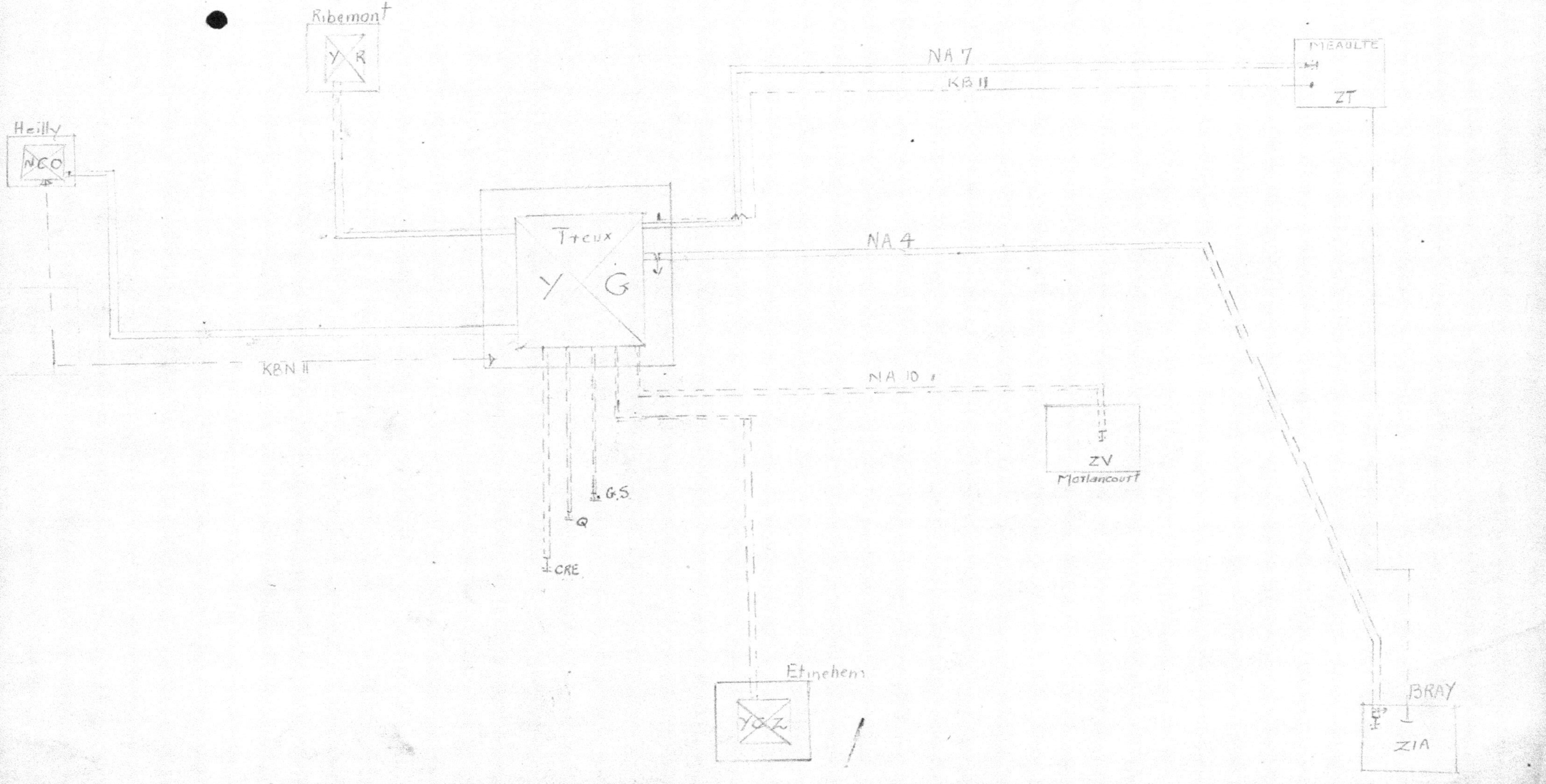

- Méaulte ZT
- Bray ZIA
- ZV Morlancourt
- Étinehem
- Treux G
- G.S.
- CRE
- Ribemont
- Heilly NEO
- NA7
- KB18
- NA4
- NA10
- KB11

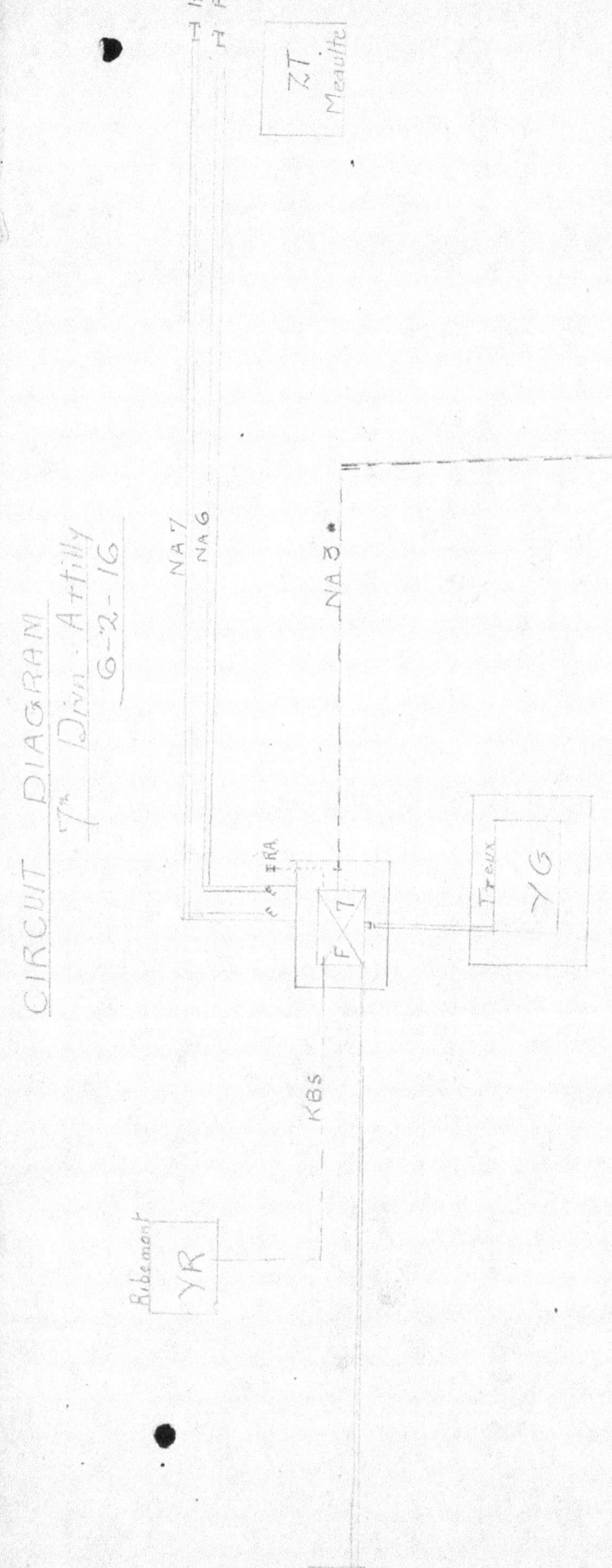

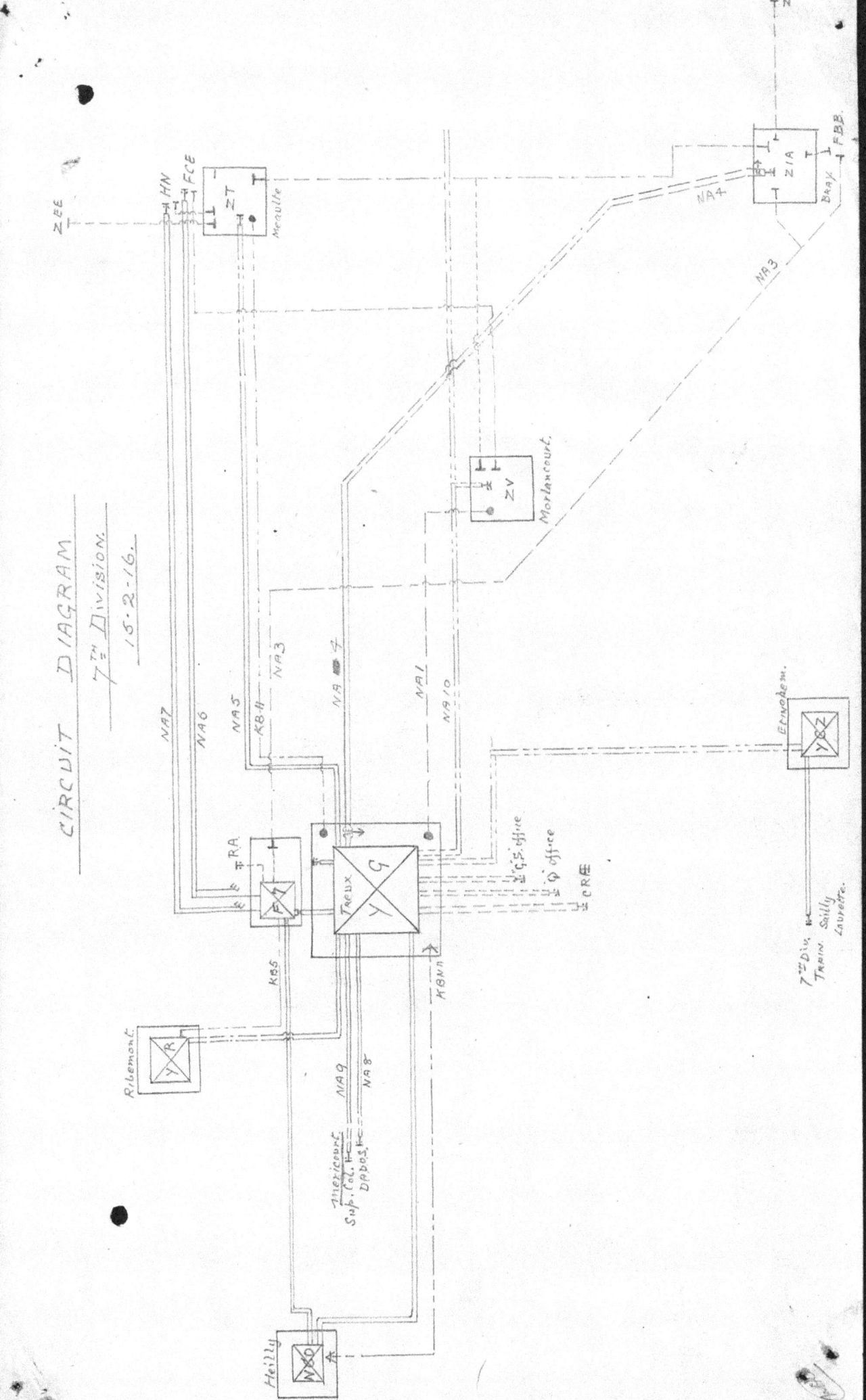

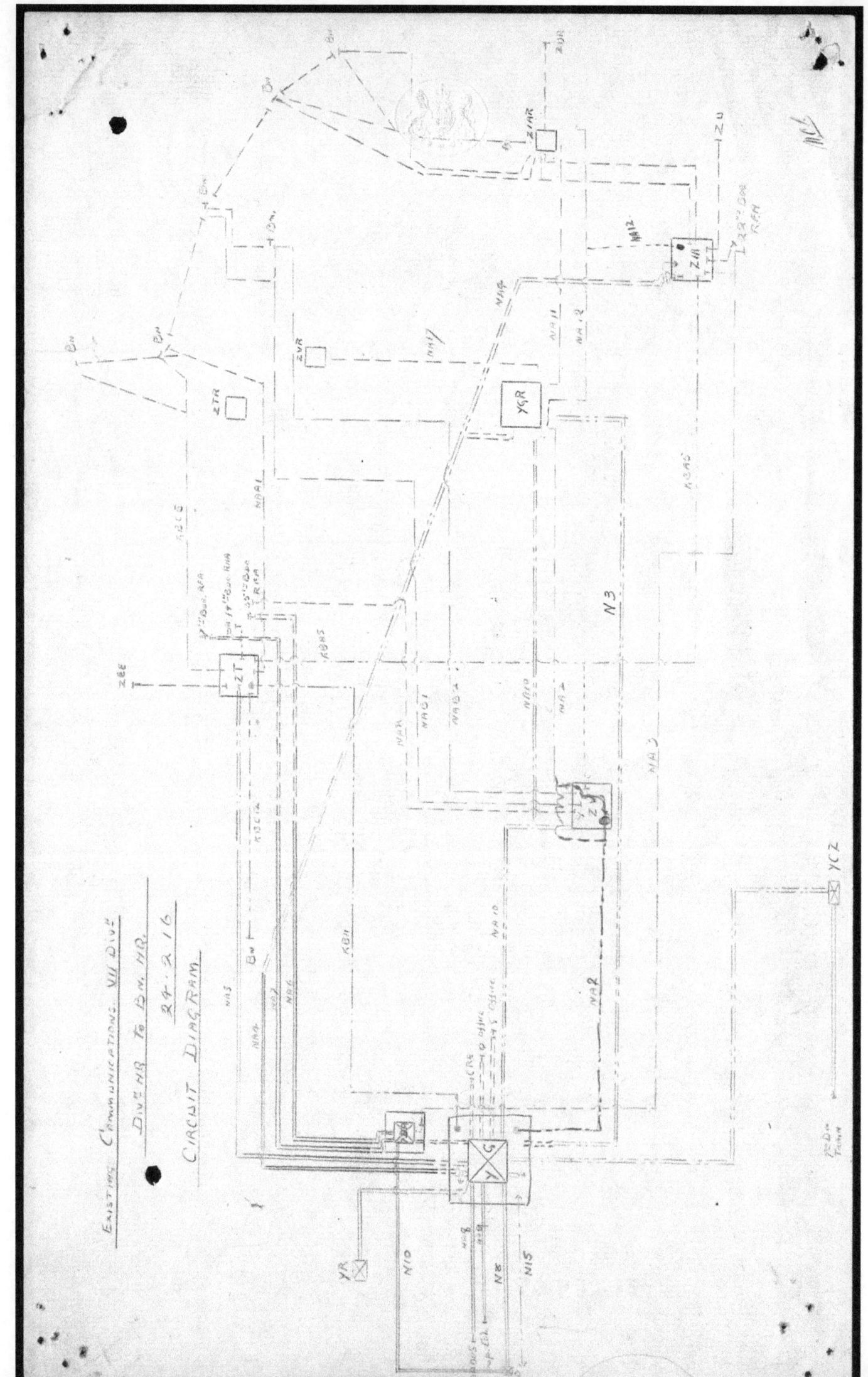

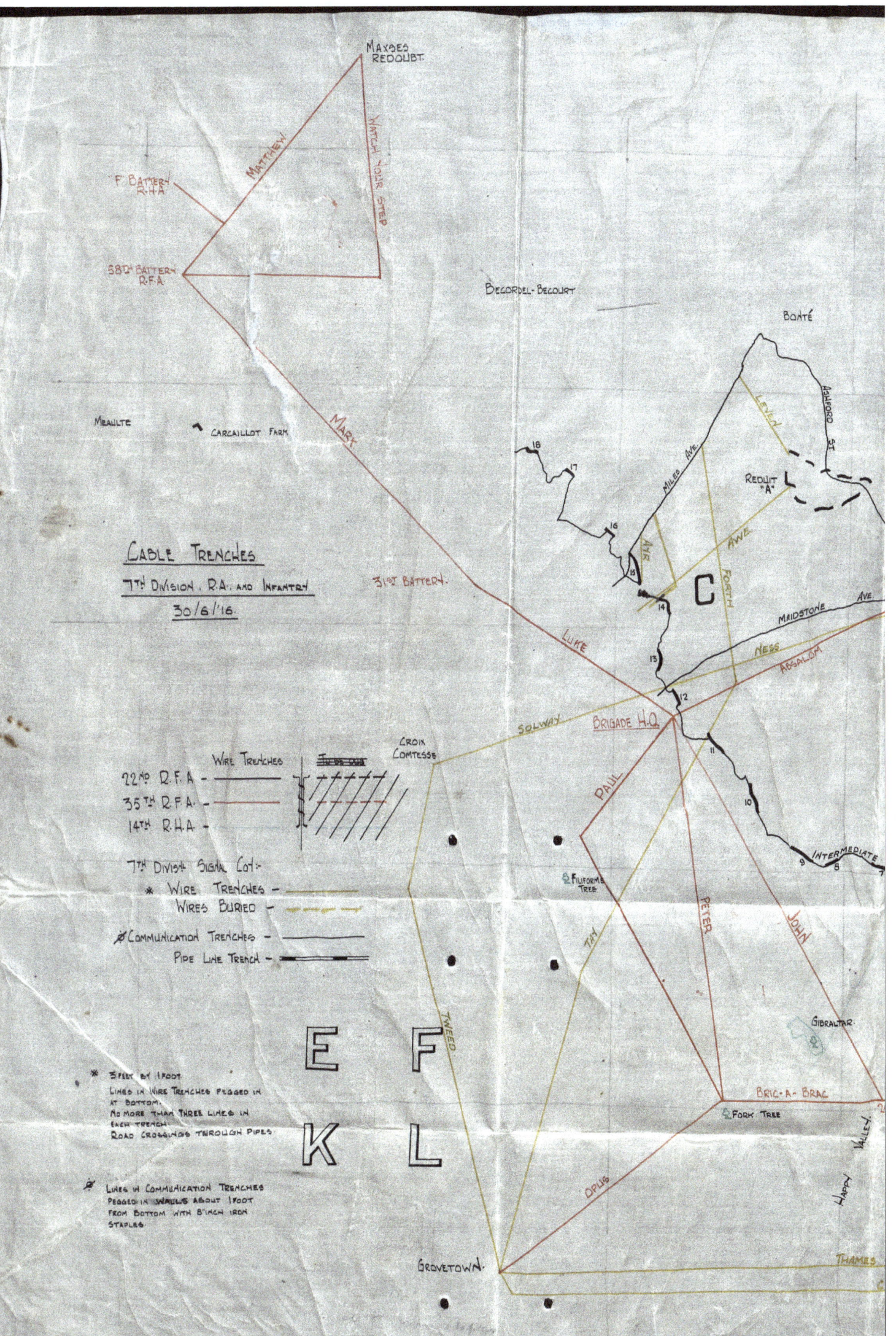

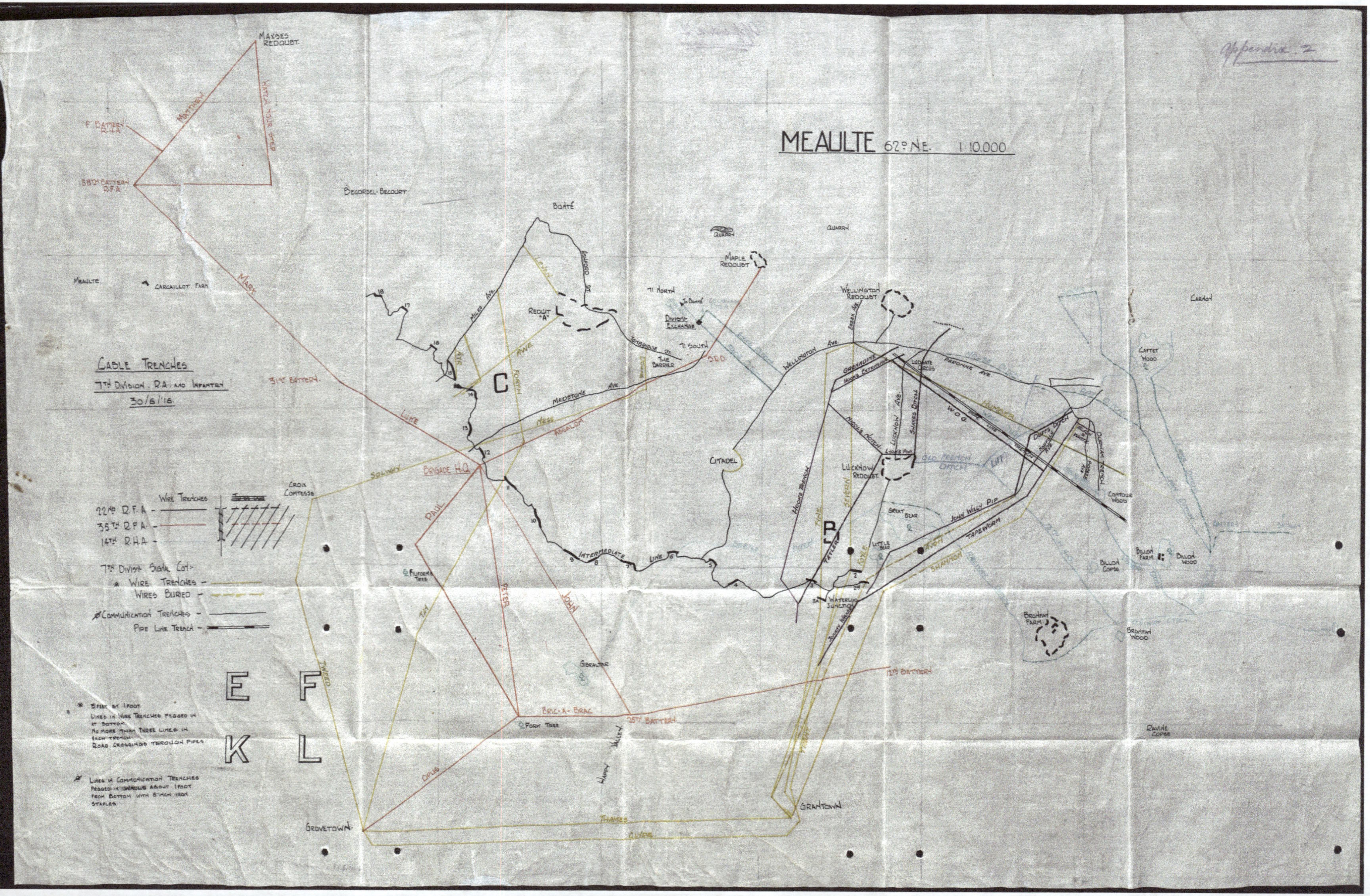
Appendix 2
MEAULTE 62º N.E. 1:10,000
CABLE TRENCHES
7TH DIVISION, R.A. AND INFANTRY
30/6/16.
22ND R.F.A. -
35TH R.F.A. -
14TH R.H.A. -
WIRE TRENCHES
7TH DIVISN SIGNAL COY:-
* WIRE TRENCHES -
WIRES BURIED -
⌀ COMMUNICATION TRENCHES -
PIPE LINE TRENCH -
* LINES IN WIRE TRENCHES PEGGED IN AT BOTTOM.
NO MORE THAN THREE LINES IN EACH TRENCH
ROAD CROSSINGS THROUGH PIPES
⌀ LINES IN COMMUNICATION TRENCHES PEGGED IN ABOUT 1 FOOT FROM BOTTOM WITH 8 INCH IRON STAPLES.
E F
K L
MAXSES REDOUBT
F. BATTERY R.H.A.
55TH BATTERY R.F.A.
MEAULTE
CARCAILLOT FARM
BECORDEL-BECOURT
BOTTOM WOOD
QUARRY
MAPLE REDOUBT
71 NORTH
71 SOUTH
DIVISNL EXCHANGE
WELLINGTON REDOUBT
CITADEL
LUCKNOW REDOUBT
WATERLOO JUNCTION
CROIX CONTESSE
BRIGADE H.Q.
GIBRALTAR
GROVETOWN
GRANTOWN
MARK
LUKE
PAUL
PETER
JOHN
BRIC-A-BRAC
TWEED
THAMES
CLYDE
MAIDSTONE AVE
WELLINGTON AVE
INTERMEDIATE LINE
REDOUT "A"
31ST BATTERY
25TH BATTERY
12TH BATTERY
C
B
BILLON FARM
BILLON WOOD
BILLON COPSE
BRONFAY FARM
BRONFAY WOOD
RAVINE COPSE
CAFTET WOOD
CARNOY

Army Form C. 2118.

WAR DIARY
or
INTELLIGENCE SUMMARY.
(Erase heading not required.)

Place	Date	Hour	Summary of Events and Information	Remarks and references to Appendices
	1916			
	March 16th		Commence digging Visual Signalling Dug Out connecting Battle Hdqrs with 91st Inf Bde Battle Hd.Qrs.	
	March 17th		Carry on with work commenced yesterday.	
	March 17th		Carry on with Visual Dugout. Dig remainder of Trenches into Battle Headquarter Dug Out	
	March 18th		Cable laid into Battle Headquarters in the pieces of Trenches Dug yesterday and then filled in.	
	March 19th		Company paraded for inspection. Squad drill with arms. All Cable wagons etc cleaned up.	
	March 20th		Lay Comic Air-line to 22nd Bde artillery. Lay out some cable for 91st Infy Bde.	
	March 21st		Commence laying lateral line in Trench from 20th to 22nd Inf. Bde Battle Hdqrs. Finish laying line to 22nd Bde R.F.A.	
	March 22nd		Complete lateral line commenced yesterday. Pick up old line to 22nd Bde R.F.A.	
	March 24th		Old VINOT Lorry changed by Supply Column for LEYLAND Lorry	

Army Form C. 2118.

7th Div Signal Coy R.E.

WAR DIARY
or
INTELLIGENCE SUMMARY.
(Erase heading not required.)

Place	Date	Hour	Summary of Events and Information	Remarks and references to Appendices
	1916 March 25th		One detachment cleaning up MEAULTE district. 2/Lt Astley-Weston 14th Bde R.H.A. and 2/Lt Baxter, 22nd Bde R.F.A arrive for Course of instruction in Signal work. Lt Keach 35th Arty Bde coming in daily for same instruction.	
	March 26th		Instruction of Artillery officers commenced.	
	March 27th		Relay line in trench from Battle Hdqrs to 91st Inf. Bde Battle Hdq is the trench having been deepened.	
	March 28th		Carry on with line of yesterday. Also instruction of arty: Officers	
	March 29th		Complete the 91st Inf Battle Hdq" line. Commence rebuilding portion of stable blown down in gale of 28th. Run lines into Battle Hdq" Dug out.	
	March 30th / 31st		Carry on with stable. Complete Battle Hdq" Dug out. Instruction of Arty Officers continues.	
	March 1st to 31st		Digging parties supplied by Northumberland Fusrs & "Cyclist Coy" for digging trenches from Battle Hdq"s to advanced 20th, 22nd and 91st Inf: Bdes and lateral trench from advanced 20th to 22nd Inf: Bde.	

A.B.C. (ms) Capt:

Comdg 7th Div Signal Coy R.E.

4

Signal Coy R.E.

Vol VI

Army Form C. 2118.

7th Div'l Signal Coy R.E.

WAR DIARY
or
INTELLIGENCE SUMMARY
(Erase heading not required.)

Place	Date	Hour	Summary of Events and Information	Remarks and references to Appendices
	1916			
	April 1st		One detachment fixing lines in Battle Headquarters Dug-out and second detachment fixing pipes in Visual Signal Dug-out for concentration of rays.	
	April 2nd		Company Parade for Baths. Squad drill for Drivers, lineman & Operators, also Lectures by C.S.M. Rodwell on care of horses. Instruction of L/t Keetch 35th City; Bde: 2/Lt Ashley Weston 4th R.H.A and 2/Lt Baxter 22nd Bde R.F.A. completed & these officers returned to their Units.	
	April 3rd		Laying line to 51st Siege Battery — Commence digging cable trench from 91st Bde to Advanced H.Qrs to PERRONE AVENUE.	
	April 4th		21st Division commence occupying RIBEMONT, BUIRE and MEAULTE.	
	April 6th		Carry on with trench commenced on 3rd inst. 20th Brigade Head'qrs move back to CORBIE from MEAULTE on being relieved by a Bde of 21st Division — Communication with 20th Inf Bde consist of one Telephone pair and a Sounder line — 35th Artillery Brigade move back to CORBIE from MEAULTE.	
	April 9th		Fine line comic airline poles being laid to BRAY to replace D.V Cable line.	Advanced Report Office

Army Form C. 2118.

WAR DIARY

or

~~INTELLIGENCE SUMMARY.~~ 7th Div'l Signal Coy R.E.

(Erase heading not required.)

Instructions regarding War Diaries and Intelligence Summaries are contained in F. S. Regs., Part II. and the Staff Manual respectively. Title pages will be prepared in manuscript.

Place	Date	Hour	Summary of Events and Information	Remarks and references to Appendices
	April 10th		Carry on putting up poles for lines to BRAY - 14th Artillery Bde leave MEAULTE for CORBIE.	
	April 11th/12th		Putting up lines on poles laid to BRAY.	
	April 13th		Carry on with BRAY lines. Diagram of communications to date attached.	
	April 14th		Carry on with Bray lines	
	April 15th		Finish Bray lines.	
	April 16th		Finish digging trench to Peronne Avenue with the exception of two road crossings.	
	April 17th		Dig trench from 91st Bde report centre to BRAY-MAMETZ road	
	April 18th		Complete trench commenced yesterday. Home Counties Brigade Heavy Artillery open Headquarters at MORLANCOURT.	
	April 19th		Lay line from TREUX to Home Counties Brigade Heavy Artillery (Field Howitzers)	
	April 21st		Continuation of trench lines to MINDEN POST marked out 20th Infantry Brigade close down their office at CORBIE and	
	April 22nd		go to 91st Infantry Brigade Report Centre. 14th Brigade R.H.A	

Army Form C. 2118.

WAR DIARY
or
INTELLIGENCE SUMMARY.
(Erase heading not required.)

7th Div. l. Sig. Coy R.E.

Place	Date	Hour	Summary of Events and Information	Remarks and references to Appendices
April	22nd		Cable open an office at CORBIE, a detachment sent to change over the offices.	
April	24th		Digging trench from Report Centre to Wellington Redoubt. Carrying on with trench to Wellington Redoubt & commence on from Report Centre to Intermediate line. Replace two lines from MORLANCOURT to BRAY-ETTINEHEM road with Airline in place of Cable.	
April	26th		Overhauling lines from advanced 22nd Report Centre to our Report Centre. Laying line in trench to intermediate lines which has been dug.	
April	29th		Digging trench across BRONFAY VALLEY to advanced 91st Bde HQrs. Cutting short pegs for laying in trenches to lay cable on.	
April	30th			

Hules
Capt
Comdg 7th Div. l Signal Coy R.E.

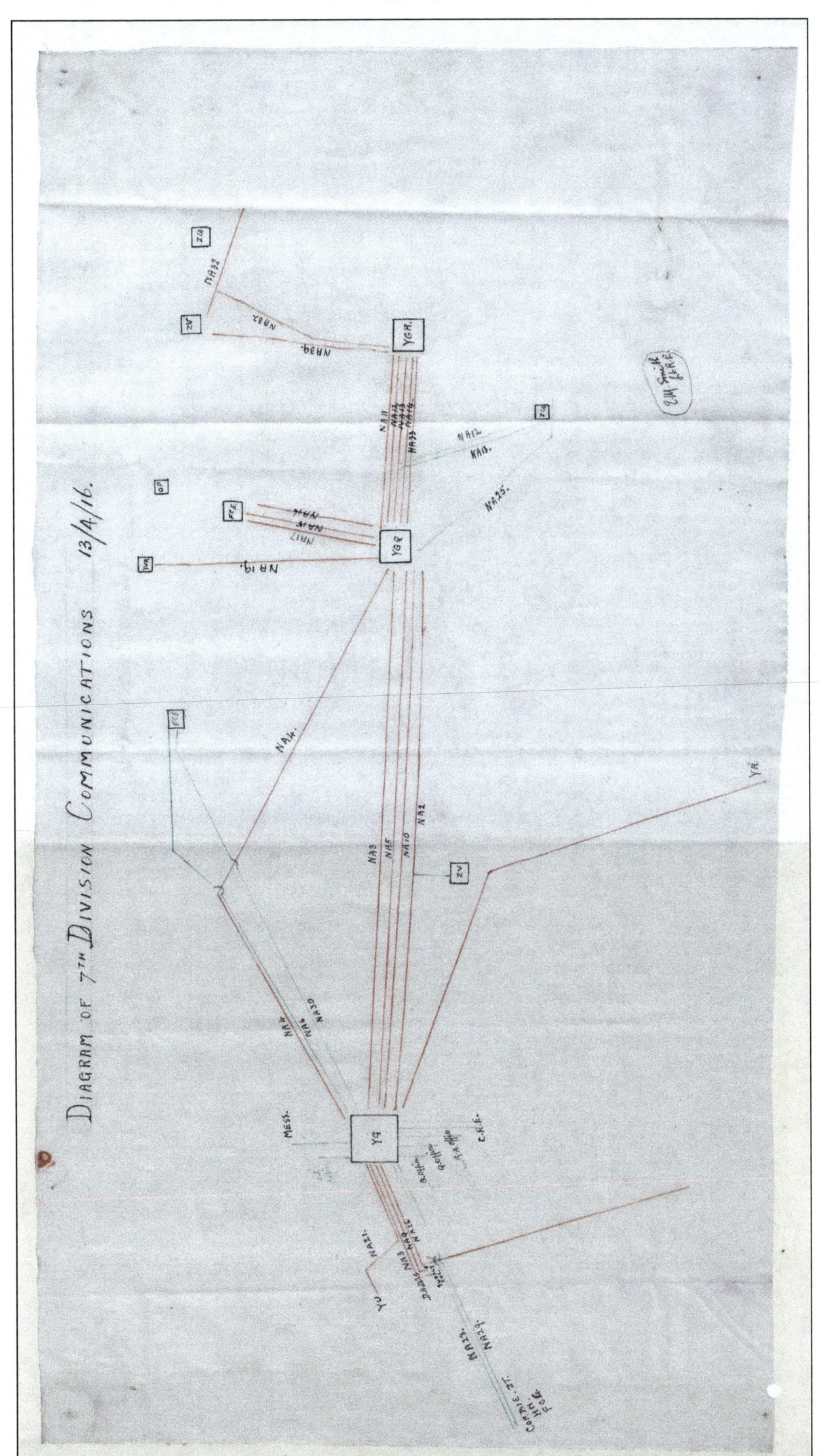

Army Form C. 2118.

7th Div.l Signal Coy R.E.

WAR DIARY

INTELLIGENCE SUMMARY
(Erase heading not required.)

Place	Date	Hour	Summary of Events and Information	Remarks and references to Appendices
	May 1st		CORBIE Office closed down. The line to Corbie was diverted to Div¹ Train who had moved to BONNAY. Seventh Division came under 15th Corps at 10·0am on April 29th who relieved the 13th Corps at HEILLY	
	May 2nd		Bury lines in pipes crossing near Railway being built by 4th Army.	
	May 3rd		Comic Cableline laid between Advanced Report Centre GROVETOWN and BOIS DE TAILLE for 1 battalion of 20th Inf: Bde. Comic Airline laid from 91st Inf Bde. via Advanced Report Centre to the BOIS DE TAILLE for 1 battalion of 91st Inf Bde. — Remainder of telephone line 22nd Bde R.7.A. made metallic.	
	May 4th		Reconstruction of the system of communication to the R.A. begun with a view to economy of stores & labour, to better co-operation throughout the Division. System of individual Battery communication directly under Battery Commander abolished, & one officer per Artillery Brigade made entirely responsible for all the communication in that Brigade, as required by the Battery	

WAR DIARY

INTELLIGENCE SUMMARY

7th Div. Signal Co.

Army Form C. 2118.

Place	Date	Hour	Summary of Events and Information	Remarks and references to Appendices
	May 5th		Commanders. Lt. Smith appointed to represent the Signal Co. & to give technical advice & general assistance wherever necessary. Vibrator line to 3rd Bde. R.F.A. at MÉAULTE partially reeled up & relaid to Corps Dump S. of MÉAULTE; previous Dump telephone pair diverted to GROVETOWN in anticipation of move of 35th Bde. R.F.A.	
	May 6th		Lateral line between 3rd Bde. R.F.A. & 22nd Inf. Bde. reeled up. — 35th Bde. R.F.A. move to GROVETOWN, & office opened there.	
	May 7th		Company parade.	
	May 8th		Line laid for Pumping Station from VILLE to MORLANCOURT.	
	May 9/10th		Line laid from Divl. Hd. Qrs. to No 3 K.B. Sect. & from there on to Divn. Battle Hd. Qrs. — 50 men digging during day (9:30am–4:0pm) on 9th/10th/11th.	
	May 11th		Line laid in deeper trench the left battalion of right sector.	
	May 12th		Night dig-ging recommenced (75 men)	
	May 13th		Line laid from the Citadel to Orchard Copse for light railway.	
	May 14th		Lt. Hook proceeded from 91st Inf. Bde. to 10th Corps to take over a	

WAR DIARY

INTELLIGENCE SUMMARY.

7th Div. Signal Co.

Army Form C. 2118.

Place	Date	Hour	Summary of Events and Information	Remarks and references to Appendices
			Cable section "W" B.G. Brig'e R.E. joined the company & was attached to No 3 (91st Inf. Bde.) section. Lt. Stevenson takes over temporary command of No 3 section vice B.G. Hosk.	
	May 15th/19th		H.Q. digging with 150 men continued & trenches to 20th Inf. Bde. Battle H.Q. finished. Cable line between Battle H.Q. of the Div. & 20th Bde. relaid in deeper trench. G.P. Exchange moved from 41 South (F.15.d.1.8) to Dombardment Trench (F.15. F.15.d.15.) to Dombardment Trench. One detachment under division o/c Lt. Grup it undertook the relifting of all men who he could be spared (including motor-cyclists orderlies 57th SI. etc.) out finishing trench from GRANTOWN to 20th Inf. Bde Battle Hd. Qrs. One detachment laying in wire as digging proceeded. Lines in trenches continued.	Maj. Ret.
	May 20th			
	May 21st		Company parades. T & as laid from existing lines into BOIS DES TAILLES. No use of 20th Inf. Bde.	
	May 22nd/23rd		Night digging continued. One detachment clearing up trenches in 91st Inf Bde area in preparation for more Tacs laid into MORLANCOURT far	

Army Form C. 2118.

1st Divn. Signal Co

WAR DIARY
or
INTELLIGENCE SUMMARY.
(Erase heading not required.)

Place	Date	Hour	Summary of Events and Information	Remarks and references to Appendices
	May 24th		2nd 20th Inf. Bde. position. Capt. Lowdon returns to Hd. Qrs., leaving Lt. Briggs in charge of No. 3 section. 50 men from the Company digging dug outs in billets to 150 Infantry men.	
	May 25th		9th Inf. Bde. moves to GRANTOWN. Lt. takes over from the 20th Inf. Bde. 20th Inf. Bde. moves to MORLANCOURT. Telegraphic communication through 22nd Inf. Bde. 1st Bde. it co-operation therewith with regard to formed dispatches etc. 2/o 2nd Bde R.T.A. move to GRANTOWN & co-operate with 9th Inf. Bde. c/o of BRAY. 2 Detachments my HQ- wiring in trenches near REDUIT "A" Y Miles	
	May 25/26th		AVENUE 75 Infantry by day- fig by night near GROVETOWN. 150 Infantry redigging trench from GROVETOWN to join up with a trench of 23rd Inf. Bde. previously made to BRAY left by by 2 Detachments.	
	May 27th		150 men start trench from GROVETOWN - GRANTOWN. 2 Detachments laying wires in trenches from	

Army Form C. 2118.

WAR DIARY
or
INTELLIGENCE SUMMARY.
(Erase heading not required.)

7th Div. l Signal Coy R.E.

Place	Date	Hour	Summary of Events and Information	Remarks and references to Appendices
	May 28th		Detachments Nos 2, 3 & 4 left for Bois des Tailles at 2·0pm under command of 2/Lt J.H. Watson where Coy are camping in order to be closer to the work.	
	May 29th		NA36 laid from YGR to ZTR & 21P.R. This runs in Cable Trench to Lucknow Redoubt.	
	May 31st		Circuit Diagram of Communications to date attached.	

MBConner
CAPT.
CMDG. 7TH DIV. SIGNAL COY. R.E.

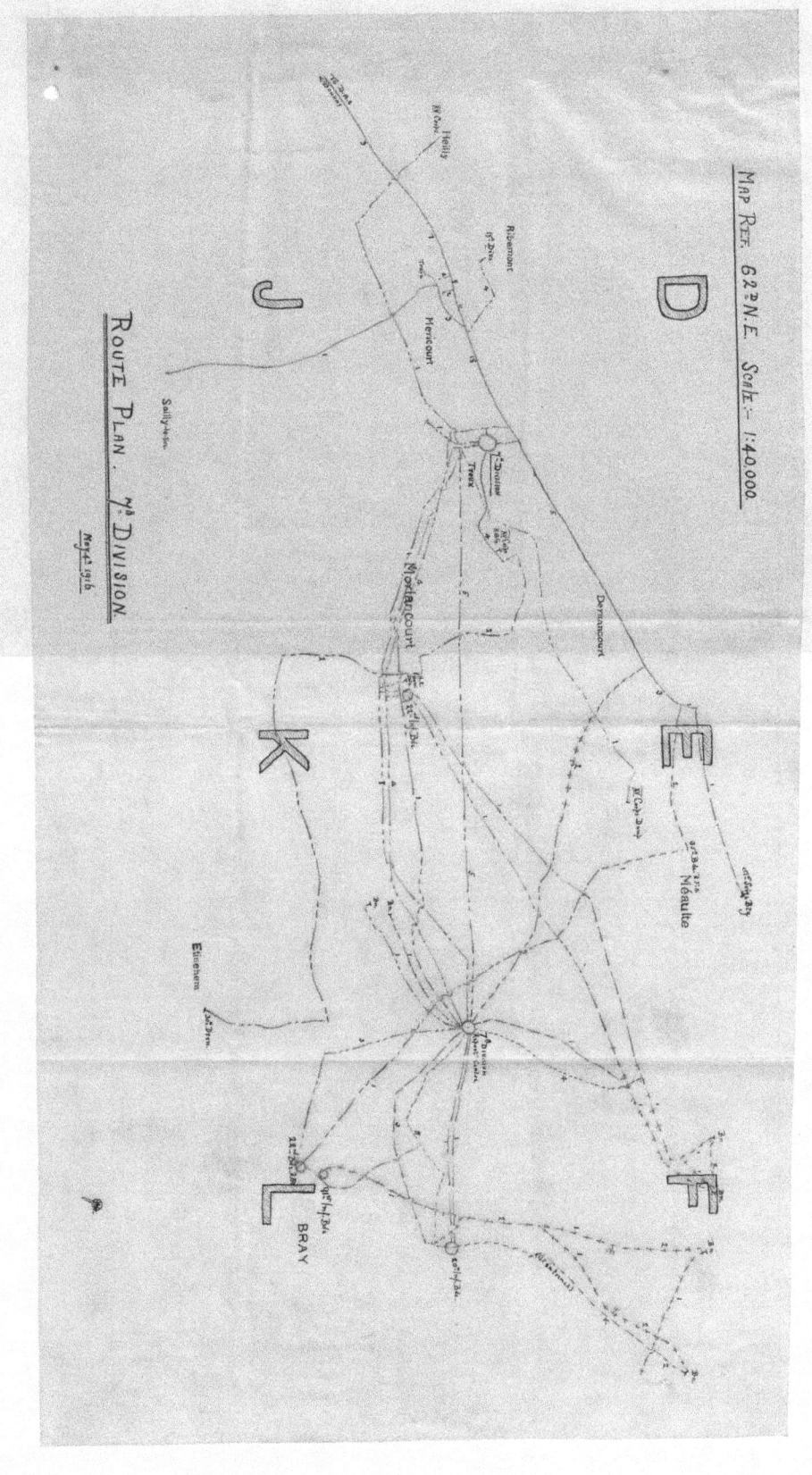

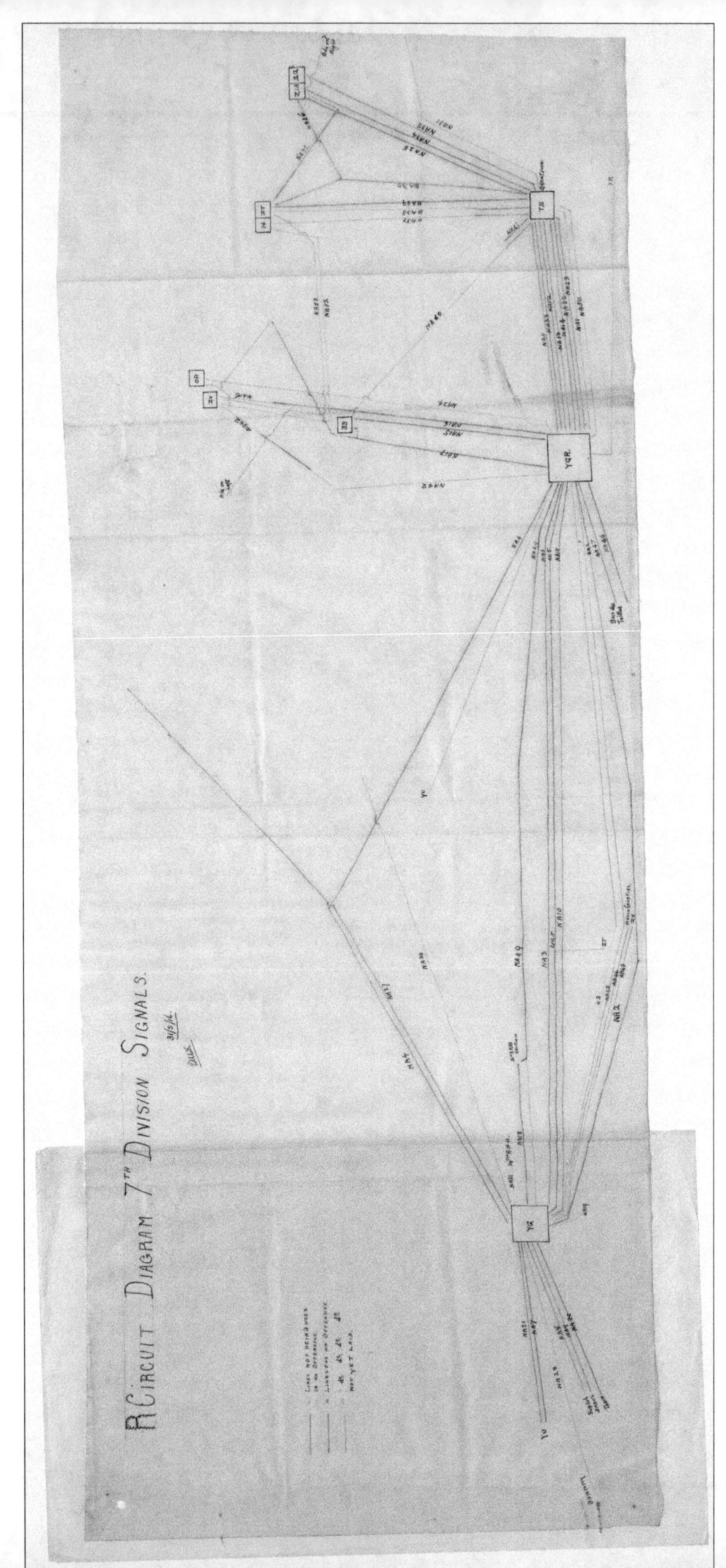

Army Form C. 2118.

WAR DIARY for JUNE 1916.

7th Div'l Signal Coy R.E.

Vol 6

or

INTELLIGENCE SUMMARY.

(Erase heading not required.)

Instructions regarding War Diaries and Intelligence Summaries are contained in F. S. Regs., Part II. and the Staff Manual respectively. Title pages will be prepared in manuscript.

Place	Date	Hour	Summary of Events and Information	Remarks and references to Appendices
1916				
June	1st		N.A.17 laid from CITADEL – REDUIT "A" – BONTÉ; Posts continued. First part of french tramway lines laid.	
"	2nd		N.A.17 continued. Tecs off lines to BRAY reeled up.	
"	3rd		Two detachments digging in lines at GROVETOWN. N.A.1 and N.A.50 laid in CLYDE	
"	4th		Digging in continued. N.A.1 and N.A.50 continued.	
"	5th		Digging in continued. N.A.1 and N.A.50 continued.	
"	6th		N.A.37 and N.A.38 laid in SHANNON to ESSEX AVE; Old N.A.1 lifted. Test boxes installed; Part of lateral brigade line to BRAY lifted.	
"	7th		N.A.37 and N.A.38 continued; line from BRAY – CITADEL lifted. N.A.17 buried near TRENCH A/12. Test boxes continued.	
"	8th		N.A.37 and N.A.38 continued; N.A.36 replaced by Armoured Twin. Tramway lines completed and telephones installed.	
"	9th		N.A.37 and N.A.38 continued. N.A.36 continued. Tramway System finished off.	
"	10th		N.A.25 (N.A.C.6) replaced in NORFOLK AVE. by Armoured Twin. N.A.36 continued. Posts	

Army Form C. 2118.

WAR DIARY or INTELLIGENCE SUMMARY

(Erase heading not required.)

7th D.vh. Signal Coy R.E.

Place	Date	Hour	Summary of Events and Information	Remarks and references to Appendices
1916	June 10th (cont'd)		Posts laid in WELLINGTON AVE.	
	11th		N.A.25. continued. N.A.52 and N.A.53 laid from ESSEX AVE. to BRAY CROSS. Posts in WELLINGTON AVE. finished.	
	12th		N.A.24 and N.A.42 laid from TRENCH 14 to BONTE'. N.A.52 and N.A.53 continued. N.A.40 laid up. INTERMEDIATE LINE to BRAY CROSS.	
	13th		N.A.24 and N.A.42 continued. N.A.40 - N.A.52 - N.A.53 continued up INTERMEDIATE LINE. Crossings at BRAY CROSS done.	
	14th		N.A.24 and N.A.42 continued. N.A.40 - N.A.52 - N.A.53 continued. N.A.24 continued. Tramway line relaid. Crossings finished.	Wireless sets against (2T and sets)
	15th		N.A.52 and N.A.53 laid from TRENCH 14 - BONTE'. N.A.51 laid into BILLON WOOD. N.A.40. finished. N.A.52 and N.A.53 continued. N.A.24 continued.	
	16th		N.A.52 and N.A.53 finished. Tees off N.A.5 embarked for 50th Brigade. Line laid from BOIS-DES-TAILLES to GROVETOWN EXCHANGE. Line laid from GROVETOWN EXCHANGE to ORCHARD CAMP.	

Army Form C. 2118.

7th Divl Signal Coy R E

WAR DIARY
or
INTELLIGENCE SUMMARY

(Erase heading not required.)

Place	Date	Hour	Summary of Events and Information	Remarks and references to Appendices
1916	June 17th		N.A 24 continued.	
"	18th		Putting in poles Cable Trench to Front Line. Finishing N.A. 24.	
"	19th		Putting poles in Cable Trench to Front Line. Continue overhauling	overhauling
			Lines from GROVETOWN to GRANTON.	
"	20th		Laying 6 pairs in deep French from RIGHT O.P EXCHANGE to Front line. French laying lines to 22nd BRIGADE ADVANCED HEADQUARTERS	
	21st		Owing to 3 pairs from TRE UX to GROVETOWN (L.1.d.4.5.) being required by Corps. Signals, a 10-Line Exchange was installed at GROVETOWN. NA4, NA10. and P17 (NA43) were used as junction lines to TRE UX Ex., Other ects were 14th Bde RHA. 22nd Bde RFA. 35th (Bde. RFA and 20th 2/1Bde. Div Bomb Store., Units in Bois des Taillas. Adv. 18th Div. Work was continued on pairs in cable trench from Right O.P. Ex. to front line.	
	22nd to 24th		Lines in deep cable trench continued. Second Junction Line from Right O.P. Ex. to Left O.P. Ex. started. Overhauling lines in Shannon trench, which had been damaged by traffic.	

Army Form C. 2118.

WAR DIARY
or
INTELLIGENCE SUMMARY.
(Erase heading not required.)

Place	Date	Hour	Summary of Events and Information	Remarks and references to Appendices
	1916 June			
	27th		35th Bde. R.F.A. moved from GROVETOWN to TRENCH 12. (Top of Maricourt Cy) worked to div's through Grovetown Ex. on MA15, and by Vibrators on N917. All lines controlled by Dinions. Arranging Grantown test office, and installing instruments. Arranging Grovetown office continued.	
	28th		Div'n H.Q. under orders to move to Rolo H.Q. at GROVETOWN. Arrangements made accordingly and move commenced. About midday owing to postponement of operations, move was cancelled. The following disposition of signal Coy. H.Q. and W.1. Section was then made.— Everybody moved to posts as previously arranged except operators and orderlies required to man TREUX Office. Maintenance of lines from TREUX to MORLANCOURT and GROVETOWN. undertaken by 17th Div. Sig Coy NE. GROVETOWN ——— 6 linemen and one office lineman BRANTOWN ——— C.S.M. Detach 13, 2 or 1 cable wagon, limber wagon & operator TRENCH 12. ——— 6 linemen (H.Q. 35th Bde RFA)	

Army Form C. 2118.

WAR DIARY
or
INTELLIGENCE SUMMARY.

(Erase heading not required.)

Instructions regarding War Diaries and Intelligence Summaries are contained in F. S. Regs., Part II. and the Staff Manual respectively. Title pages will be prepared in manuscript.

Place	Date	Hour	Summary of Events and Information	Remarks and references to Appendices
	1916 June.			
	29th		Position on evening of 28th. All lines patrolled and proved. Arrangements in Grovetown Office completed.	
	30th		Drn. H.Q. moved to Adv. H.Q. at Grovetown. All Sdns moved to Bdes. H.Qs. as previously arranged. Arrivals working on circuit diagram. No. Her attached circuit diagram. K. Wilson circuit which ods P1 and P.J. moved to 202 Bde. H.Q. at Essex Av. P.J. erected. Signals to Corps ect (P.J.) very good. Attentions attached.	App. 1. 1. Circuit Diagram on 30th. 2. Diagrammatic plan of cable trenches, giving names. 3(A) Route plans of Bde section systems. (B) (C)

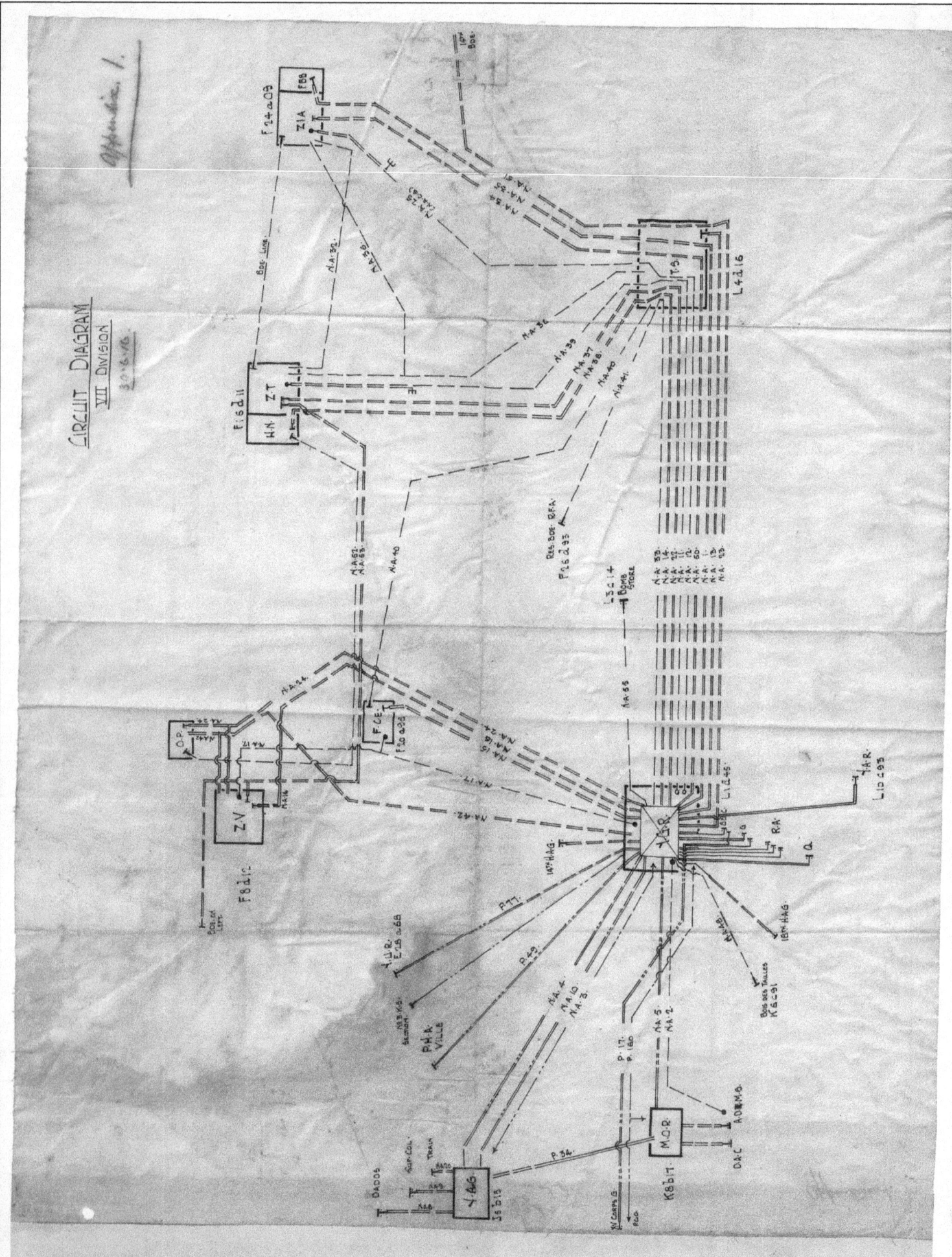

WAR DIARY for July 1916.
INTELLIGENCE SUMMARY

Army Form C. 2118.

7th Divl Signal Coy. R.E.

Vol 9

Place	Date	Hour	Summary of Events and Information	Remarks and references to Appendices
Map reference:— Albert Combined Sheet 1/40000 and MONTAUBAN 1/20,000.	1916 July 1st		All lines tested, lineman starting at 4 a.m. Two again patrolled at midday and 8 p.m. This arrangement was carried out daily. Telephone and Telegraph (vibrator) communication was continuous throughout the day. At 11 pm one Wireless set (P¹) was ordered to Mametz. P⁶ removed and erected at Essex Av.	
	2nd		35th Bde R.F.A. moved to Stafford St⁶ in Fricourt. (F.11.2) Telephone office was in old Bn. Signal dugout. Ble. worked to dinn on NAC6, an old Bn. line, NAC6 was gone to NA25 to SHANTOWN (T5) Test office and then to GROVETOWN by MA12. Instrument working was Tel. pat. DIII. to Bigger Ex. NA15. joined to NA40 giving another line to Grandon (T5 from Grovetown) (D9) operator withdrawn from O.P. station at Bowl Redoubt. Wireless set at Mametz in operation at 4 a.m. and continuously throughout the day. Magneto messages were sent, as Telephone communication was maintained throughout. 91st Inf. Bde. worked vibrator on NA36. On 3rd, when 22nd Inf. Bde. moved, NA17 was joined to NA52, which was joined to NA32. 20th Bde and 91st Bde then worked vibrator on this circuit.	

WAR DIARY
INTELLIGENCE SUMMARY

Army Form C. 2118.

Place	Date	Hour	Summary of Events and Information	Remarks and references to Appendices
	July 1916 3rd		22nd Inf Bde. moved in afternoon to Mametz near HALTE on Fricourt - Bronfay Rd. just west of MAMETZ. Communication was established by extending a Bn. line of 22nd Bde. (Z.T.2.) through old German trenches and Hidden Wood to Bde Reports. Extension was made with single D5. Jegged to wall of trenches with 8" bare poles. Cable was laid out from 1 mile drum carried in rafter by two men. Two linemen were left at 22nd Inf Bde. H.Q. to maintain this new line. Also two linemen were sent to H.Q. 91st Bde to maintain N906 to 35th Bde. Three linemen were drawn from attached D5. on treeandphones at GRANTHAM. 80th Bde R.F.A. moved from GIBRALTAR to CARNOY line. Laid and joined to NA36.	
	4th		As 20th Bde Bns. were withdrawn from the line on night 3rd/4th inst, a line 273. from Essex Av. to our old front line became spare. This line was extended to 22nd Inf. Bde. The extension was laid in the same trench as the one laid on 3rd inst. and labelled PA2. A teeoff 273 was led into 35th Bde. 273 was used as reliable line to 22nd Inf. Bde. and 35th Bde. NAG and 273 were used as telephone lines. Tel. Port DIII. being added.	

WAR DIARY
or
INTELLIGENCE SUMMARY
(Erase heading not required.)

Army Form C. 2118.

Place	Date	Hour	Summary of Events and Information	Remarks and references to Appendices
	July, 1916 4th (Monday)		Two detachts laid a single D5 line from 22nd Inf Bde H.Q. to Bn. H.Q. at Quens Nullah. x.29.d.97. for use of Bde. Scots. who had not time to lay the necessary lines themselves, for an attack on evening of 4th inst. P.J. wireless set moved 22nd Infy Bde H.Q. Set in operation about 9 p.m. P.I. wireless set moved to Quens Nullah Westend, erected and working about 6.30 p.m. Latter set was heavily shelled throughout the operations during the night and aerial frequently broken, but this was quickly repaired and communication maintained. No operation messages were sent as Telephone communication was maintained was established.	
	5th		P.I. wireless set moved to 22 Infy Bde H.Q. near HALTE but was not erected. PJ maintained communication with P.V. the Cypress. Tea off NA51 laid to Durham French 91st Bde. Line laid- G.P. in Shannon. This line was laid as spare to Durham Fr. as all units were moving into that sector. 113th Infy Bde relieved 91st Bde. Divnl Operators and Linemen remained with 113th Bde till the 6th inst.	

Army Form C. 2118.

WAR DIARY
or
INTELLIGENCE SUMMARY.
(Erase heading not required.)

Instructions regarding War Diaries and Intelligence Summaries are contained in F. S. Regs., Part II. and the Staff Manual respectively. Title pages will be prepared in manuscript.

Place	Date	Hour	Summary of Events and Information	Remarks and references to Appendices
	July 1916 6th		38th Divn relieved 7th Divn. Signal Coy. moved to old billets at TREUX during the afternoon. Lt. Smith and I cable detachts were left with 38th Divn to assist with maintenance. Lt Watson and wireless set also remained with 38th Divn. Office linemen at Grovetown and Grovetown also remained. Linemen at Grovetown was withdrawn on 7th inst. All lines were handed over, working well, as per circuit diagram attached. All exchanges and test board at Grovetown were left in use at Grovetown; only wibratos and DII telephones and bell telephones were relieved.

Up to this date, there was no interruption in telephone or telegraph communication with Bdes., though when Bdes. moved esty. was sometimes caused by insufficient or too late information being given about new position. The ble lines were very useful and were extended for divnl not intercom possible. The wireless sets were not used for messages, transmission of, but were always available, and ready for immediate use. The system of lines in 3' cable trenches with several routes to each Bde. proved invaluable for offensive operations. Coupled with | App. 1. |

T./134. Wt. W708–776. 50(090. 4/15. Sir J. C. & S.

Army Form C. 2118.

WAR DIARY
or
INTELLIGENCE SUMMARY.
(Erase heading not required.)

Instructions regarding War Diaries and Intelligence Summaries are contained in F. S. Regs., Part II. and the Staff Manual respectively. Title pages will be prepared in manuscript.

Place	Date	Hour	Summary of Events and Information	Remarks and references to Appendices
	July 1916		filled in trenches. They have the advantage of being easy to follow by day or night, and if the lines are carefully laid in the same order throughout and kept in. They are easily repaired. Metallic circuits must be used. Shallow trenches, with several routes, give sufficient protection from shell fire for offensive operations, and giving as safe a system as one with depth of 5ft trenches and fewer routes, with less labour.	
	7th		Divn M.G. at Treux. Communication was as under:— Telephone line to DD field in Treux. Telephone line & 91st Bde & Brine. Telephone through 15th Corps Ex. to 222 Woll at Holly. L.R.A. and C.R.E. remain at GROVE TOWN.	
	8th		Overhauling waggons and equipment. Company resting. 25 mls D 5 cable selected by Bn. Sclm Electd. to 38th Div W. NA 72, 24 formed Relin at 16 & 17 were lifted.	

T.2134. W.t. W708-776. 500/000. 4/15. Sir J. C. & S.

Army Form C. 2118.

WAR DIARY
or
INTELLIGENCE SUMMARY.
(Erase heading not required.)

Instructions regarding War Diaries and Intelligence Summaries are contained in F. S. Regs., Part II. and the Staff Manual respectively. Title pages will be prepared in manuscript.

Place	Date	Hour	Summary of Events and Information	Remarks and references to Appendices
	July 1916.	9ᵃᵐ	Nos 2 and 4 cable detachts moved from GRANTOWN to TREUX, and No 1 detacht moved out to GRANTOWN instead. In addition, Capt O'Connor and Capt Lawson, 6 linemen and 12 operators moved to GROVETOWN to assist 38th Divl Signals. On the evening of 9th, BF cable section from XV Corps installed the armoured twin NAC 7, by two D5s, to 113th Bde. at DANTZIG ALLEY. This was completed about 3 p.m on 10th. No 1. Detacht. overhauled a single D5 line from GRANTOWN to POMMIERS REDOUBT. The 7th Divl Linemen and operators were distributed at Divl H.Q. and Bdes. to assist the 38th Divl linemen and operators. PJ wireless set moved from HALTE, to DURHAM TRENCH. Lt. SMITH established visual stations, manned by 7th Divl Signallers, at DURHAM TRENCH, DANTZIG ALLEY, and POMMIERS REDOUBT. 38th Divl Signals laid a single D5 line across country from HALTE (115th Bde) to DANTZIG ALLEY (113th Bde) and POMMIERS REDOUBT (114th Bde) (By 38th Divn.) His line was joined to the cross country line which had previously been laid from GROVETOWN to GRANTOWN in THAMES Cable trench, and then across country to HALTE. Between 6 p.m. and 9 p.m., the following alterations in H.A. Bde. H.Q. took place.	

WAR DIARY
or
INTELLIGENCE SUMMARY.
(Erase heading not required.)

Army Form C. 2118.

Instructions regarding War Diaries and Intelligence Summaries are contained in F. S. Regs., Part II. and the Staff Manual respectively. Title pages will be prepared in manuscript.

Place	Date	Hour	Summary of Events and Information	Remarks and references to Appendices
	July 1916	9th (contin)	122nd Bde. R.F.A. (36th Div Arty) went into action with H.Q. at DALE STREET near MANSEL COPSE, and 120th Bde. R.F.A. (38th Div Arty) with their H.Q. at junction of HIGH ST. and CROSS STREET. 38th Div Signals laid a single D5 line to 122nd Bde. who arranged to join them through to 150th Bde.	
		10th	Beaucle Station extended 11h35 from old British front line to POMMIERS REDOUBT and from D5 stopped in old German trenches. 39th Div'n attached MAMETZ WOOD and 3pm. Telephone and telegraph communication was maintained to all Bdes and auxiliary means were not used, though constantly available.	
		11th	38th Div'n was relieved by 7th Div'n. 7th Division H.Q opened at DURHAM TRENCH at 5pm. TREUX Office closed at 1pm. Cable detacht arrived at Durham TRENCH about midday and were employed till dark establishing office and local lines to staff offices at Minden Post. Communication as per attached diagram.	App. 2.

WAR DIARY
or
INTELLIGENCE SUMMARY.

Army Form C. 2118.

Place	Date	Hour	Summary of Events and Information	Remarks and references to Appendices
	July 1916.			
	12th		22nd Bde. R.E.O. moved from DURHAM TRENCH to VALLEY TRENCH. (Appx.1.1.) Communication established by extending RA2. one of the lines from RIGHT O.P. Ex. to front line, in 7ft cable trench. Circuit working DIII, exit return.	
			14th Bde. R.H.A. moved to front near BULGAR Pt. (F.14.b.9.0.) NBC7, (metallic) Ziz'd off via Bulgar Pt.	
			31st Bde. R.F.A. occupied old H.Q. in Billon Wood and worked on NA51. NA35 and NBC7. extension in front of old British front line were overhauled. Also single D5 line to Pommiers Redoubt, which was relayed in communication trenches. Visual station at DANTZIG ALLEY withdrawn. Also Div2 operator and linesman at rear of 122nd Bde R.F.A. and laid in Queens Rd and Cross St. to 1202 Bde R.F.A.	
			(3.25.b.7.3)	
			Detach'd started at 5am to lay lines to WHITE TRENCH for 22nd Inf.Bde. which moved there during the afternoon.	
	13th		No 4. detach't. laid Ladder line D5. on ground, from 20th Bde. Pommiers Redoubt to White Tr. This line was later joined to a single D5 line laid straight across country from Durham Tr. to Pommiers Redoubt. by 22nd Bde. R.F.A. (P.43)	
			No 3 detacht. Extended RA1 from front end of 7ft cable trench, to 27th Bde H.Q. This line (PRA)	

Army Form C. 2118.

WAR DIARY
or
INTELLIGENCE SUMMARY.
(Erase heading not required.)

Place	Date	Hour	Summary of Events and Information	Remarks and references to Appendices
	July 1916 13th		Line was laid in communication Trenches, stapled to wall, running past E. end of MAMETZ village to NW end of White Trench & thence to Bde H.Q. No 1 detach. completed relaying N°4.3 to Pommiers Redoubt and laid Tee (PP5) off it, via Montauban alley and White Trench to 22nd Inf Bde H.Q. No 2 detach. laid single D5 line PA6, from 4th Bde R.H.A. to Durham Tr. This line was stapled in communication Trenches to Mindin Post and then poled to Signal Office. B.F. section. laid a single D5 line from our old front line, teeing into PA6. The line was laid via B.Gn. Alley, Fritz Trench to 22nd Bde R.F.A. and thence across country to 22nd Bde, at White Tr. The line from Halte to Pommiers Redoubt was joined to this line. The Corps. Wireless Set. (PV) moved to DURHAM TRENCH, and PJ moved to 22nd Bde. at White Tr. P1 remained at Pommier Redoubt. Visual stations at Durham Trench, Pommiers Redoubt and White Trench. Communications on evening 13th, as per attached diagram.	Appx 3.

Army Form C. 2118.

WAR DIARY
or
INTELLIGENCE SUMMARY.
(Erase heading not required.)

Place	Date	Hour	Summary of Events and Information	Remarks and references to Appendices
	July 1916 14th		7th Divn attacked German second line, and BAZENTIN-LE-PETIT. at 3.25 a.m., and all objectives reached. (S.19.d.8.8.) C.S.M. Rodwell and H/R. and A. Ritchie, proceeded to the South corner of Mametz Wood. The proposed H.Q. of the 91st Infl.Bde. arriving there about 9 a.m. They laid two single lines about 200 yds apart to White Trench near the 22nd Bde H.Q. One line was teed to P94. and the other to P95. The Bde. M.G. did not move till about 6 p.m. The C.S.M. remained out with detacht. till 7 p.m. and maintained the lines they had just laid, with difficulty. The valley south of Mametz Wood was heavily shelled. The 91st Bde. moved about 8 p.m. to the East corner of Caterpillar Wood. (S.20.d.9.9.). The tee off P94. already laid was extended along the top of Caterpillar Wood by "B" substitute by two aun- Linesmen, Corp. Ford. and Mugglestone. No 3 detacht. laid a line from 22nd Bde at White Trench. to 81st Bde R.F.A. at W. end of Caterpillar Wood. (S.20.c.3.7.). Line was single D5. laid on ground. At 23rd Bde. it was joined to P93. 122nd Bde. R.F.A. who had moved to White Trench at same place as 22nd Inf.Bde. were also put on this line (P93) No 3 detacht. also laid a tee off P95. from junction of White Trench and	

WAR DIARY
or
INTELLIGENCE SUMMARY.
(Erase heading not required.)

Army Form C. 2118.

Place	Date	Hour	Summary of Events and Information	Remarks and references to Appendices
	July.1916 14th (contd)		and Montauban Alley. This line was laid alongside Montauban Alley, as the details fell rather short of Longueval, then down East trench, and along top of Caterpillar Wood to 35th Bde. R.F.A. at 2.27. a.2.5. A te off was taken in 91st Bde. The line worked intact, for 35th and 91st Bdes to D.H.Q. Two wire buries were left with 91st Inf.Bde. to maintain lines from 91st and 35th Bde.	
			Visual stations did not work.	
			One operated and linesman were disposed as under.	
			Formation H.Q. Operators. Linesmen.	
			22nd Inf.Bde. 3. 4.	
			20th Inf.Bde. 3. 4.	
			91st Inf.Bde. 2. 2.	
			1st Bde. RHA 2. 1.	
			22nd Bde. RFA. 2. 1.	
			35th Bde. RFA. 2. 1.	
			120th Bde. RFA. 2. —	
			P.1. Wireless set moved to Mametz Wood in morning, and later moved to Caterpillar Wood with the 91st Bde. H.Q.	

Army Form C. 2118.

WAR DIARY
or
INTELLIGENCE SUMMARY
(Erase heading not required.)

Place	Date	Hour	Summary of Events and Information	Remarks and references to Appendices
	July, 1916 15th		No. 2 Detachment laid new Tee to 35th Bde R.F.A. along Montauban Alley to S.27.c.3.9. then along a new trench to Bde Office, and picked up old overhead wire between 35th Bde and 91st Bde. The same detacht. then laid a line (PA7) from the 35th Bde. to the 120th Bde R.F.A. at the Briqueterie S.22.C.0.5. This line was stapled in new trench to Montauban Alley, then along Montauban Alley to just S. of Briqueterie then across the ground to the HQ. The line was extended from there across the ground to the 80th Bde R.F.A. who had moved to about S.22.a.1.6. Two linesmen from No. 2 detacht. were left with the 120th Bde R.F.A. No. 1 Detacht. picked up the Tee of PA4 to Waterlot wood and used the Tee off PA5 to ladder the line to 8/14th Bde. R.F.A. This detacht then laid a ladder tee off PA4 near S.22.d.4.6., to 91st Inf Bde., to 91st Inf Bde. in East trench, just behind their old position in Caterpillar wood. The ladder line was laid on the ground and stapled frequently. Nos. 3 and 4 detachments, laid an extension to the line to Zn, 80th Bde H.Q. at Carnoy. This line PA10. was a single D.5. poled cable line. The route followed was from N. end of Carnoy to Pommiers Redoubt, then just S. of Montauban Rd. to about	

Army Form C. 2118.

WAR DIARY
or
INTELLIGENCE SUMMARY.
(Erase heading not required.)

Instructions regarding War Diaries and Intelligence Summaries are contained in F. S. Regs., Part II. and the Staff Manual respectively. Title pages will be prepared in manuscript.

Place	Date	Hour	Summary of Events and Information	Remarks and references to Appendices
July 1916	15th (Cont'd)		About S26.d.9.1., then straight to 35th Bde. H.Q. No.2 detacht. laid out and jumped holes for the poles, and No.3 detacht. laid out the cable and erected the line. This line was put through very quickly, and was only broken once during the next few days. Wireless and Visual Stations r.o. on 18th inst.	
	16th		91st Inf. Bde. moved to HALTE in early morning. T.1 wireless set opened to White Trench but did not exist. Two own linemen with 91st Bde. were attached to 35th Bde. No.3 detacht. changed over the forked line. PAID. to the line to old 120th Bde. position at junction of HIGH ST. and CROSS ST. and extended line to old 80th Bde. position in Carnoy. This new extension was also joined D5. laid about 200 yds. E. of Carnoy - Montauban road, as far as Breslau Alley at A.3.c.1.7. From there the line was extended by No.1 detacht. up communication trenches through Montauban to Montauban Alley, at S.27.v.55 and was there laid to PP7. This line in Montauban was frequently cut by shell fire	

T.J134. Wt. W708—776. 500000. 4/15. Sir J.C. & S.

Place	Date	Hour	Summary of Events and Information	Remarks and references to Appendices
	July 1/16 16th (contd)		in the village. About this time during the operations, constant trouble was caused to the lines by the infantry during in the communication trenches. They cut the lines when digging holes in the walls of the trench, they burnt off the insulation, and sometimes cut it off to use as firelighters. They also removed the iron staples. Trouble was also caused by lines being broken by parties clearing the roads, but in many places the trenches were carefully filled in without breaking the lines.	
	19th		The 20th & 33rd Div were under orders to move up to BAZENTIN le GRAND WOOD during the afternoon. To provide communication to them the following arrangements were made. (a) Lines. No 2 detacht under Lt Smith laid a tee off PAA to the proposed H.Q. The line started at the N end of White trench and was laid in Wood trench and along the edge of the wood to track running through centre of wood Torride Wood. The line was stopped on the ground alongside this track to the N end of wood, then along N edge to point about S.13.d. 59. and then straight across country to N corner of	

WAR DIARY or INTELLIGENCE SUMMARY

Army Form C. 2118.

Place	Date	Hour	Summary of Events and Information	Remarks and references to Appendices
	July 1916 17th (contd)		of Bazentin le Grand wood. A loop was laid back to the corner of Mametz Wood. This line was laid under great difficulties, as a constant barrage was maintained on the western corner of Mametz wood. No. 3. Detacht. under Sgt. Downes, laid an extension to one leg of MA.35, from Pommiers Redoubt. This line was a single D5. to White Trench and then a ladder line to Bazentin le Grand wood. The whole line was stapled on the ground, except where it crossed Caterpillar valley, where it was overhead for one long bay. No. 4. detacht. under C.S.M. Rodwell, extended the tee off PA5 down East trench across Caterpillar valley to Marlboro' Trench, and thence to the "Snout", then through the wood to the Bde. H.Q. at S.19.b.2.3.. The line was stapled in communication trenches, and on the ground in the wood. It was looped across Caterpillar valley and through Bazentin wood. No. 4. detacht also laid a new line to the 80th and 120th Bdes from 35th Bde. This line was laid along some shelter trenches on N. side of Caterpillar valley. Four linesmen &c were left at the 30th Bde.H.Q., in Bazentin le Grand wood.	

Army Form C. 2118.

WAR DIARY
or
INTELLIGENCE SUMMARY.
(Erase heading not required.)

Place	Date	Hour	Summary of Events and Information	Remarks and references to Appendices
	July 1916 17th (contd)		**Wireless.** P.I. set moved to Bazentin le Grand wood and P.J. moved to 30th Bde A.F.A., H.Q. P.J. was heavily shelled from time to time, but no important message was sent through when the telephone communication was interrupted for a short time. **Visual.** A visual station was established at 30th Bde H.Q., this station worked to one at junction of Caterpillar Alley and Montauban Alley, which was in communication with Pommiers Redoubt. This station at Durham Tr. was closed. It was intended to send a station to the "Front," but owing to the move of 20th Inf Bde H.Q. being postponed, the orders were cancelled. As the move of 20th Bde was postponed, the linesmen were left out at Bazentin wood and one operator was sent from the 20th Bde, to Bazentin to keep the lines tested.	

WAR DIARY
or
INTELLIGENCE SUMMARY.
(Erase heading not required.)

Army Form C. 2118.

Instructions regarding War Diaries and Intelligence Summaries are contained in F.S. Regs., Part II. and the Staff Manual respectively. Title pages will be prepared in manuscript.

Place	Date	Hour	Summary of Events and Information	Remarks and references to Appendices
	July 1916			
	18th		In consequence of further postponement of the move forward of 25th Div. P1. wireless set was withdrawn to White Trench. Two detachments overhauled lines PA4, PA6 and PA9. And linemen made careful patrols of all other lines. 9th Hy. Bde. moved to Becordel. Messages were delivered by D.R. only. No.1 detacht. laid an extension to the leg of NAC7, to Pommiers Redoubt.	
	19th		Further overhauling of all lines N. of White Trench. P1. wireless set moved out to Bazentin-le-Grand wood. A visual station was established at the "Snout" in the evening working direct to Pommier Redoubt. The 20th Iny. Bde. H.Q. moved to Bazentin-le-Grand wood, about 7 p.m. and the 19th Bde. RHA. HQ. moved to Pommiers Redoubt. Communication on evening 19th, was as per attached circuit diagram	App 4.

Army Form C. 2118.

WAR DIARY
or
INTELLIGENCE SUMMARY.
(Erase heading not required.)

Instructions regarding War Diaries and Intelligence Summaries are contained in F. S. Regs., Part II. and the Staff Manual respectively. Title pages will be prepared in manuscript.

Place	Date	Hour	Summary of Events and Information	Remarks and references to Appendices
July 1916	20th		20th H.Q.R. attacked at 3.35 a.m. Throughout the day the lines to 20th Bde. and 20th Bde. R.F.A. were very frequently broken by shell-fire, but owing to the very excellent work of the linemen at these H.Qs. and at 35th Bde. H.Q. constant telephone communication was maintained. The aerials of the wireless sets were frequently broken, but were quickly repaired and communication reopened with the Corps set (R.V.) Visual communication was maintained throughout. All R.A.Bdes were relieved in the evening by the Div. arty. 5th Div. and lines taken over by them.	
	21st		Division H.Q. closed at 1 WINDEN POST at 10 p.m. Signal Coy moved off, under Lt Smith at 10.30 a.m. and proceeded to QUERRIEUX. Lt Watson with the 30 cwt lorry and Electric Lamp proceeded in advance. The wireless sets were handed over to O.C. Signals 5th Div. Div. H.Q. Report Centre opened at H.Q. of Div. Supply Col (at MERICOURT) at 10 a.m. A motorcyclist was stationed there. All by Bdes moved to DERNANCOURT. All communication was by D.R. All lines of Rec to 5th Div were taken over by them. Those or parts not required	

T2134. Wt. W708-776. 50000. 4/15. Sir J. C. & S.

Army Form C. 2118.

WAR DIARY
or
INTELLIGENCE SUMMARY.
(Erase heading not required.)

Instructions regarding War Diaries and Intelligence Summaries are contained in F.S. Regs., Part II. and the Staff Manual respectively. Title pages will be prepared in manuscript.

Place	Date	Hour	Summary of Events and Information	Remarks and references to Appendices
	July 1916 21st (contd)		By them were left, and a charger handed over to a Signals 352 Div., who took over the Divl. M.G.n. The principle difficulties experienced in maintaining telephonic communication were (a) faults caused by infantry Coys using our & the back communication trenches and (b) Shell fire on the forward lines only. This was reduced to a minimum by carefully avoiding the places where a barrage was most frequently put. No definite rules & plans can be laid down as to what type or types of lines should be used. Practically all types were tried, and each worked successfully if the proper conditions for its use were present. Most circuits were made up of several types of line, varying as the conditions changed throughout the route. Telephone communication can be maintained during and operations, but the success with which it can be done depends to a great extent on the efficiency and gallantry of the linesmen and on the proper organisation of their position at definite Test Points,	

WAR DIARY
or
INTELLIGENCE SUMMARY

Army Form C. 2118.

Place	Date	Hour	Summary of Events and Information	Remarks and references to Appendices
	July 1916 (contd)		Lines should be arranged so that each can be tied into several signal offices. This arrangement provides spare lines for everybody and simplifies the localisation of faults. Lines tested & adjusted = be tested at Bde HQrs thereby facilitating the delivery of orders, & the distribution of orders and instructions between forward & rear stations.	
			It is a decided advantage to have civil operators at R.A. as well as Bde HQ. The civil operator takes more interest in and understands the testing of lines arranged for and he is available to work a telegraph circuit which should always be available.	
			A separate telephone circuit to each Bde should be aimed at but if it is necessary to put more than one office on a line, the offices should be all R.A. or all Infy. Telegraph lines should be provided as well, whenever possible, but one line can easily take two offices, though they should preferably be all R.A. Bdes or all infy Bdes. Above all, every effort should be made to avoid having telegraph work on telephone circuits.	
			Have twice telegraph circuits for converse lines. Each circuit. D3 telephones connected to Bell telephones were used on the front offices, ring 10th difficulty of ringing them off the exchange with want of attention of ifs went out of order, & its difficulty of ringing though on faulty line.	

WAR DIARY or INTELLIGENCE SUMMARY

Army Form C. 2118.

Place	Date	Hour	Summary of Events and Information	Remarks and references to Appendices
	July 1916		Our vibrators were in possession of Spencer for the Games when Fullerphones would have been used, but the P.O. type gets easily out of adjustment, & does not appear to work well though in Sully but used.	

If telephone communication had broken down, visual communication by lamp or flag was always available, between the more isolated H.Qrs. and could always have been used. The country was very suitable for visual signalling, and arrangements were always made for its use.

Wireless

The workdone by the officer i/c the wireless Sets (2nd Lieut ----) was excellent throughout. Before the operations he perfected the training of the operators and had the sets adjusted to a workable condition. Both sets maintained constant communication with each other and with the Corps set. This means of communication would have been invaluable if telephonic communication had failed.

Pigeons.

Pigeons were distributed to all H.Qrs. and Battns when on the O.O. but few

Army Form C. 2118.

WAR DIARY
or
INTELLIGENCE SUMMARY.
(Erase heading not required.)

Instructions regarding War Diaries and Intelligence Summaries are contained in F.S. Regs., Part II. and the Staff Manual respectively. Title pages will be prepared in manuscript.

Place	Date	Hour	Summary of Events and Information	Remarks and references to Appendices
	July 1916		messages were sent by them, or by other means of communication being available. Some messages sent took rather a long time to reach the addressee, sometimes as much as three hours, but there is no doubt pigeons would be very useful to battns if other means of communication failed.	
	22nd		Divl. H.Q. opened at Billon-s-Somme at 3pm. Signal Coy. arrived about same time, having marched from GUERBIGNY. The evening of 22nd spent establishing Office and local Telephones.	
	23rd		Lines to Bdes arranged. Communications them as far as pigeons Communications arranged.	Apps.5.
	24th to 31st		Overhauling waggons and equipment. Cleaning harness and clothing. By resting generally.	

O.C. Penn. Capt.
O.C. 7. Div. Sig. Coy. R.E.

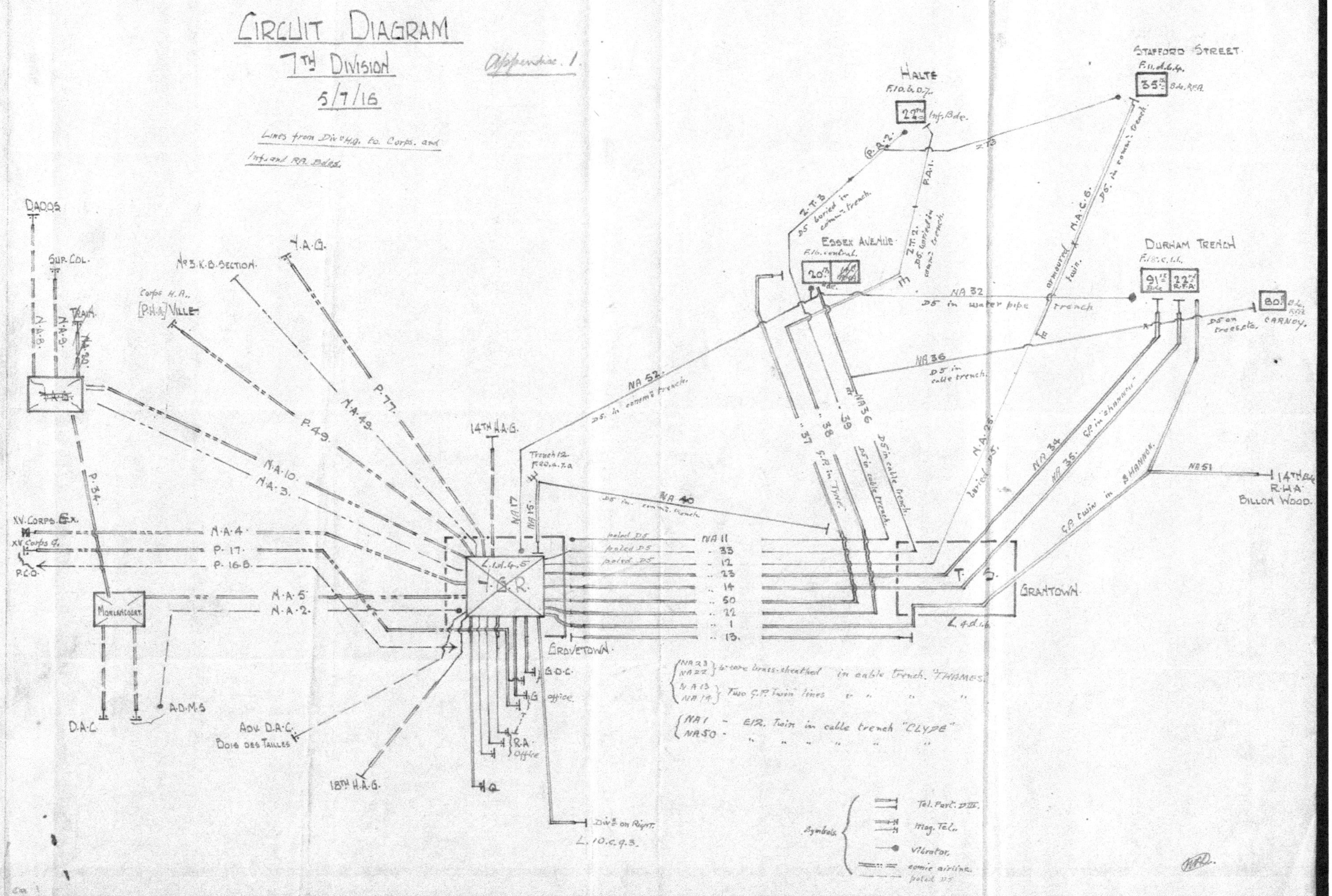
CIRCUIT DIAGRAM
7TH DIVISION
5/7/16
Appendix 1.
Lines from Divl H.Q. to Corps. and Inf. and RA. Bdes.
HALTE
F.10.b.0.7.
22nd Inf. Bde.
STAFFORD STREET
F.11.d.6.4.
35th Bde. RFA.
ESSEX AVENUE
F.16. central.
20th Bde.
DURHAM TRENCH
F.18.c.1.1.
91st Bde.
22nd R.F.A.
80th Bde. RFA
CARNOY.
14th Bde. R.H.A.
BILLON WOOD.
GRANTOWN.
GROVETOWN.
DADOS.
SUP. COL.
TRAIN.
No 3. K.B. SECTION.
Corps H.A.
[P.H.A.] VILLE
14TH H.A.G.
18TH H.A.G.
XV. CORPS. Ex.
XV. Corps G.
P.C.O.
MORLANCOURT.
D.A.C.
A.D.M.S.
ADV. D.A.C.
BOIS DES TAILLES
G.O.C.
G office.
R.A. Office
H.Q.
Divl. on Right.
L.10.c.9.3.
Trench 12
F.20.a.7.a
P.77.
N.A.49.
P.49.
N.A.10.
N.A.3.
N.A.4.
P.17.
P.16.B.
N.A.5.
N.A.2.
P.34.
N.A.B.
N.A.9.
NA 52.
D5. in comm. trench.
NA 40
D5 in comm. trench.
NA 17
NA 15
NA 11
33
12
23
14
50
22
1
13.
poled D5
NA 36
D5 in cable trench.
39
38
37
S.R. in TYNE.
NA 32
D5 in water pipe trench
D5 in cable trench.
NA 25.
buried D5.
NA 34.
NA 35.
C.P. in "SHANNON"
C.P. twin in SHANNON.
NA 51
D5 on trestles.
Z.T.3.
D5 buried in comm. trench.
Z.T.2.
D5 buried in comm. trench.
R.A.2.
R.A.1.
Z.T.3
N.A.C.6.
armoured twin.
D5. in comm. trench.
L.14.d.1.5.
L.4.d.1.6.
NA 23 } 6-core brass-sheathed in cable trench "THAMES"
NA 27
N.A.13 } Two C.P. twin lines
NA 14
NA 1 - E/R. Twin in cable trench "CLYDE"
NA 50 -
Symbols
Tel. Port. D III.
Mag. Tel.
Vibrator.
comic airline.
poled D5

Appendix 2

7th Division.
Circuit Diagram.
11.7.16.

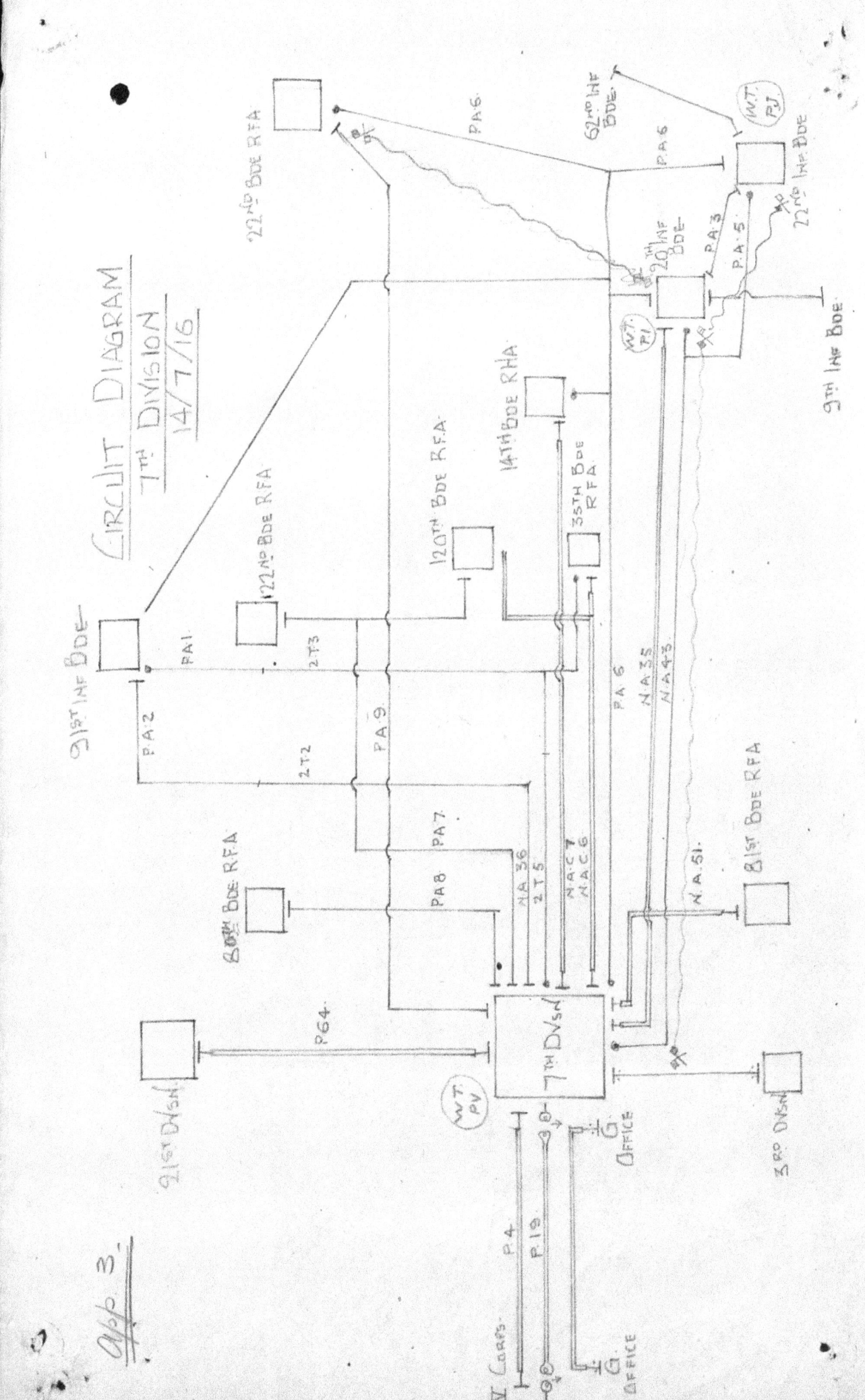

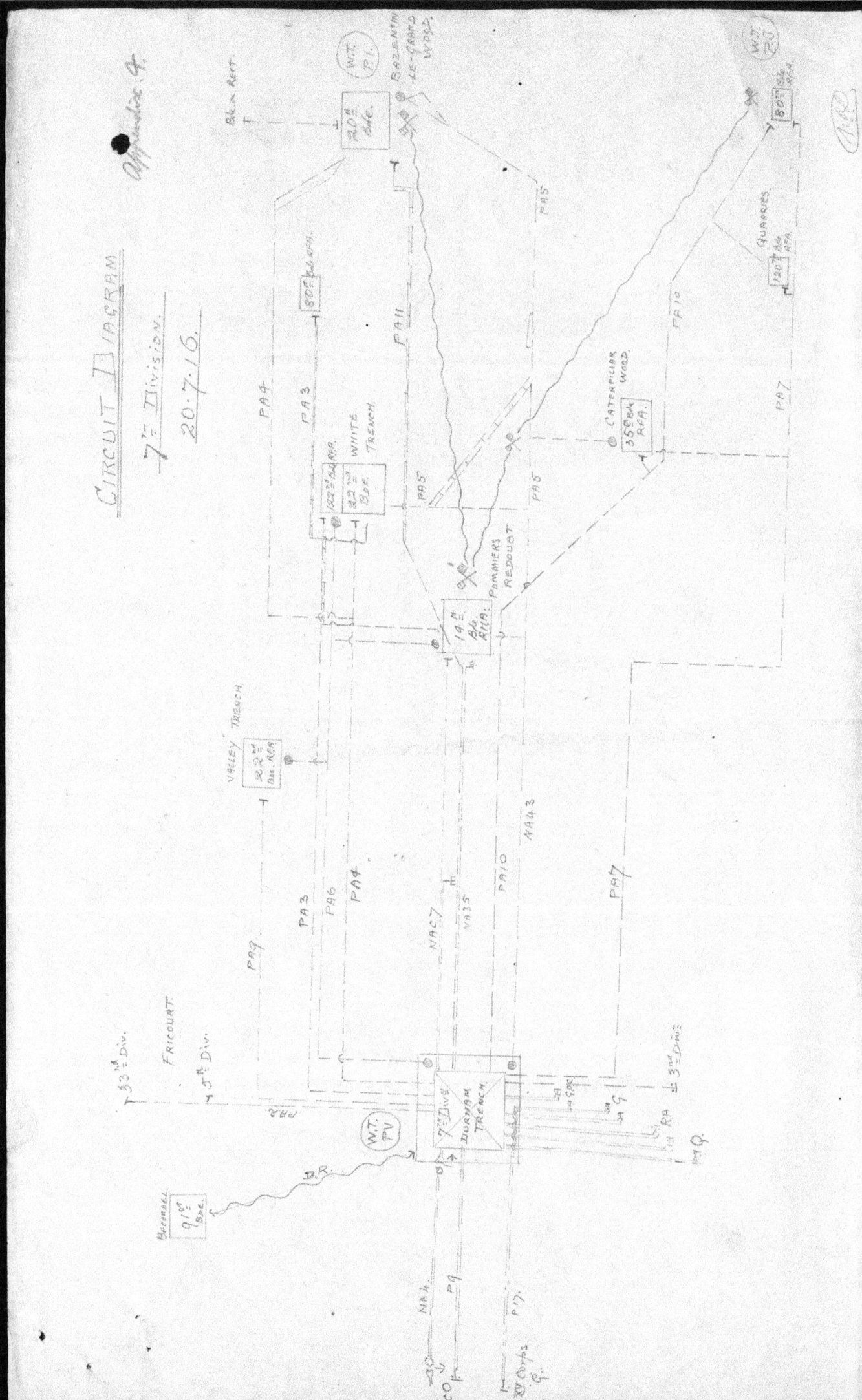

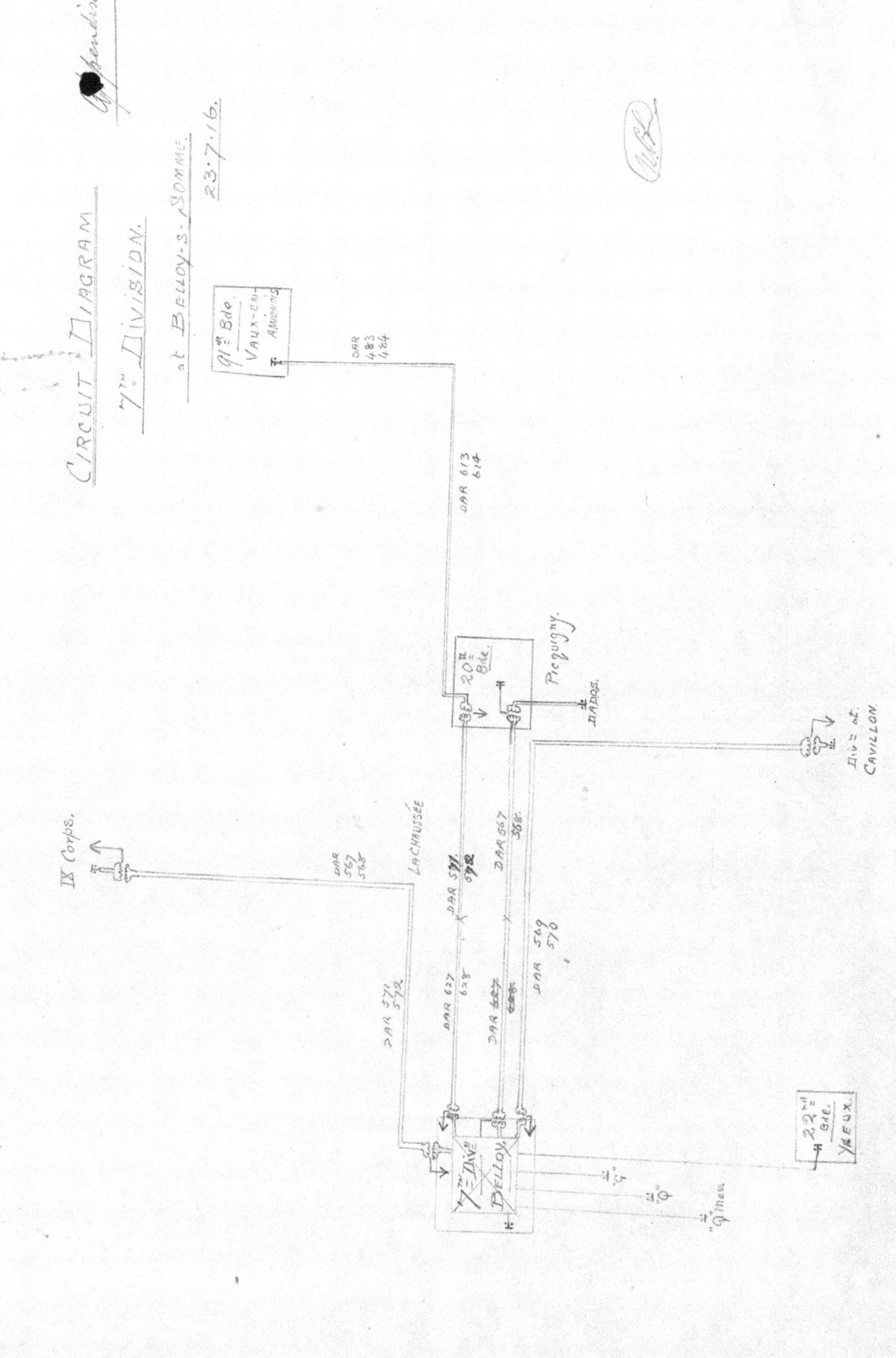

7th Divisional Engineers

7th DIVISIONAL SIGNAL COMPANY R. E.

AUGUST 1 9 1 6

Vol 10 Army Form C. 2118.
7th Divn Signal Coy. R.E. Vol 2

WAR DIARY
or
INTELLIGENCE SUMMARY
(Erase heading not required.)

Place	Date	Hour	Summary of Events and Information	Remarks and references to Appendices
	August 1916			
	1st to 6th		Does still nothing. A certain amount of signal drill and smoke helmet practice carried out.	
	7th		Coy. was present dismounted at inspection of 22nd Infbde. by Army Commander. No. 3 + 4 Sections inspected by O.C. Company in "marching order".	
	8th		No. 2 Section inspected. + HQo + No. 1 Section.	
	9th		General parade in the morning. Swimming etc in the afternoon.	
	10th		General Inspection of Harness in the afternoon.	
	11th		HQo + No 1 Sec. less office staff. and 30 men under Lieut C.M. SMITH moved off to QUERRIEU at 10.30 am by march route. Capt LAWSON R.E. proceeded to RIBEMONT to make arrangements about lines with XV Corps SIGNALS. LCpl. J. PORTELLI + GROUBER made arrangements about Coys offices with Brins about to the night.	watson

Army Form C. 2118.

WAR DIARY
or
INTELLIGENCE SUMMARY
(Erase heading not required.)

Place	Date	Hour	Summary of Events and Information	Remarks and references to Appendices
	11th and		Money again to HQrs. Again despatched to QUERRIEU with a further load of Stores where he was in effort with LT. SMITH + pick up the Company orders for the 13th.	
	12th		Party under LT. SMITH continued march from QUERRIEU to RIBEMONT. Party of 30 men under Cpl. HUGHES entrained HANGEST, detrained MERICOURT. Div. HQrs. opened at RIBEMONT 4 pm.	
	13th and 14th		Communication with Bdes. established. All lines being on railway, and allotted by XV Corps. Signals. Communication as per attached diagram.	App. I.
	15th		Lines to Bdes. carefully patrolled and a considerable amount of earth removed.	
	16th		MI9. put through as per diagram to 22nd Inf. Bde.; communication then being as per diagram.	App. II.

T./134. Wt. W708—776. 500,000. 4/15. Sir J. C. & S.

Army Form C. 2118.

WAR DIARY
or
INTELLIGENCE SUMMARY.
(Erase heading not required.)

Instructions regarding War Diaries and Intelligence Summaries are contained in F. S. Regs., Part II. and the Staff Manual respectively. Title pages will be prepared in manuscript.

Place	Date	Hour	Summary of Events and Information	Remarks and references to Appendices
August, 1916	17th	—	Survey made of all lines in Ribemont and pole diagrams made.	
	18th		Lt. SMITH moved to 14th Divl. Signals, and is attached for R.A. duties. Instrt. Repairer attached to XV Corps Signals to make test board and test out. All lines to Boies labelled. No. 1 Detachlt. joined Lt. SMITH at 14th Divn. also sent to 14th Divn.	
	19th		Rearranging and overhauling 10-line Cordless Switchboards stated. 2 telephone operators and 10-line cordless switchbd	
	20th		Lt. WATSON proceeded to DAOURS, to attend course of instruction in "Ground Induction Buzzer Sets".	
	21st		—	

Army Form C. 2118.

WAR DIARY
or
INTELLIGENCE SUMMARY.
(Erase heading not required.)

Instructions regarding War Diaries and Intelligence Summaries are contained in F. S. Regs., Part II. and the Staff Manual respectively. Title pages will be prepared in manuscript.

Place	Date	Hour	Summary of Events and Information	Remarks and references to Appendices
	August 1916			
	22nd		Just spares returned from Capt. Squales with test set, and terminal plug board. No. 2 detacht sent to 12th Divn "Afox Airsupport"	
	23rd		No. 3 detacht laid line for 12th Divn from R.A. exchange at POMMIERS REDOUBT to No. 4 Kite Balloon Section.	
	24th		Line to No. 4 Kite Balloon Sectn continued and finished.	
	25th		No. 3 and No. 4 Detachts commenced pooled cable route from Fricourt chateau to Pommiers Redoubt. Line to take 2 pairs, PC 21 and PC 22, and runs from S corner of Fricourt wood just N. east of Mametz, and then runs about 200 yds S of Mametz-Montauban road. No. 1 and No. 2 detachts overhauled lines, PC 5, PC 6 and PC 7, between Pommiers Redoubt and Fricourt, and relaid pair PC 5 and PC 6 forward to 35th Bde R.C.P. Line renewed PC 2G. Line runs along parapet of Montauban Alley.	

T.134. Wt. W708-776. 50C000. 4/15. Sir J. C. & S.

Army Form C. 2118.

WAR DIARY
or
INTELLIGENCE SUMMARY.
(Erase heading not required.)

Place	Date	Hour	Summary of Events and Information	Remarks and references to Appendices
	August, 1916			
	26th		PC22 bent through temporarily by laying out cable on ground.	
			No. 4 detachment laid twin poled D5. from Pommiers Redoubt to 3rd of Breslau Alley.	
			No. 1. detacht. extended that line with armoured twin to H.Q. 22nd Inf. Bde. (S.28.a,4,0)	
			Line was laid along parapet of Breslau Alley, then across open to trench at S.27.d.41	
			and then along new trenches through Montauban.	
			No. 2. detacht. laid route flag twin pairs + 3 single lines from Bridge at F.4.a.3.6 to	
			Fricourt Chateau to lead in. PC.5, PC.6, and AM1. and pair to cols. 14th Divn.	Apx III
			Divn H.Q. opened at FRICOURT CHATEAU at 5 pm. Communication that evening	
			as per diagram. Divn R.A. moved from Belle Vue Farm to Fricourt at 7 a.m.	
			Communication to R.A. Btys remained as from Belle Vue Farm except that lines	
			to Pommiers Redoubt were diverted to Fricourt Chateau.	
	27th		No. 3 detacht. completed PC 21 and PC 22.	
			No. 4 detacht. replaced poled cable in PC 23. with armoured cable laid in	
			Pommiers Lane, Pommiers Trench, and Mine Alley.	

Army Form C. 2118.

WAR DIARY
or
INTELLIGENCE SUMMARY
(Erase heading not required.)

Instructions regarding War Diaries and Intelligence Summaries are contained in F. S. Regs., Part II. and the Staff Manual respectively. Title pages will be prepared in manuscript.

Place	Date	Hour	Summary of Events and Information	Remarks and references to Appendices
August, 1916	30th		No 1. detacht. overhauled lines to 19th Bde. R.F.A. (YA9, 151 and 152.)	
			No 2. detacht. overhauled extention of line to 156th Bde. R.F.A.	
			No 4. cleared earth fault on PC23.	
			No 3. detacht. lifted spare lines in H.Q. dug outs.	
			Line overhauled by No 2 detacht was an extension laid by the 150th Bde when they moved forward to a new position. The line was very badly laid over a badly chosen route and only worked for a few hours. The line was abandoned.	
			The tee off G.V.I. laid on 29th inst. to new position 156th Bde. R.F.A. was also abandoned as it crossed a valley which was constantly bombarded and could not be properly maintained. Communication on 30th so per diagram attached	App. II.
	31st		No 3. detachment laid a tee of YA9152. to the 156th Bde. R.F.A. This line ran in old trenches most of the way, and worked well.	
			No 4 detacht controlled PE26 and PC23.	
			No 1 and 2 picked up spare lines at H.Q.	

Army Form C. 2118.

WAR DIARY
or
INTELLIGENCE SUMMARY.
(Erase heading not required.)

Instructions regarding War Diaries and Intelligence Summaries are contained in F. S. Regs., Part II. and the Staff Manual respectively. Title pages will be prepared in manuscript.

Place	Date	Hour	Summary of Events and Information	Remarks and references to Appendices
August, 1916.	31st (contd.)		The enemy made a strong counter attack today and heavily barraged the valley between 22nd Bde and 156th Bde. AFA, and 19th Bde RHA. Communication by telephone was never a trial this to all Bdes. PC25 was always through to the 19th Bde, and was only cut once during the night to the 22nd Bde. PC23 was not cut by shell fire though trouble was experienced with earth faults. PC27 was only cut twice in the forenoon. Communication was good to the 156th Bde after new line was laid, but had shocking from then was experienced at night, due to a bad telephone, and to the personnel wearing out gas helmets. There were a frequent source of trouble with them.

As other operations are still in progress, no comments are made on the methods of communication used. | |

G.G.C.
Capt.
O.C. 7th Div. Sig. Coy. R.E.

Circuit Diagram
7th Division
13th August 1916

Appendix I

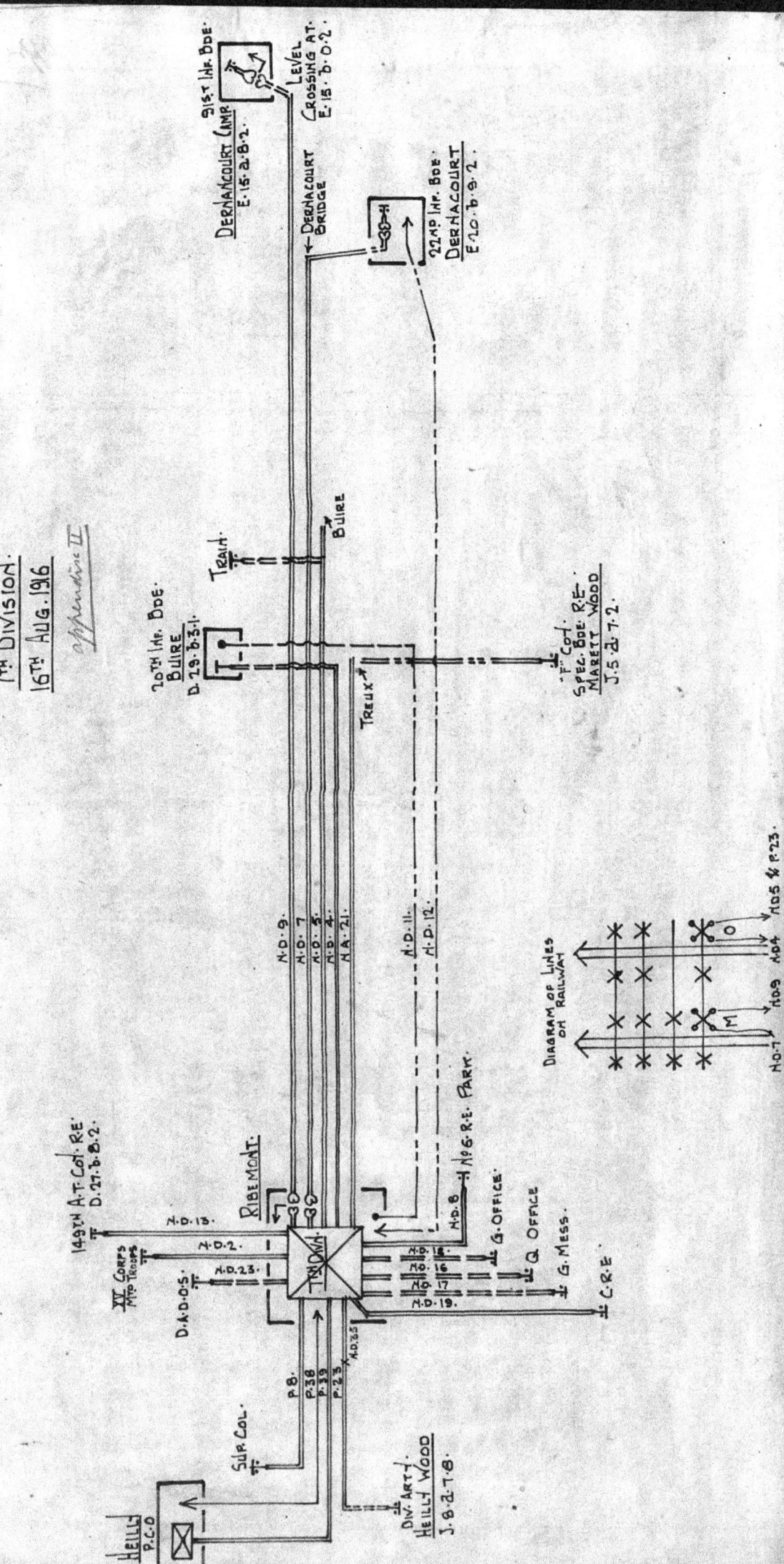

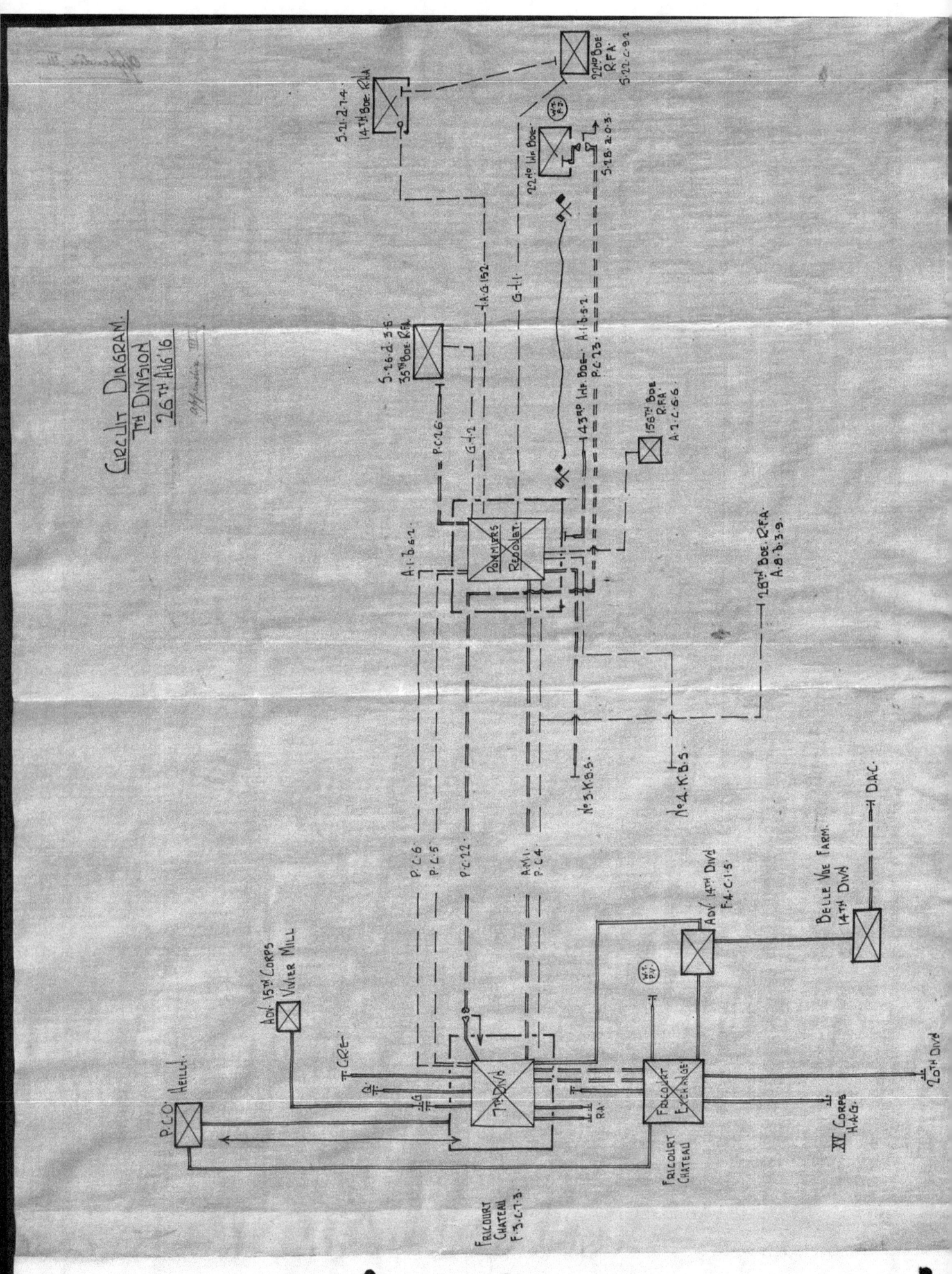

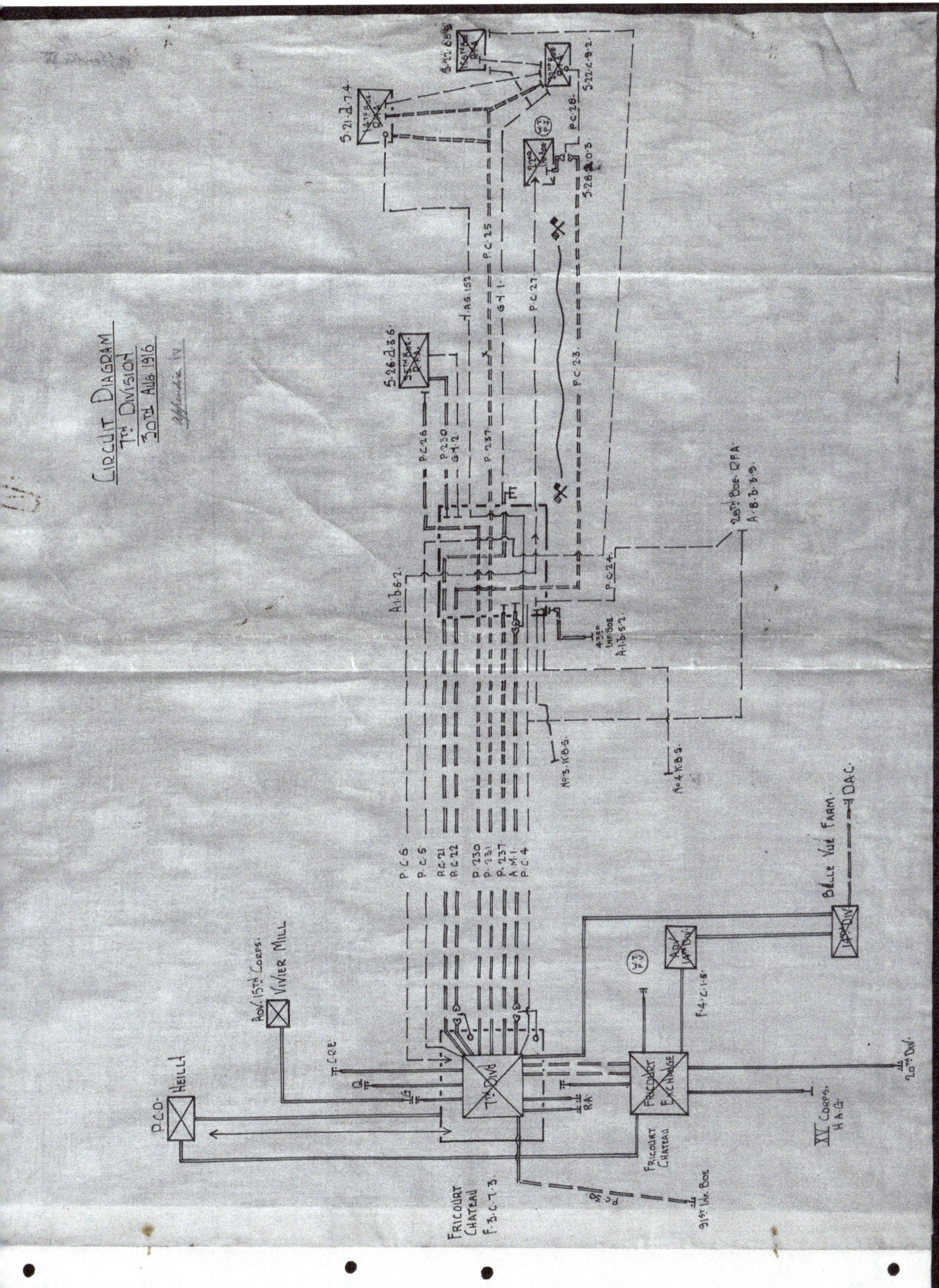

Army Form C. 2118.

Signal Coy 7 ? FC XI

WAR DIARY
or
INTELLIGENCE SUMMARY
(Erase heading not required.)

Instructions regarding War Diaries and Intelligence Summaries are contained in F.S. Regs., Part II. and the Staff Manual respectively. Title pages will be prepared in manuscript.

Place	Date	Hour	Summary of Events and Information	Remarks and references to Appendices
September, 1916.	1st		Earth fault again cleared on concentric cable in PC23. A loop was laid at Y9Q.152 and at AQ.151. Found a battery which was frequently shelled. No 1 and 3. detachments laid in afternoon a line (PC31) single D5, from Pommiers Redoubt to Inf. Bde H.Q. in Montauban. Line runs from the Redoubt to junction of Pommiers lane and Pommiers trench, then straight across country to corner of hedge at A.3.a.55.95, then along hedge to trench at 9.27.d.2.2, and then in fire trench of Montauban defences round S and E. of village to Bde H.Q.	
	2nd		No 3. detacht. lifted armoured cable of NA16 and 52 laid in June in Mules Coy. No 4. detacht used this cable to replace concentric cable in PC23. No 1. detacht. strengthened PC31 and installed PC27. No 2. detacht. replaced some broken poles on PC4. Hostile shelling much less today, and lines were not often cut. Wireless at P.J. was erected at H.Q. 156th Bde, R.F.A. in evening. P.J. remained at 29 ?/?/?	

T/134. Wt. W708—776. 50000. 4/15. Sir J. C. & S.

Army Form C. 2118.

WAR DIARY
INTELLIGENCE SUMMARY.
(Erase heading not required.)

Instructions regarding War Diaries and Intelligence Summaries are contained in F. S. Regs., Part II. and the Staff Manual respectively. Title pages will be prepared in manuscript.

Place	Date	Hour	Summary of Events and Information	Remarks and references to Appendices
	September 1916			
	3rd		22nd Sig. Bde, attached Ginchy at midday. Two detachments with cable waggons under Sgts. Tigan and Stannard, were sent to Rommiers Redoubt, but were not required, and returned to H.Q. in evening. Throughout the day very little trouble was experienced with the lines. Only about four breaks occurred, and communication was never interrupted to any Bde. Linemen and operators were distributed as follows:—	

H.Q. or Office.   Linemen   Operators.
28th Bde (rf)   2   2
14th Bde RHA   2   2
22nd Bde RFA   1   2
35th Bde RFA   -   2
156th Bde RFA   2   1
28th Bde RFA   1   -
Rommiers Redoubt Post Office, 4 t.Nco.ple. 2.

In the evening the linemen at the 28th Bde was withdrawn and 2 extra were sent to Rommiers Redoubt.

T2134. Wt. W708-776. 500,000. 4/15. Sir J. C. & S.

Army Form C. 2118.

WAR DIARY
INTELLIGENCE SUMMARY
(Erase heading not required.)

Place	Date	Hour	Summary of Events and Information	Remarks and references to Appendices
	September, 1916.			
	3rd (contd.)		Diagram of communications is attached, and Route plan of lines.	App. I. App. II.
			In the evening the 30th Inf Bde. relieved the 22nd Inf Bde. and took over their headquarters. The 22nd Inf Bde. moved to a camp beside the 91st Bde., and used their line, PC 30, for communication to division.	
	4th		Very few faults occurred, and there were no movements of H.Q. All lines forward from Ronviers Redoubt were batyelled in the enemy. No 2. detacht replaced some shot poles in PC 30. to 9.12 and 27th Inf Bde. or The 55th Divn took over Belle Vue Farm, and were allotted PZ01 by Corps. signals. The YDAC.line was put on 55th divn. exchange.	
	5th		No 1 detacht overhauled some track crossings on PC27, and 9.11, which had given slight trouble owing to the ground being softened by heavy rains. The 22nd Inf Bde moved to Bruire. Communication was	

Army Form C. 2118.

WAR DIARY
or
INTELLIGENCE SUMMARY.
(Erase heading not required.)

Instructions regarding War Diaries and Intelligence Summaries are contained in F. S. Regs., Part II. and the Staff Manual respectively. Title pages will be prepared in manuscript.

Place	Date	Hour	Summary of Events and Information	Remarks and references to Appendices
	September 1916			
	6th (cont.)		established through Corps office at Ribemont, by telephone and vibrator, using the lines which had been used to 29th Bde, while 3rd was ", 7th 15th Bde RFA relieved the 28th Bde RFA and took over their H.Q.	
	6th to 8th		Communications remained unaltered during this period, and worked satisfactorily.	
	9th		7th Div. H.Q. closed at FRICOURT CHAU at 11 am. and opened same hour at RIBEMONT. The wireless sets were withdrawn and handed over with personnel to Corps Wireless Officer. PC 27 and PC 23 were handed over to 55th Div2 who took over Bde H.Q. at Mortauban. All artillery communications were handed to same. 7th Div Arty remained in action, Lt. Smith and 2 detacht with extra operators were left to maintain communication	

Army Form C. 2118.

WAR DIARY
~~INTELLIGENCE SUMMARY.~~
(Erase heading not required.)

Instructions regarding War Diaries and Intelligence Summaries are contained in F. S. Regs., Part II. and the Staff Manual respectively. Title pages will be prepared in manuscript.

Place	Date	Hour	Summary of Events and Information	Remarks and references to Appendices
September 1916	9th		Ribemont office closed 11am; reopened Hallencourt at 3 p.m.	
	10th		Both lorries with some linemen and operators went on ahead and opened office. Horse transport moved by road on 9th and 10th.	
			Lt. Smith's section. — Made arrangements for move of 22nd R.F.A. Bde Hqrs. but they did not move.	
	11th		Instruments put on existing lines to 22nd W. Bde. at Yonville, and arrangements made for communication with 20th Bde. through Airaines and Hallencourt P.O.s.	
			Lt. Smith's section. — All lines installed.	
	12th		Line to 91st Bde at Huppy, rebuilt by I Corps ago. Sounders superimposed to 22 & 24 gph. Diagram of communications attached.	App. III.
	13th		Part of coy at Hallencourt reequipping and cleaning waggons etc. Capt. Lowson relieved Lt. Smith with detachment with 7th D.A. Lt. Smith proceeded to 20th Inf. Bde to relieve Lt. Muirhead, who has been appointed Staff Captain 91st Inf. Bde.	

T.J.134. Wt. W708—776. 50000. 4/15. Sir J.C. & S.

Army Form C. 2118.

WAR DIARY
or
INTELLIGENCE SUMMARY.
(Erase heading not required.)

Instructions regarding War Diaries and Intelligence Summaries are contained in F.S. Regs., Part II. and the Staff Manual respectively. Title pages will be prepared in manuscript.

Place	Date	Hour	Summary of Events and Information	Remarks and references to Appendices
September, 1916	14th		Detacht with 7th D.R. — Arrangements made for probable forward moves of R.O. 15ters. Two pairs in cable French from Bazenier Redoubt to York French allotted for R.A. use. Diagram of communications on this date attached.	App. IV.
	15th	5 a.m.	Detacht with 7th Div Arty. — XV Corps attached at 6:30 a.m. C.S.M. Rockwell, and M.T. detacht (N.C.O. 2 men, and 3 attached men of N.Z.E.A.) and No 2 detacht (3 men) moved to Bazenier Redoubt at 5 a.m. No 2 detacht extended two pairs thro to Bazenier Office from Cpl No 4 detacht cable French, and No 4. tested through from York French at 7 a.m. started to lay line to front of Delville wood at same time as 35th Bde and NZ FA Bde. Failed to move up. One pair D5. on ground was laid round the end of Delville wood to Bde. H.Q. This line was badly knocked about, and did not last long. Another pair was laid up valley in front of Delville wood and in to N.Z. Bde. at old Bri. H.Q. then to York French. This line worked well to N.Z Bde. and fairly well to 35th Bde. Very heavy shelling was experienced round the wood. The detacht laying line under C.S.M. Rockwell	

WAR DIARY
or
INTELLIGENCE SUMMARY

Army Form C. 2118.

Place	Date	Hour	Summary of Events and Information	Remarks and references to Appendices
	September 1916		Splendidly.	
			Considerable trouble was experienced during this day with on P.C.4 which was badly damaged by cavalry and waggon lines. PC 31 was also damaged several times. Otherwise communication to Bdes was good. No.2 and No.9 detacht. remained at Pommiers Redoubt during night. Lt Jones and Muggleston remained out with N.Z. F.A. Bde.	
	16th		Detacht with 7th Div. Arty ———— No.2. detacht started at 4:30 am to York Tr. to extend a pair to 15th Bde. Maj. HQ. This was not close as Bde did not move. Took over 3rd pair in corps cable trench. (P.313, P.350) One 5 line magneto unit and one 4+3 line buzzer unit, taken from Pommiers Redoubt and sent to York Tr. One 4 line French exchange pnt in Pommiers Redoubt. Adv. exchange opened in old Runner post dug out in York Trench. 2 Operators (Howard & Longfort) sent for present to Pommiers and Gillingham and Brewer sent forward to York Trench. Detachr employed fixing up exchange at York Tr.	

Army Form C. 2118.

WAR DIARY
or
~~INTELLIGENCE SUMMARY.~~
(Erase heading not required.)

Place	Date	Hour	Summary of Events and Information	Remarks and references to Appendices
	September 1916			
	16th (contin.)		14th Divn. again attacked at 10.15am. Cables at York Trench working by 1pm with 2 full circuits to Fricourt and one back to 35th and N.Z. Bde. (Buzzers ect.). N.º 2 detacht. laid single line through Delville Wood to 35th Bde. This line was through about 6pm and work well through the night. One pair was laid to 52nd Bde. RFA at S.23.a.26 and to 14th Bde at S.17.a.23. (afternoon) to which places they moved during the day. These worked bugger to York Trench. PC4, PC31 and GYI. all gave trouble being badly damaged by traffic. AM1. also attached to G.P. Cpl End. I/c York R. En. Linemen I/c 1st and 2nd	
			called in to En. Communications as per diagram.	App. V
	17th		Office at HALLENCOURT closed at midnight 17th=18th Septr. Detach² with 7th Divn Arty. - PC+5 extended by poled cable to York Trench. from old 16th Bde. H.Q.. Pc 4. abandoned as working line. Laid connection between York Trench Ex. and My 13 Bde in same Trench. PC 31 and GY1 very bad between Bernains and W. end Montauban 21st Divn. relieved 14th Divn. and took over Fricourt chateau.	

Army Form C. 2118.

WAR DIARY
or
INTELLIGENCE SUMMARY.
(Erase heading not required.)

Instructions regarding War Diaries and Intelligence Summaries are contained in F. S. Regs., Part II. and the Staff Manual respectively. Title pages will be prepared in manuscript.

Place	Date	Hour	Summary of Events and Information	Remarks and references to Appendices
	September 1916			
	18th		7th Divn H.Q. arrived at FLETRE. Office opened at 3.30 p.m. Circuit to IX Corps only. H.Q. Sig Bde. at moor. Communication by D.R. only. 20th Inf Bde. PONT NIEPPE. 91st Inf Bde. La Petite Munque Farm. 22nd Inf Bde. Meteren. Linesmen sent out to Nieppe, to 19 Divn Sig. Coy. Detail[?] with 7th Divn Arty. PC 25 patrolled only and earth fault cleared but it developed again. 35th Bde moved back to dugouts near 19th Bde. QM Find got tie off single line to them. No 2 detacht. Relaid part of PC 31. along parapet of Corps cable trench. No 4 rebuilt A.M.1. All lines to Bdes from York Fm overhauled by linesmen. QY 1. diverted into P 230 (forward of Pommery) thereby cutting out last part of QY 1. Ravied heavily all day. Pricourt Church shelled, Couplines broken.	

Army Form C. 2118.

WAR DIARY
or
INTELLIGENCE SUMMARY
(Erase heading not required.)

Instructions regarding War Diaries and Intelligence Summaries are contained in F. S. Regs., Part II. and the Staff Manual respectively. Title pages will be prepared in manuscript.

Hour, Date, Place	Summary of Events and Information	Remarks and References to Appendices
September 19th, 1916.	20th Inf. Bde. relieved 56th Inf Bde., H.Qr. at Pont Nieppe. 91st Inf Bde relieved 57th Inf Bde., HQ at Little Mongin Vue. Communication arranged by Sigs 19th Div. as Bdes under command. 9 a.m. 19th Div. Lt. Bayne joined coy. Detacht with 2nd D.A. ——— PC.21 & PC 22 carefully overhauled by No 4 detacht. Earth fault on PC 25 cleared by laying new cable along Montauban alley, about 500 yds.	
20th.	Nos. 1 & 3 detachts moved to Nieppe and took over cables from 19th Division. 7th Div. Office opened at Bulluck and Adv. Office at Nieppe at 6 p.m.	

Army Form C. 2118.

WAR DIARY
or
INTELLIGENCE SUMMARY.
(Erase heading not required.)

Instructions regarding War Diaries and Intelligence Summaries are contained in F. S. Regs., Part II. and the Staff Manual respectively. Title pages will be prepared in manuscript.

Hour, Date, Place	Summary of Events and Information	Remarks and References to Appendices
September 20th 1916. (contin)	Detachts with 7th D.A. ——. No. 2 overhauled and poled G/1. and extended to 15th Bde, R.F.A. who moved to W. edge of Berafay wood. PC 31 also extended to 15th Bde. No. 4. poled East of PC 25. and fort men, new poles in PC 6 and PC 25. and G/1. Bad overhearing developed on lines in Corps Trunk. This was reported to the Corps Sigs. and cleared by them following day.	
21st.	Lineamen out Nights out all day, going over lines. 22nd Bde (Inf) relieved 56th Inf Bde. Lt. Baynes proceeded to Niepp. HQrs. Detachts with 7th Div Arty. —— PC 40 and PC 45. poled by No. 4. detacht. No. 2 Detacht finished up PC 31. MM1 + G/1.	

Forms/C. 2118/11.

Army Form C. 2118.

WAR DIARY
or
INTELLIGENCE SUMMARY.
(Erase heading not required.)

Hour, Date, Place	Summary of Events and Information	Remarks and References to Appendices
September 22nd 1916.	Telephone and cameden line to 20th Bde. carefully patrolled lines from 20th Bde. to T.P. and from adv. 20th Bde. to T.P. overhauled. 23rd Inf Bde moved to new H.Q. at B.10.A.5.4. (Sheet 36.). DeTache with 7th Aus Divy. — 4th N.Z. Bde. moved up and joined 3rd N.Z. Bde. Tee, cut off 9V1 and Pc25. 5 N.Z. F.A. mm. and cable wagon worked with 31st Div Sigs. Laying poled route to York Rd. from Montauban. PC 41. and PC 43 poled by onbined DeTach? Circuit diagram attached.	
23rd.	9.15 N/ Bde. moved to H.Q. recently vacated by 22nd Bde. Lines which were patrolled on 22nd inst. were labelled. One telephone pair working from Y.G.R. to each Bde. and a sounder circuit from Y.G. to each Bde.	Appendice #VI.

Army Form C. 2118.

WAR DIARY
or
INTELLIGENCE SUMMARY.
(Erase heading not required.)

Instructions regarding War Diaries and Intelligence Summaries are contained in F. S. Regs., Part II. and the Staff Manual respectively. Title pages will be prepared in manuscript.

Hour, Date, Place	Summary of Events and Information	Remarks and References to Appendices
September 23rd 1916 (contd)	Detach'ts with 7th D.A. —— PC6. PC21. PC22. AM1. Patrolled by party. D is one by PC15 cleared. Pair from Pommero to Montauban point through by Coys. for private BG CRA line to Fricourt.	
24th	22nd Inf. Bde. made intermediate on Sounder line between 91st Bde. & Div. — The ditched cable part of route between T.P. & 91st Bde. was overhauled & re-labelled. Detachments with 7th D.A. —— Cpl. (Game & Smith) joined PC27 & PC30 at (CATERPILLAR TRENCH, repaired PC27, & joined G/14 & PC97 to LV4 (21st Div. line). —— LV4 led h.t. C.A. + PC99 leed into 22nd Bde R.F.A. — Waggons greased.	
25th	Linemen spent whole day in tracing out buried routes & ditched cable, & in patrolling local lines on the	

WAR DIARY
INTELLIGENCE SUMMARY
(Erase heading not required.)

Army Form C. 2118.

Hour, Date, Place	Summary of Events and Information	Remarks and References to Appendices
Sept 25 (cont'd)	Nieppe Exchange. Relieved with 7th D.A. — 21st Div. moved to Advr H.Q. at Montauban & attacked Gueudecourt at 12.35 p.m. — 6y1.— PC 27 cut, otherwise lines good to 4 p.m. reo/. at P & 6 actual wire again cut over railway — 2 detachments under Capt. Ward J.C. York Trench [ ] at 11.0 a.m. & returned at 8 p.m. 2 operators came in from Pommiers Redoubt to Fricourt. L.I. to 21st D.A. at Pommiers Redoubt laid early & 14th DA. line connected. — PC 6 again broken, otherwise no trouble.	
262.	Linesmen sent out to learn the 19th D.A. lines — officer & three Lt Wilkinson arrived & disposed of his detachment as follows :- 1 NCO & 3 men at Cinder f.m. (T.19.c.15.7.), Advr 22nd (m) Bde HQ; 2 men to Le Bizet Convent (B.12.a.5.6), Advr 20th (m) Ble HQ; remaining two with himself at Advr. Divn HQ (B.9.d.8.2)	

Army Form C. 2118.

WAR DIARY
or
INTELLIGENCE SUMMARY.
(Erase heading not required.)

Hour, Date, Place	Summary of Events and Information	Remarks and References to Appendices
26/9/17 (contd.)	Details with 7 Bde A. — Lines patrolled, detachments not sent up. LV & TCb disn. G.T. Command detachment sent to YORK TRENCH at 2.0 p.m. returned at 7.0 p.m. 21 Divn continued attack.	
27.	Enemy continued [shelling] lines. Cct's with 7 Bde A. — Advanced party 33 Divn arrived, operators & linesmen sent to PANTHER REDOUBT & YORK TRENCH at 3.0 p.m. Attachments except phones & al. B.M. clerks & R.A. mess changed over. 33rd Divn. operators on with 7th Divn. ops., & lines shown round lines.	
28.	Patrolling of R.A. lines continued. Cct's with 7 Bde D.A. — Enemy arty 3 Divn. again shown over lines. 3rd Divn personnel left YORK TRENCH at 7.0 a.m. & PANTHER REDOUBT at 9.0 a.m.	

Army Form C. 2118.

WAR DIARY
or
INTELLIGENCE SUMMARY.
(Erase heading not required.)

Hour, Date, Place	Summary of Events and Information	Remarks and References to Appendices
Sept 28th (cont)	Detachments with 7th DA moved off to BONNAY in the morning.	
29th/30th	Detachments moved to LONGUEDY & entrained early morning of 30th, arriving at CAESTRE early morning of 1st.	
October 1st		

M Johnson Captain.
O.C. 7th Dn Sig Cy. R.E.

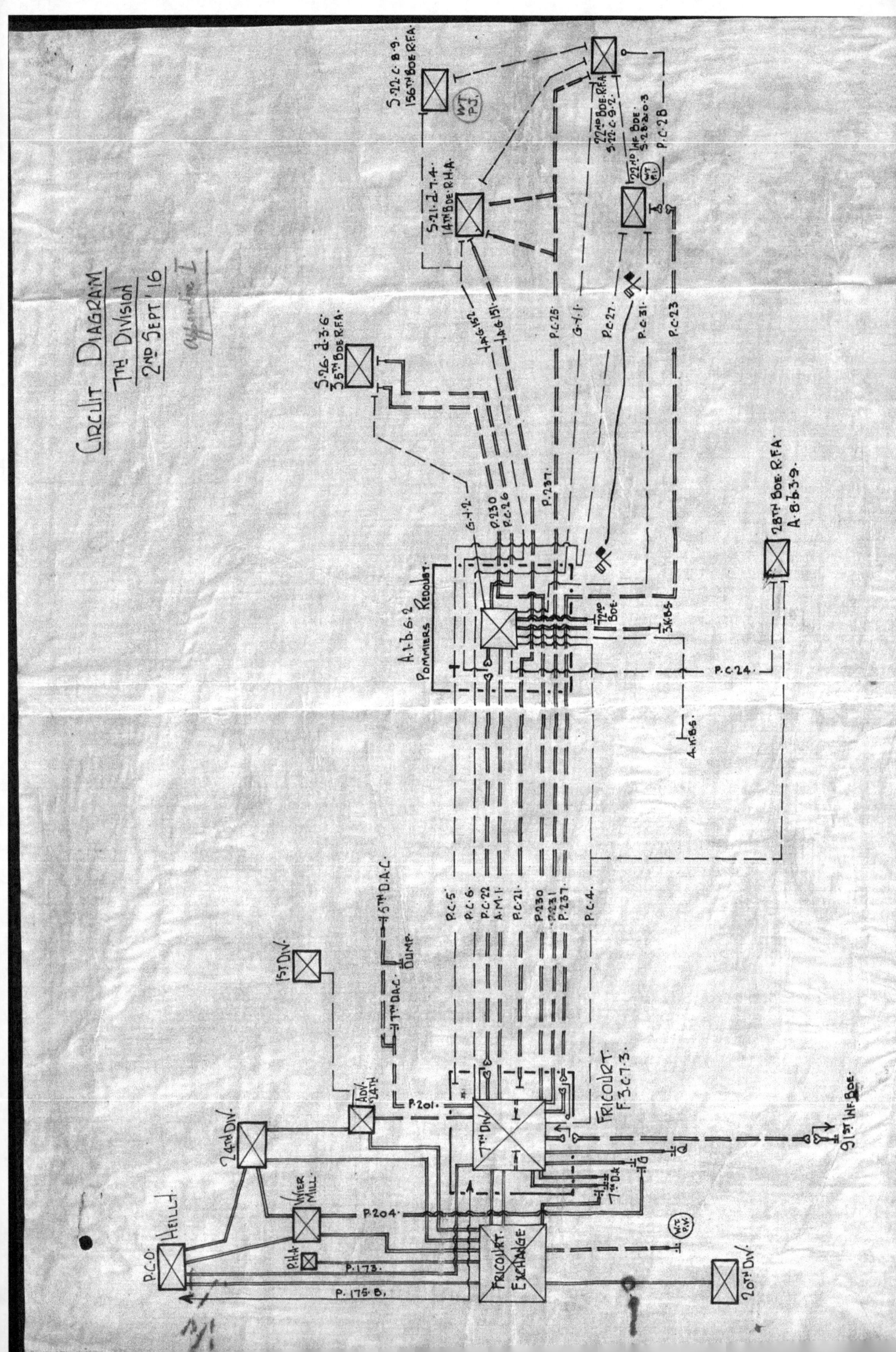

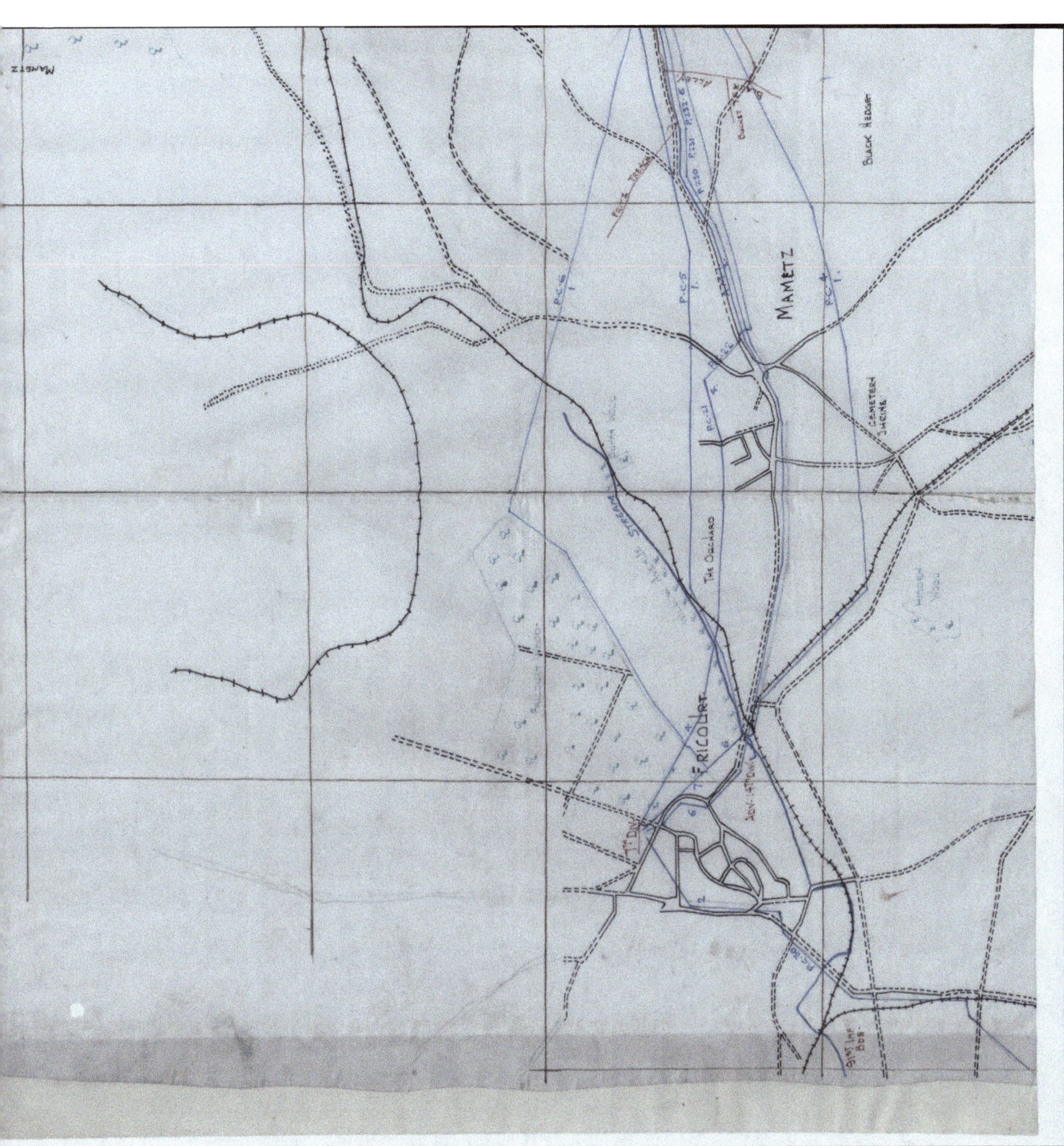

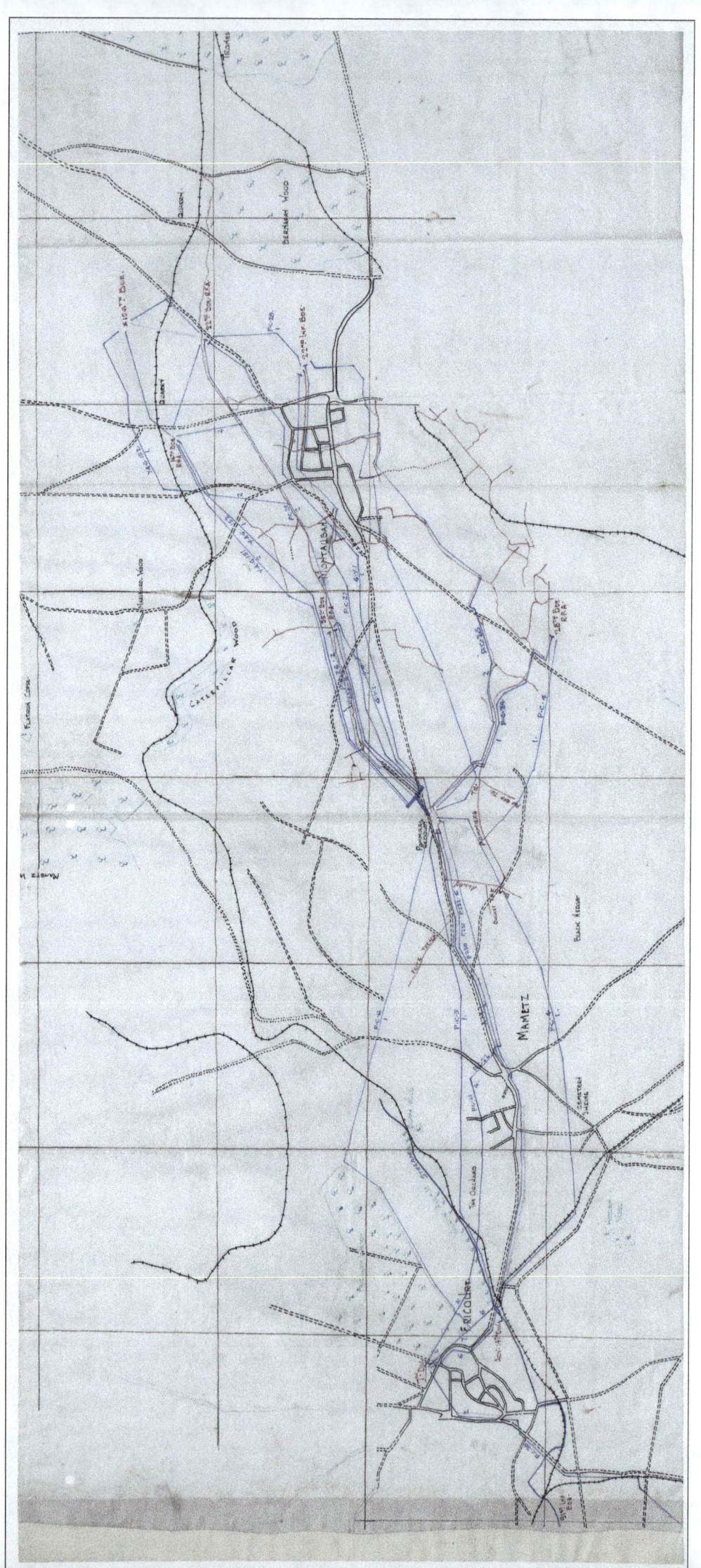

Appendix IV

Lines in No. 5 Area (HQ. Hallencourt)

7th Division
13th September 1916.

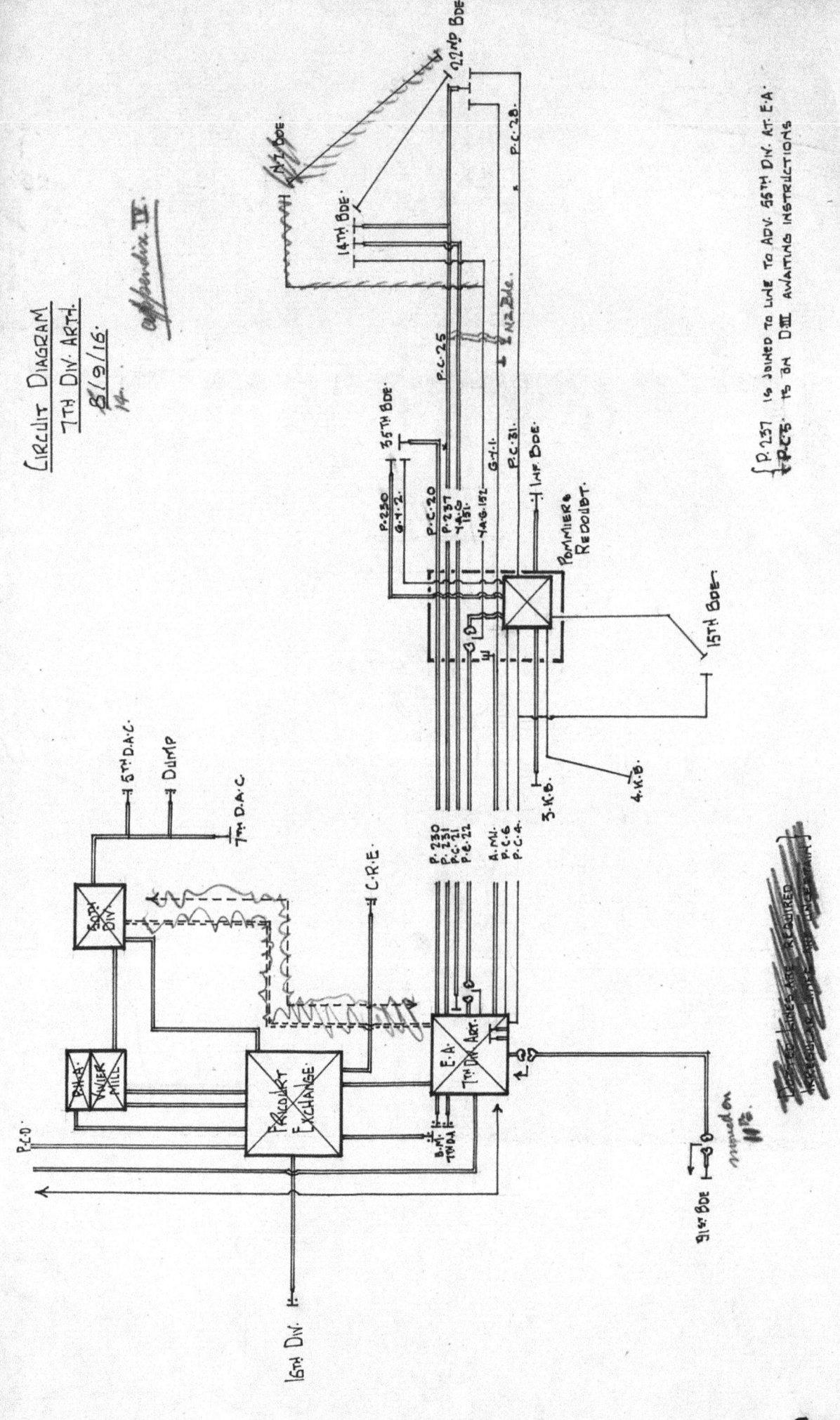

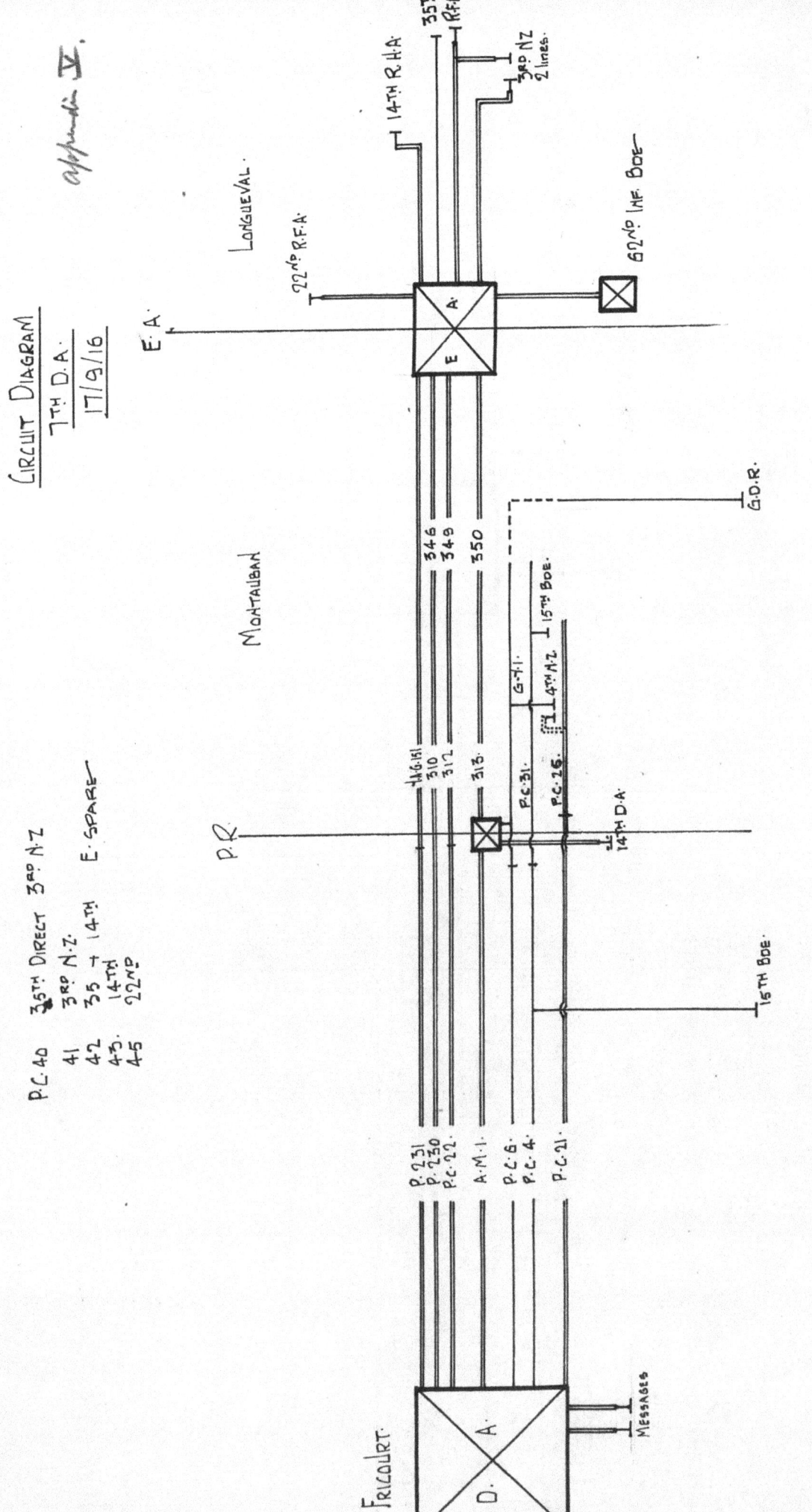

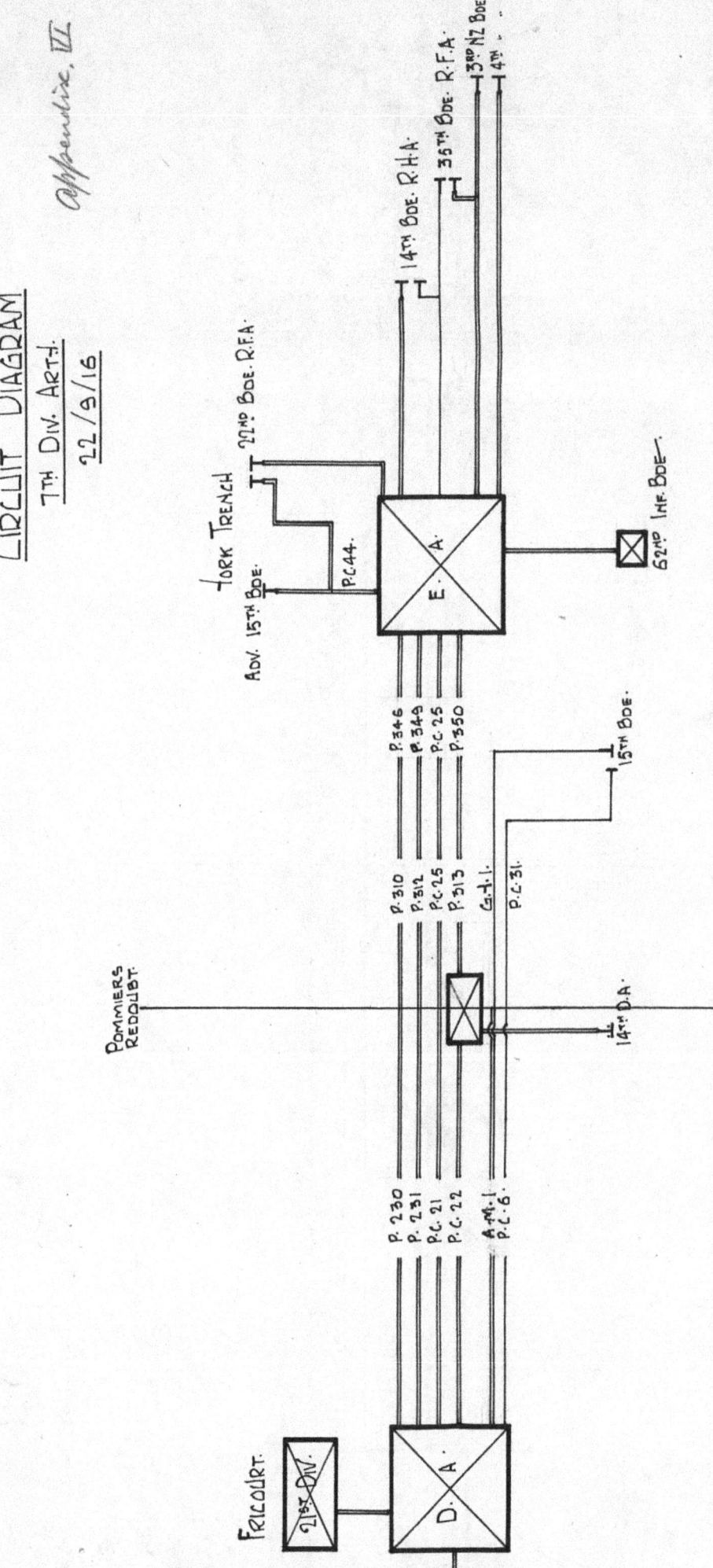

Army Form C. 2118.

Signal Coy 7? Vol 2

WAR DIARY
or
INTELLIGENCE SUMMARY.
(Erase heading not required.)

Instructions regarding War Diaries and Intelligence Summaries are contained in F. S. Regs., Part II. and the Staff Manual respectively. Title pages will be prepared in manuscript.

Hour, Date, Place	Summary of Events and Information	Remarks and References to Appendices
October 1916.		
1st	No 2 and 4 detachts who arrived early morning unpacking and arranging billets. Capt. O'Connor left on leave.	
2nd	7th Divl Arty relieved 19th Divl Arty. 19th Div. Arty. lines taken over, as working and all instruments relieved.	
3rd	R.A. 2nd Office at Armignet closed and R.A. lines taken on exchange at Nieppe. Test Station at Pontigneal, only used now as Cinema post.	
4th	Lt. Baynes spent time going over R.E.9. Boles lines. to see what state they were in. Most of coy employed making camp habitable, by laying trench boards, clearing mud etc.	

Army Form C. 2118.

WAR DIARY
or
INTELLIGENCE SUMMARY.
(Erase heading not required.)

Instructions regarding War Diaries and Intelligence Summaries are contained in F. S. Regs., Part II. and the Staff Manual respectively. Title pages will be prepared in manuscript.

Hour, Date, Place	Summary of Events and Information	Remarks and References to Appendices
October 1916		
5th	No 3 detacht. overhauled 8-line comic airline route from English Farm to Bde H.Q. at Ronarin and started to overhaul trestle route from English Farm to La Petite Munque Farm.	
6th	No 3 detacht. continued to overhaul trestle route. Capts. airline section rebuilding semi-permanent lines from M/offre office to Ronarin and from Ronarin to T.P.	
7th	No 4 detacht. overhauled 5-line semi-permanent route from M/offre office to T.P. Two linesmen sent to 35th Batty, to assist them to repair on C.P. line. Started to build stables.	
8th	Work on 7th continued	

Forms/C. 2118/11.

Army Form C. 2118.

WAR DIARY
or
INTELLIGENCE SUMMARY.
(Erase heading not required.)

Instructions regarding War Diaries and Intelligence Summaries are contained in F. S. Regs., Part II. and the Staff Manual respectively. Title pages will be prepared in manuscript.

Hour, Date, Place	Summary of Events and Information	Remarks and References to Appendices
October 1916.		
9th	Several unknown lines traced through and direct line between Right Bde and centre Bde arranged.	
10th	Picked spare lines round about Nieppe. Arrange new circuit to Adv. H.Q. H.A.S. exchange. Part of old circuit having been used for lateral line between Bdes.	
11th	Work on tables and cleaning camp continued. Capt O'Connor returned off leave.	
12th	Picked up spare cable on Ploegsteert-Romarin road. Capt. O'Connor joined 9th Inf. Bde. acting Bde Major.	
13th	Picking up spare cable on Ploegsteert road continued. Pair from Le Rou to D/14 battery near Cinder Farm put through in preparation for proposed move of it to RHA Bde HQ.	

(9 20 6) W 2794 100,000 8/14 H W V Forms/C. 2118/11.

Army Form C. 2118.

WAR DIARY
or
INTELLIGENCE SUMMARY.

(Erase heading not required.)

Instructions regarding War Diaries and Intelligence Summaries are contained in F. S. Regs., Part II. and the Staff Manual respectively. Title pages will be prepared in manuscript.

Place	Date	Hour	Summary of Events and Information	Remarks and references to Appendices
	October 1916			
	14th		No 2 detachmt. started the retwire and laid in lines at 91st Bde. office.	
	15th		Corps. built B. lines on form. route from 91st Bde. to Le Don. for 1st D.B.KM.A.	
	16th to 19th		Picked up some old ditched lines between N. office and T.P.	
			Work of 14th continued.	
	18th			
	19th to 21st		Line to 25th Battery waggon lines joined up.	
	22nd		Blowing up cable in trench area.	
			Gas helmets tested.	
			Started renewing T.P. office.	
	23rd		Renewing of T.P. continued.	
			Lt. Whishaw joined.	
	24th		Arranged lateral lines between batteries of left and centre groups	
	25th and 26th			
	27th		Renewing T.P. finished. Commenced renewing lines Div. Signal office	

2353 Wt. W2544/1454 700,000 5/15 D. D. & L.   A.D.S.S./Forms/C. 2118.

Army Form C. 2118.

WAR DIARY
or
INTELLIGENCE SUMMARY.
(Erase heading not required.)

Place	Date	Hour	Summary of Events and Information	Remarks and references to Appendices
	October 28th to 30th		Picked up cable in area, round Petite Munque Farm and adjoint W of Ploegsteert Wood	
	31st		10th Bde. R.H.A. moved to new headquarters at Le Doux. All lines had previously been prepared.	

W. Roberts Capt RE.
D.C. 9th Div. Sig. Cy. RE.

Signals 7th Div
Vol 13

Army Form C. 2118.

WAR DIARY
or
INTELLIGENCE SUMMARY.

(Erase heading not required.)

Instructions regarding War Diaries and Intelligence Summaries are contained in F.S. Regs., Part II. and the Staff Manual respectively. Title pages will be prepared in manuscript.

Place	Date	Hour	Summary of Events and Information	Remarks and references to Appendices
	November			
	1st		Officers and licences of 25th Div. Sig. Coy. billeted over Sleep.	
	2nd		Licences and NCOs of 25th Div. sent to T.P.	
	3rd		Arranged communication to Steenvoorde Bttln. for Bde. relieved. 7th Division relieved by 25th Div.	
	4th		Coy. moved from Nieppe to FLETRE. Lt. Whichelow with 30 cart loggy proceeded in advance to establish office. Larry Lumsdon & H. Whichelow and 3 operators went on in car. 7.9. closed at Bailleul at 9am. in Bailleul. H. Whichelow & optical FUC. same time. Communication as follows:— Div. Hd. Coys. — Telephone pair, superimposed sounder. Div. to 20th Bde. (GOTTAS) — Telephone pair. Div. to 91st Bde. (MEEEREN) — Telephone pair, superimposed sounder. Div. to 22nd Bde. (STEENVOORDE) — Telephone pair to eastings at 91st. Sounder superimposed with 91st intermittent. Lt. Weston went on leave.	

Army Form C. 2118.

WAR DIARY
or
INTELLIGENCE SUMMARY.
(Erase heading not required.)

Instructions regarding War Diaries and Intelligence Summaries are contained in F.S. Regs., Part II. and the Staff Manual respectively. Title pages will be prepared in manuscript.

Place	Date	Hour	Summary of Events and Information	Remarks and references to Appendices
	November 5th		Waggons cleaned and painting started. 3-line exchange installed at 20th Bde. (Caestre), and extension lent to Ordnance office.	
	6th		Party employed opening up lines in village. About 30 men went for a route march in afternoon.	
	7th 8th		Waggon painting and opening up lines in village continued.	
	9th		Division H.Q. moved from Flêtre to Renescure. Electric light went on in advance. Lt Kirwan established went by car to St Omer, and arrange lines. Communication established by one pair, remainder superimposed to 2nd Army. D.R. runs only to Bdes.	
	10th		Divl H.Q. remained at Renescure. Bdes continued their march.	
	11th		Divl H.Q. moved from Renescure to Tilques. 15-line exchange and wonder set taken over in signal office, working to St. Omer. Lines to 20th Bde. Moulgres and 22nd at Eperlecque put into use. No 2 detacht. stationed at head of column at Ganspette. Line through about 5 p.m. and extended in line to 91st Bde. at Ganspette.	

2353 Wt. W2544/1454 700,000 5/15 D. D. & L. A.D.S.S./Forms/C. 2118.

Army Form C. 2118.

WAR DIARY
or
INTELLIGENCE SUMMARY.
(Erase heading not required.)

Instructions regarding War Diaries and Intelligence Summaries are contained in F. S. Regs., Part II. and the Staff Manual respectively. Title pages will be prepared in manuscript.

Place	Date	Hour	Summary of Events and Information	Remarks and references to Appendices
	November 1916			
	12th		Three line exchange installed at 2273.B. and Div. Train connected to it. Cable laid by M.L. Rostadt in previous evening overhauled.	
	13th		Visual scheme carried out by H.Q. Signallers and 185 on Tilques - Zudausques and Moringhem roads.	
	14th		Similar signal scheme carried out of Tilques Quelmes road. Lecture on Telephone given by Lt Williams 2nd Wg Sgnls. to Div. HQrs and Battn. signallers. Supplies Stores requisitioned to establish, to be sent by rail to new area. Lt Watson rejoined from Line. Our continued to march. Div. HQ moved to Lumbres. HQ details hitched up cables to 9th S. Bde. and moved to Lumbres independently. Electric Lgt to lorry and 17 Wireless proceeded in advance, and opened communication with St Omer.	
	15th		Div. HQ moved to Bomy. The same arrangements were made with the lorries for next days march. The E.L. lorry moved in advance, both arriving to open office. The 30 cwt lorry remained till office closed, and took on office staff. Communications at Bomy were established on arriving.	

Army Form C. 2118.

WAR DIARY
or
INTELLIGENCE SUMMARY.
(Erase heading not required.)

Instructions regarding War Diaries and Intelligence Summaries are contained in F.S. Regs., Part II. and the Staff Manual respectively. Title pages will be prepared in manuscript.

Place	Date	Hour	Summary of Events and Information	Remarks and references to Appendices
	November 1916		Comms. to 3rd Army and part way to 29th Bde and to 91st Bde. No 1 and No 4. laid extensions to their Bdes.	
	17th		The Divn H.Q. remained at Bovey.	
	18th		March continued to Flers. Some arrangement of lorries. Communication to 3rd Army and to the Bdes. An existing single line was test off to new Bde H.Q. No 1. and No 4. details picked up cable laid on 16th, and moved independently to Flers.	
	19th		Div.l H.B. moved to Frotan-le-Grand. No 1 detacht. laid single line from 91st CBde in Allies to Div.n on way in. No 4. Detachmn and laid cable from Frotan to 22nd Bde at Renault. Communication with Doullens exchange established with superimposed on line direct to 3rd Army.	
	20th		Div.n H.Q. moved to Doullens. Signal office taken over from 2nd Div.l Direct telephone, with superimposed sounder to 4th Corps. Also lines to Doullens Ex. 91st Bde. connected to Gapamant Exchange, which is connected to Doullens. 20th Bde. connected direct on existing line. 29th Bde joined to Doullens 3rd Army through at Frotan-le-Grand. Cable laid 6 x 17th and Exch. & Doullens.	

2353 Wt. W2544/1454 700,000 5/15 D. D. & L. A.D.S.S./Forms/C. 2118.

WAR DIARY
or
INTELLIGENCE SUMMARY

Army Form C. 2118.

Place	Date	Hour	Summary of Events and Information	Remarks and references to Appendices
	November 1916			
	21st		No 1. Details packed up cable from Villers L'Hopital. Lieut on 19th inst. Lt. Smith went sick to hospital.	
			Division HQ moved from Doullens to Marieux.	
			20th Bde. moved to Beaucourt, and came on 32nd Div. Exchange.	
			91st Bde moved to Lealvillers and came on 51st Div Exchange.	
			22nd A moved to Raincheval and came on Raincheval Exchange.	
			Direct communication to 5th Corps through Marieux exchange. Superimposed work.	
			Lt. Watson joined 20th Bde. vice Lt Smith.	
			Lt. Whitlow and 10 pioneers went in lorry to 32nd Div for attachment to learn lines.	
	22nd 23rd 24th		Div= HQ remained at Marieux. Arrangements made for relief of 32nd Div=. One office relief, with instruments sent on 24th.	
	25th		Division HQ moved to Bertrancourt and took over from 32nd Div. at 9 pm.	
			2nd Div= Artillery remained in.	
			20th Bde HQ at 9.B.4.5. 91st Bde HR at White City, and 22nd Bde in reserve at Beaussart.	
			2nd Div personnel manned Beaussart Ex, which was mostly R.E. mints.	

Army Form C. 2118.

WAR DIARY
or
INTELLIGENCE SUMMARY.
(Erase heading not required.)

Instructions regarding War Diaries and Intelligence
Summaries are contained in F. S. Regs., Part II.
and the Staff Manual respectively. Title pages
will be prepared in manuscript.

Place	Date	Hour	Summary of Events and Information	Remarks and references to Appendices
	November 1916			
	26.		Overhauling and rearranging local lines, and offices. Register keeper added to office staff for D.R.S. work. Forward lines traced through by linesman at H.Q.	
	27th		Lines from rebate Cty. Muirelly gone through. Lines fr. certy. test leads in bad order, about three unreliable. Written locals and office continued. System of recording D.R's post in operation.	
	28th		Traced out and tested H.D. lines from Bertrancourt at ofound faulty. Borrowed one post to & Argent from Heavy Artillery. Obtained list of lines allotted to divs in Corps Reserve routes from Corps Officer I/c Divigl Routes.	
	29th		Put through pair from Q.Q. to Cat Tunnel for 20th Bde.	
	30th		91st Inf Bde. H.Q. moved back to Mailly Mavillet. Commn. rearranged accordingly. Bde worked forward on divn lines.	

M.P.Shown - Capt R.E.
O.C. 91st Div Sig Coy R.E.

Army Form C. 2118.

Signal 7D

Vol 14

WAR DIARY
or
INTELLIGENCE SUMMARY.
(Erase heading not required.)

Instructions regarding War Diaries and Intelligence Summaries are contained in F. S. Regs., Part II. and the Staff Manual respectively. Title pages will be prepared in manuscript.

Place	Date	Hour	Summary of Events and Information	Remarks and references to Appendices
December. 1916.	1st		Lt. PRENDERGAST joined as supernumerary for duty.	
			1/2 Lamas (Primus) started rebuilding test magnets in buried routes from office at Gd.45.c. west city.	
			Internal wiring in Mailly Maillet signal office renewed.	
			37th Div. Arty. relieved 2nd Div. Arty. 37th D.A. signal officer took over all lines in use by 2nd D.A.	
			Div Train connected to Div. Exchange.	
			Temporary cable lines to L.P. dugouts finished.	
	2nd		Lt. Prendergast was attached to Signal Officer 37th D.A. to assist him and to learn lines and routes.	
			Cable to assist 72nd D.A. on arrival.	
			Lt. Colston commenced making line diagrams etc	
			Power party continued on test boxes.	
			Communication by telephone was reported unsatisfactory to all battalions from G.O.C. front line. This is the most front ever taken over by this divn. & its signals from Beth- thines. They had practically all to be laid	

Army Form C. 2118.

WAR DIARY
or
INTELLIGENCE SUMMARY.
(Erase heading not required.)

Instructions regarding War Diaries and Intelligence Summaries are contained in F.S. Regs., Part II. and the Staff Manual respectively. Title pages will be prepared in manuscript.

Place	Date	Hour	Summary of Events and Information	Remarks and references to Appendices
	December, 1916			
	2nd		H.P. buried route from Bertrancourt to G.B.4's. Tested out and found to be very earthy. An effort was made to clear earth but it was found to be a general leakage. Div. School at Vauchel connected to Exchange at Do. M.B.	
	4th		Clearing party on lines in Bertrancourt. All old cables picked up. F.B.S.T. route overhauled from Beaussart to 94th Lancs. and S.A.A. dumps. Line from Toutencourt to old British Front Line traced out and tested for use to G.1/1 a S.S. The runs adv. H.Q. of night B.L.G.	
	5th		Line from Toutencourt tested on 4th, extended to adv. Bde. H.Q. through armoured tunnel. Clearing party started in Beaussart. (N2 detail) 91st Inf Bde relieved 70th Inf Bde in left sector.	
	6th		Clearing party continued in Beaussart. Two airlines to hire exchanges installed at adv. H.Q. instead of D5 line above which is very faulty.	

Army Form C. 2118.

WAR DIARY
or
INTELLIGENCE SUMMARY.
(Erase heading not required.)

Instructions regarding War Diaries and Intelligence Summaries are contained in F.S. Regs., Part II. and the Staff Manual respectively. Title pages will be prepared in manuscript.

Place	Date	Hour	Summary of Events and Information	Remarks and references to Appendices
	December 1916.			
	7th		Clearing partly in Beaumont continued. W.BST. lines re-laid to W. dugout	
	8th			
	9th		Pioneer party completed testing outs on White City route. 22nd Inf. Bde. moved M.B. from Minty Miniert to Beaumont and 20th Inf. Bde. moved to Beaucourt.	
	10th		No 32 detacht. laid pair 705 from T. dugout to Q.17 a 88. Work started on White City lines, endeavouring to trace them out.	
	11th		Another pair laid from T. dugout to Q.17 a 88. main Featherstone wiring on old pair extracted. Clearing and relaying wiring in Beaumont finished and laid an extra pair WBSTR Lineman at Beaumont started to wiring office and Lewis gun. 20th Inf.Bde. relieved 22nd Inf./Bde.	
	12th		Earth faults cleared on first line from T to Q.17 a 88. No 2 detacht. and Lt Baynes attached with J=D-2 mG.	

2353 Wt. W3544/1454 700,000 5/15 D. D. & L. A.D.S.S./Forms/C. 2118.

Army Form C. 2118.

Instructions regarding War Diaries and Intelligence
Summaries are contained in F. S. Regs., Part II.
and the Staff Manual respectively. Title pages
will be prepared in manuscript.

WAR DIARY
or
INTELLIGENCE SUMMARY.
(Erase heading not required.)

Place	Date	Hour	Summary of Events and Information	Remarks and references to Appendices
	December 1915			
	13th		Lt Watson went to Applefies HQ and Capt Wilkinson returned to div HQ.	
	14th		Line from Ex Nugent to R17.a.88. which had been laid by Bn cents was lifted and relaid in old trenches and disused tunnel. Diagram of communications attached, showing lines to inf Bdes etc.	Appendix I.
	15th		Brigade unit distributor to RA batteries & Bdes. Magneto unit installed.	
	16th		7th Divn Arty relieved 37th Div Arty. Diagram of communications to RA Bdes attached. Stables completed and all roads put under cover.	Appendix II
	17th		Pair of D5 cable was laid direct from Beaumont to 14th Bde RHA. HDS. Head wire 12th Cd. to provide a heliographic forward for 14th Bde.RHA. and cct to Beaumont via BST. HQ. Rewiring of W. Nugent carried out. Terminal boards rearranged and proper "jumpers" arranged. New trestle route from W. Nugent to H. Nugent started. Trestles were made up ready to erect. Picked up BST 3a, 4 & 6. I.C. bottom arm on this conit route from Beaumont. There were too many lines on this route for the weight of poles used.	
	18th		Continued with cable route. and rewiring W. Nugent. Relaid lines in orchard behind Beaumont office. Diagram attached showing lines to inf Bde and buried lines in use by Bdes.	Appendix III

Army Form C. 2118.

WAR DIARY
or
INTELLIGENCE SUMMARY.
(Erase heading not required.)

Instructions regarding War Diaries and Intelligence
Summaries are contained in F.S. Regs., Part II.
and the Staff Manual respectively. Title pages
will be prepared in manuscript.

Place	Date	Hour	Summary of Events and Information	Remarks and references to Appendices
	December 1916			
	19th		Comic airline route. PST. 1 + 2 + HR Bay route relaid. H.W. Bonz continued.	
	20th		Relabelled HD route to BT/9.2.6. route. Relaid line from M.Boisgente to 25th Bde R.F.A.	
	21st		Completed put up trestles on WWI route. Lofed in BT. Feb. 3 to 14th Bde R.F.A. Marked forward from Beaurest to G.S. (offsetline) and back. 19th Bde. R.F.A. buzzer line to divis"	
	22nd		Laid WW1 @ and WW2 twisted D5 and put additional stays on trestles. New permanent route to B dugout from BT. Taken into use. Line to DPC. Laid, using one pair on some route.	
	23rd		Cable in Ben transcent thrown spare by use of new route to G. picked up. Clearing party in Mailly Maillet village completed work. Lt. Davenport started working with Sound ranging section under orders from Fifth Army Sigs. Laid WW3. on trestle route.	

Army Form C. 2118.

Instructions regarding War Diaries and Intelligence
Summaries are contained in F. S. Regs., Part II.
and the Staff Manual respectively. Title pages
will be prepared in manuscript.

WAR DIARY
or
INTELLIGENCE SUMMARY.
(Erase heading not required.)

Place	Date	Hour	Summary of Events and Information	Remarks and references to Appendices
	December 1916			
	24th		Rewiring of signal office at D.H.Q. E.8 started and terminal board installed.	
			T.M.H. 1 and 2 and 3. Ex-H.H. 1 exchanges and labelled.	
			Notice boards "All lines to be answered HERE" placed in Mailly Mallet.	
			Fullerphone set arranged from Divn. to Lonsdownt, superimposed on School Telephone line, for messages to battery waggon lines of the Divl. Arty. Lonsdownt set manned by one signaller from each R.F.A. Bde.	
	25th		7th Divnl. Depot Battalion. connected to Divisional Exchange. Wiring etc of limited lines ability to get completed, but all my T.G. Boxing Day. By using of Corps Commander as little work as possible was done. No working parties were sent out.	
	26th		D.H.Q. by Bus relieved 32nd by 1 Bde in the line. Escorts & Battalions in Mailly Mallet arranged. Rewiring of dugout at D.H.Q. completed. Motor Garage just myself to Lonsdowne arc weton during absence of 1st Bde on leave.	
	27th		Second line from E5 dugout to D.H.Q. B laid (Ex-H.H.2) following the same route as exH.H.1. Relaying of cable lead in to Beaumont office from orchard carried out. Ringing Telephone installed to 54th Manchesters and connected to Beaumont Exchange. Diagram of communications to inf/Bdes and buried lines to Bns. attached and diagram of artillery communications resume last	Appendix IV Appendix V

2353 Wt. W2544/1454 700,000 5/15 D. D. & L. A.D.S.S./Forms/C. 2118.

Army Form C. 2118.

WAR DIARY
or
INTELLIGENCE SUMMARY
(Erase heading not required.)

Instructions regarding War Diaries and Intelligence Summaries are contained in F. S. Regs., Part II. and the Staff Manual respectively. Title pages will be prepared in manuscript.

Place	Date	Hour	Summary of Events and Information	Remarks and references to Appendices
	December 1916			
	28th		Patrol line from 22nd Bde RFA to 33rd Bde RFA overhauled. Line 87/87/A1 between Barbamont and ? overhauled.	
	29th		BST. 3, 4 and 5, 6 overhauled, also N-BST. 11, 12, 13. White City lines to Appletrees retested & by it clear overbearing.	
	30th		New testboard installed at A.D.G.S. Office.	
	31st		Laid line in Martby Mallet. Fr 32nd Div. Bdes who are reported living here an armoured guard along back of road and walk to 35th Bde RFA and 155th Battn. Buzzer lines to 35th Bde extended to 168th Bde AFA & 161 Bde RFA. Cont. D5 pair from ? extent	

M Thomson Capt RE
O.C. 7th Divn Sig Coy RE

2353 Wt. W2544/1454 700,000 5/15 D. D. & L. A.D.S.S./Forms/C. 2118.

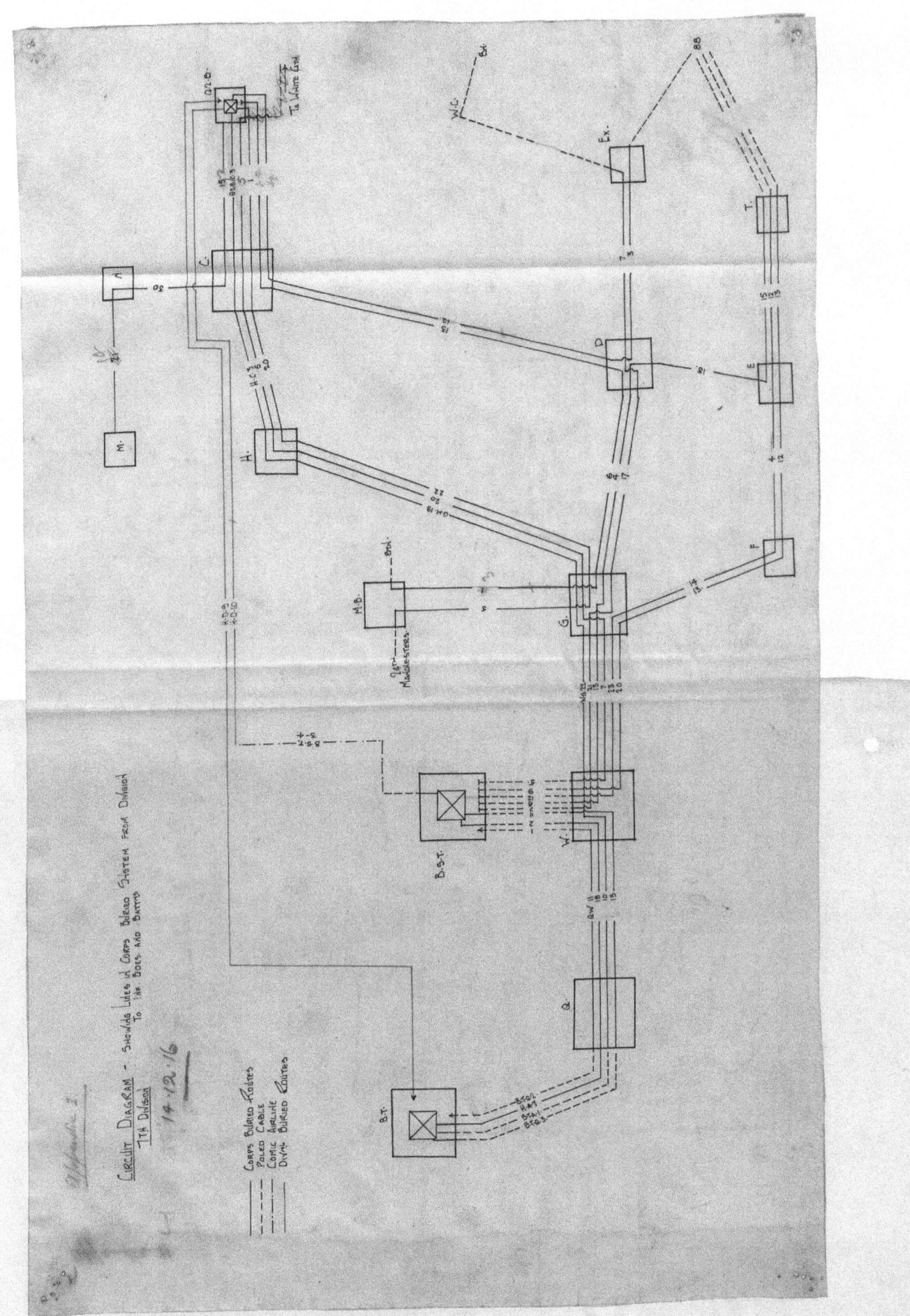

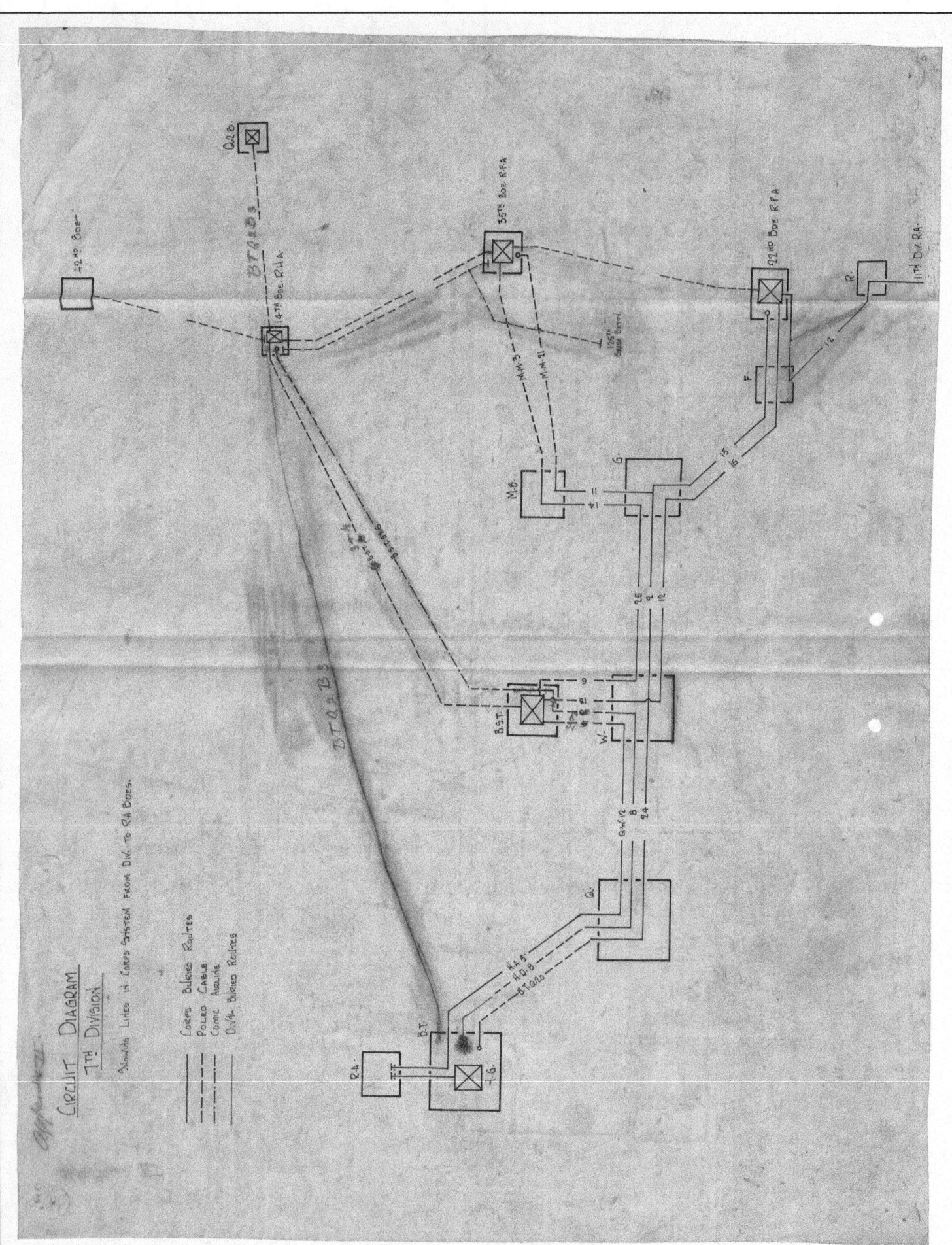

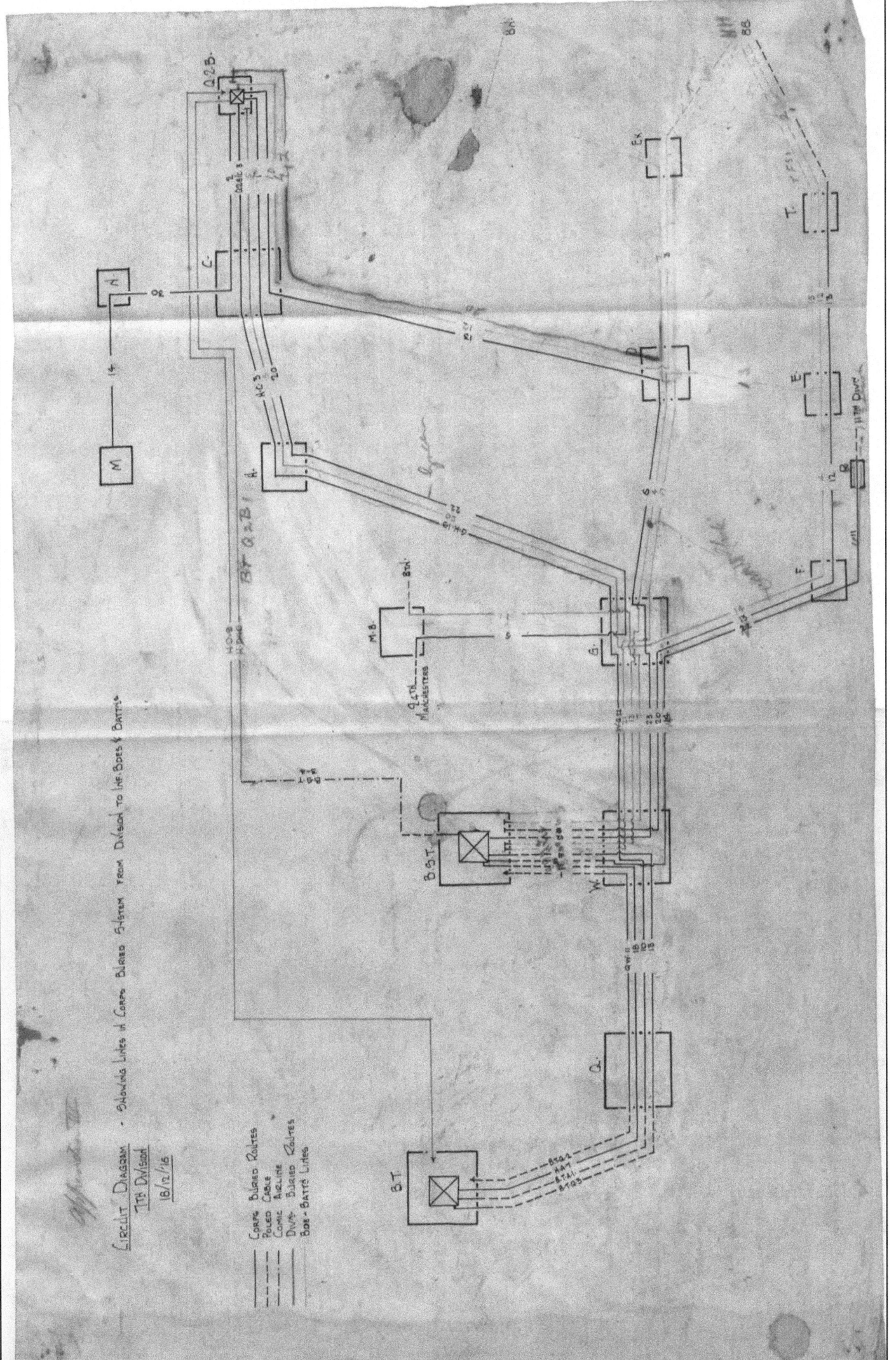

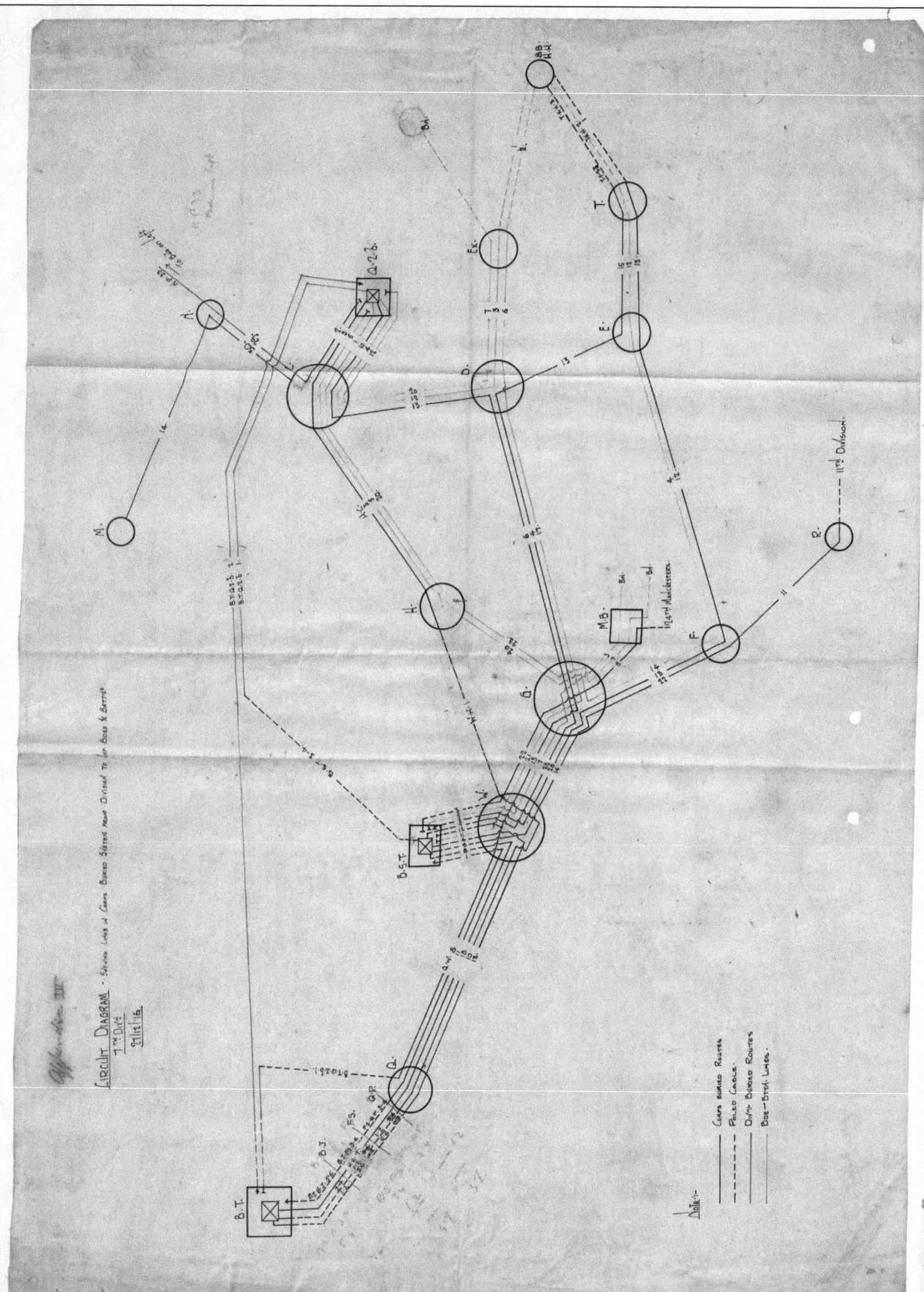

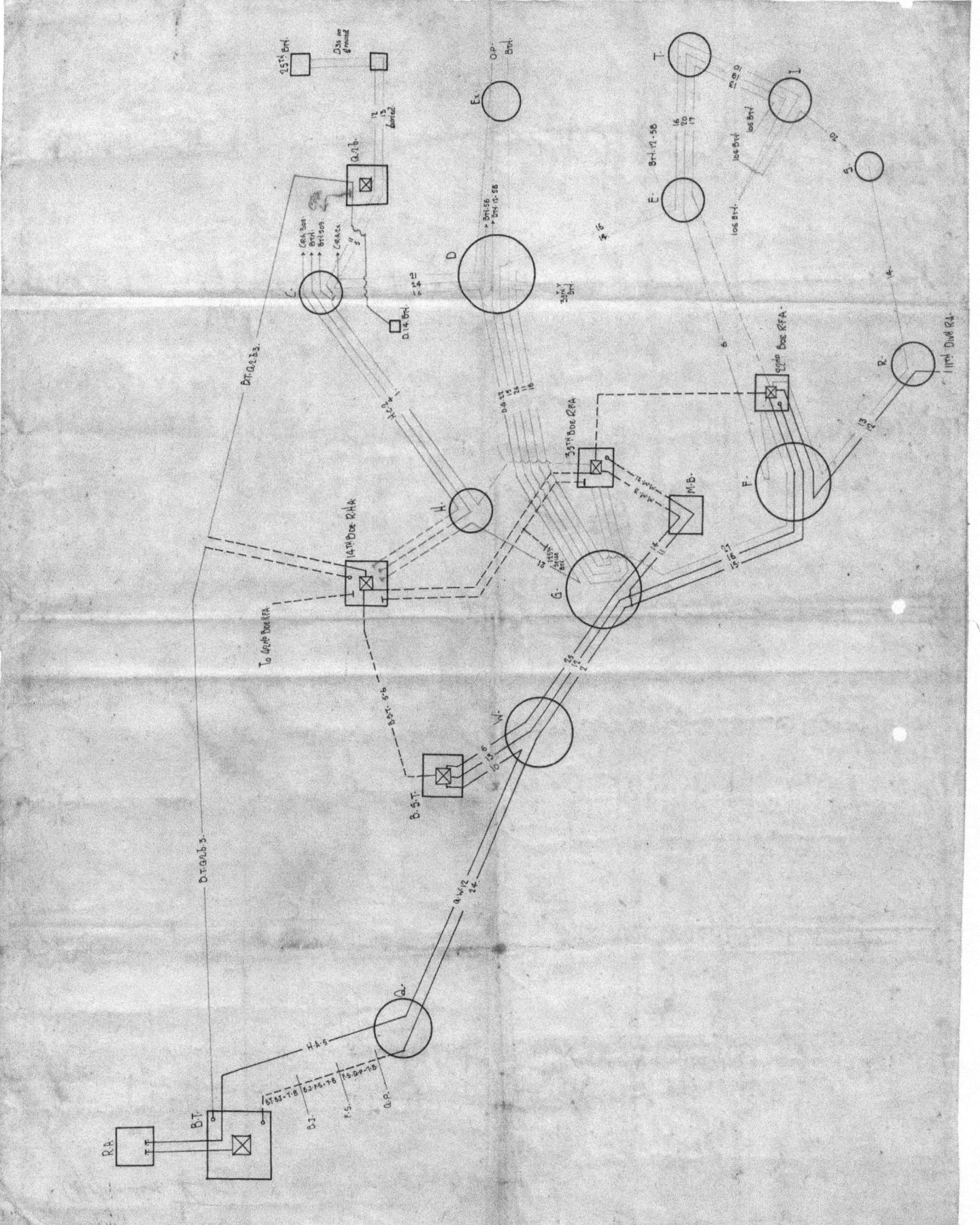

7th DIVISION.

7th DIVISIONAL SIGNAL COMPANY.

JANUARY 1917.

A. Branch
7th Div[?]

Herewith Jan 17
war diary for
7th Div Sig Coy.
Appendices attached.

[signature]
Capt[?]
for OC 7th Div Sig Coy
4/2/17

Army Form C. 2118.

WAR DIARY
or
INTELLIGENCE SUMMARY.
(Erase heading not required.)

7 DM Signal Vol 15

Instructions regarding War Diaries and Intelligence Summaries are contained in F. S. Regs., Part II. and the Staff Manual respectively. Title pages will be prepared in manuscript.

Place	Date	Hour	Summary of Events and Information	Remarks and references to Appendices
	January 1st 1917		Exchange opened at Mailly Maillet. RA Boles and proven stations connected to it. Traveller switchboard put in Beauvort. One cable detail from 32nd Div. Sig. Cy. arrived, to prepare line & 32nd Div. & Ty Boles.	
	2nd		Laid the following lines in preparation for communication to 39th Div Arty Bgns.— (a) Pilot cable pair from Hedgepost to Sillet No 50 fr 161st Bde 1st, (b) " " " " " No 22 fr 153rd Bde RA. (c) Completed armoured cable line station – 31st bde & 155th bde. Divl School Vandelicourt required to open Lillets about 3/4 mile distant line extended.	
	3rd		Average line from Mailly Ex. office to 14th Bde. and ted off then buzzer line to 10th RFA and extended to 155th Bde RFA. Picked up cable in Mailly, which was interfered with 1657 f.4. & 516. Connected Mailly Pigeon Loft to exchange.	

2353 Wt. W2544/1454 700,000 5/15 D. D. & L. A.D.S.S./Forms/C. 2118.

Army Form C. 2118.

Instructions regarding War Diaries and Intelligence Summaries are contained in F. S. Regs., Part II. and the Staff Manual respectively. Title pages will be prepared in manuscript.

WAR DIARY
or
INTELLIGENCE SUMMARY.
(Erase heading not required.)

Place	Date	Hour	Summary of Events and Information	Remarks and references to Appendices
	January 1917			
	4th		Three Orty Bdes from 32nd Div. joined MB in Shelley Mallet and joined up on lines previously laid. 7th Divn. Depot Battalion move from Rancheval to Vaudelles. Telephone tried in on school line. Lt Colton + 3 hirers tried + found done. German cables S of Beaumont Hamel but had no success will try lines opposite BP. Cable lines inspected, maintained. Capt. Whicker left on leave.	
	5th		Lt Newton returned to Divn. MQ. 168th Bde. RFA moved MQ to new position, lines extended. Lt Remigart guides 32nd Div Arty Bdes now to 32nd Div Sig Off. by m/c.	
	6th		Relieved 24th Manchester and IMA. Lui. Whicker to Hospital.	

Army Form C. 2118.

WAR DIARY
or
INTELLIGENCE SUMMARY.
(Erase heading not required.)

Place	Date	Hour	Summary of Events and Information	Remarks and references to Appendices
January 1917	7th		Put through line to Battalion at Pt 7a. (FRST 1+2) El Watzan posted to 20th Infantry Brigade.	
	8th		Lt Colston and detachment went to man Headquarters at Point 86 (MH). Saw OEXA lines on account of earth faults on cables. Lt Pendergast reported to 22nd Bde RFA. to assist with their communications.	
	9th		Further work at OEXA lines – final preparations for the attack	
	10th		20th Infantry Brigade attack at 2am.	
	11th		9.163 Infantry Brigade attack at 6.40 am. Drum office at Point 86 handed over to 11th Bde. Lt Colston returns to Division and is sent on G.H.Q. wireless course for 4 days.	
	12th			
	13th			

WAR DIARY
or
INTELLIGENCE SUMMARY.
(Erase heading not required.)

Army Form C. 2118.

Place	Date	Hour	Summary of Events and Information	Remarks and references to Appendices
	Jan 1917			
	13th		(continued) Dr Brindeyer Transferred to 11th Divisions -	
	14th		Work in camp.	
	15th		Sgt Regan's detachment employed on welding up cable. The men employed by S. School villages are further used in Camp. The village of Mailly itself is almost nearly up.	
	16th		Starting other huts in camp.	
	17th		do	
	18th		The welding up still carried out gently. Huts used by snow.	
	19th		Exchange moved from MAILLY MAILLET to BEAUSART on account of (1) 32 Div Arty moving out. (11) advantage of concentrating personnel life.	
	20th		when Division moves out. Whilst handing over to 32nd Division (32nd Infantry only) general preparations for move being put into force following division. Orders thought to at date visit changes 19th inst.	

Army Form C. 2118.

WAR DIARY
or
INTELLIGENCE SUMMARY.
(Erase heading not required.)

Instructions regarding War Diaries and Intelligence Summaries are contained in F. S. Regs., Part II. and the Staff Manual respectively. Title pages will be prepared in manuscript.

Place	Date	Hour	Summary of Events and Information	Remarks and references to Appendices
	21st		Much improvement in Brigades in follows: [illegible]	
	22nd		[illegible handwritten entries]	
	23rd		[illegible handwritten entries]	

Communications – 7th Division
24th Jan. 1917 – 31st Jan. 1917

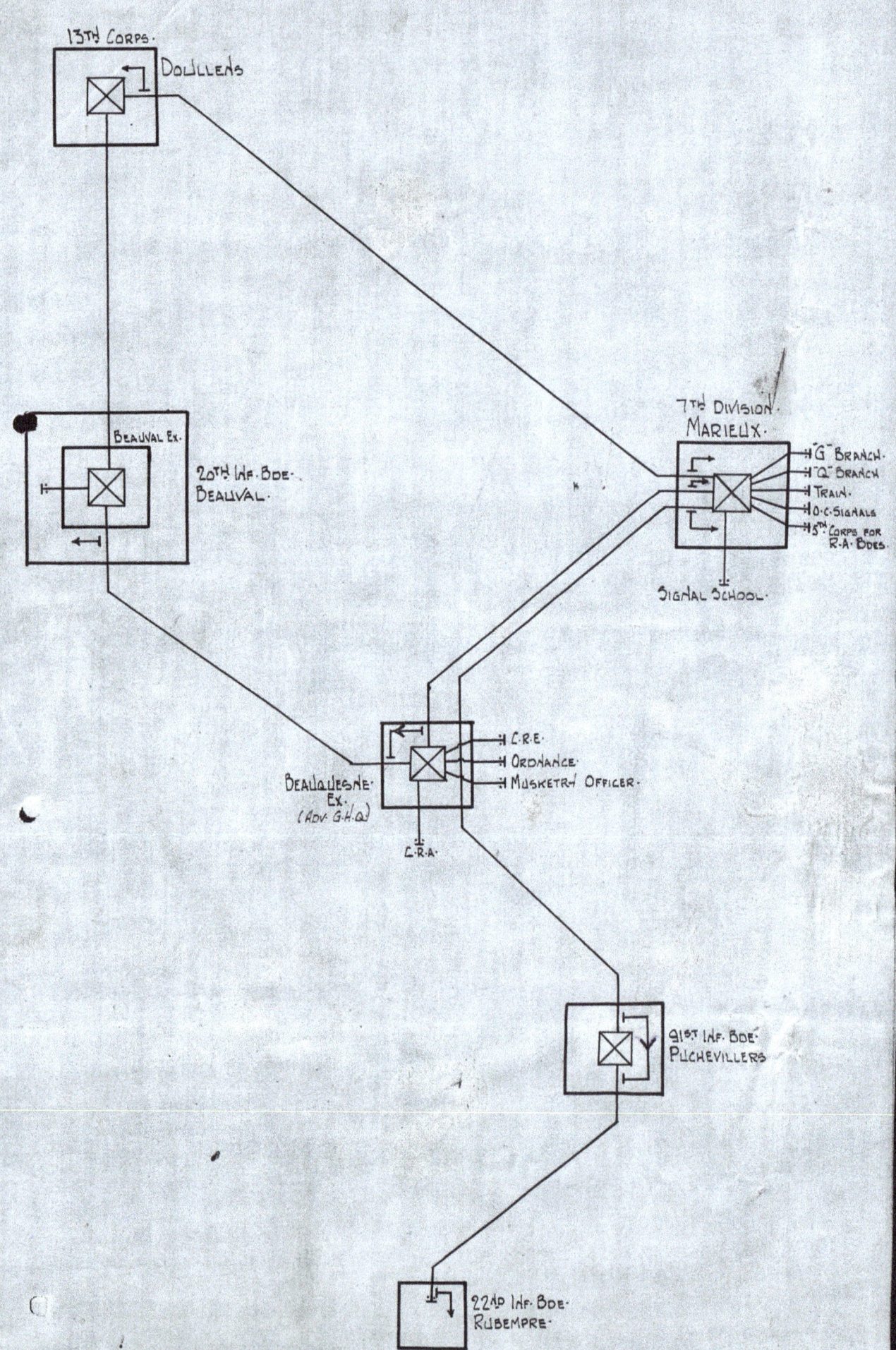

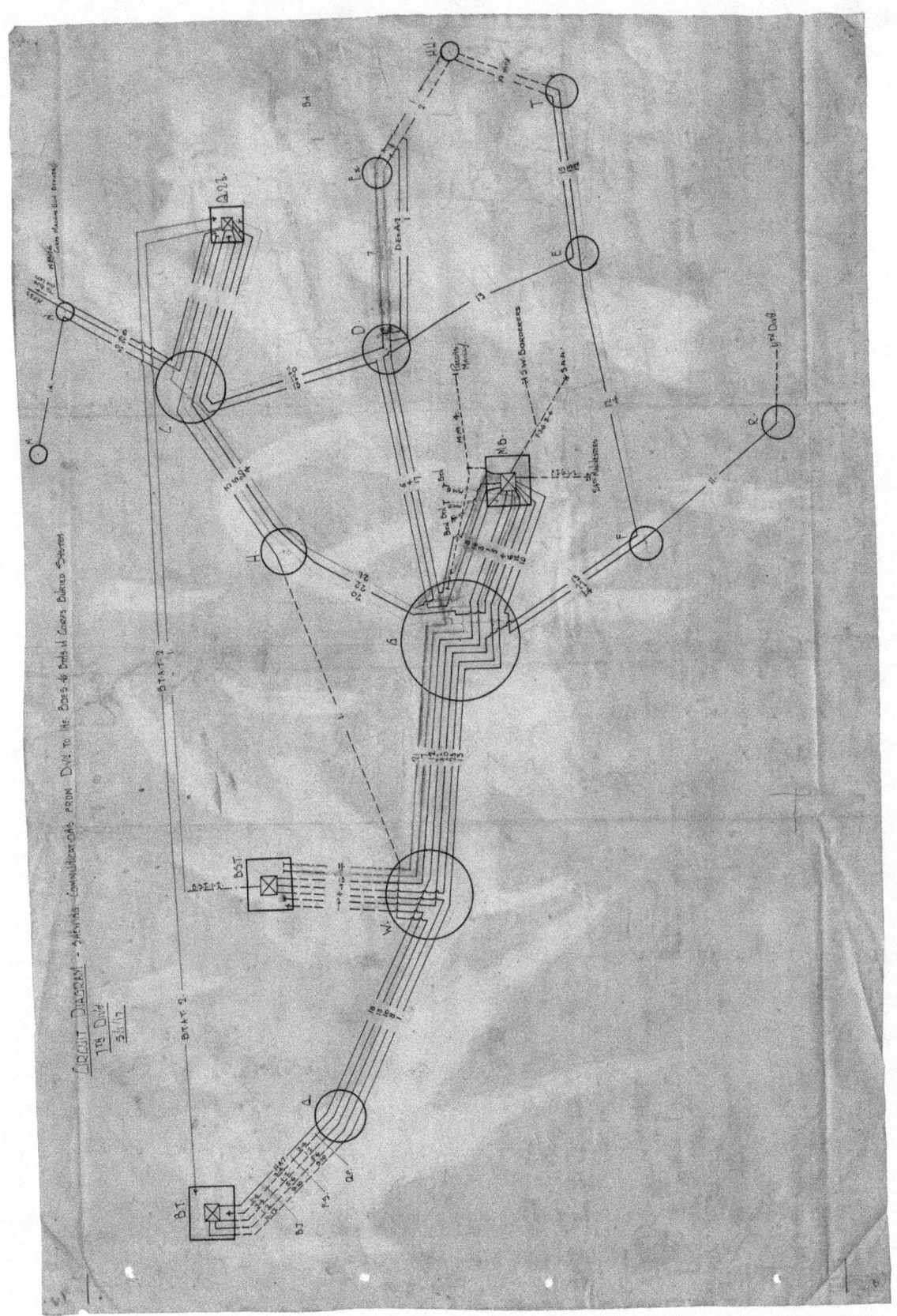

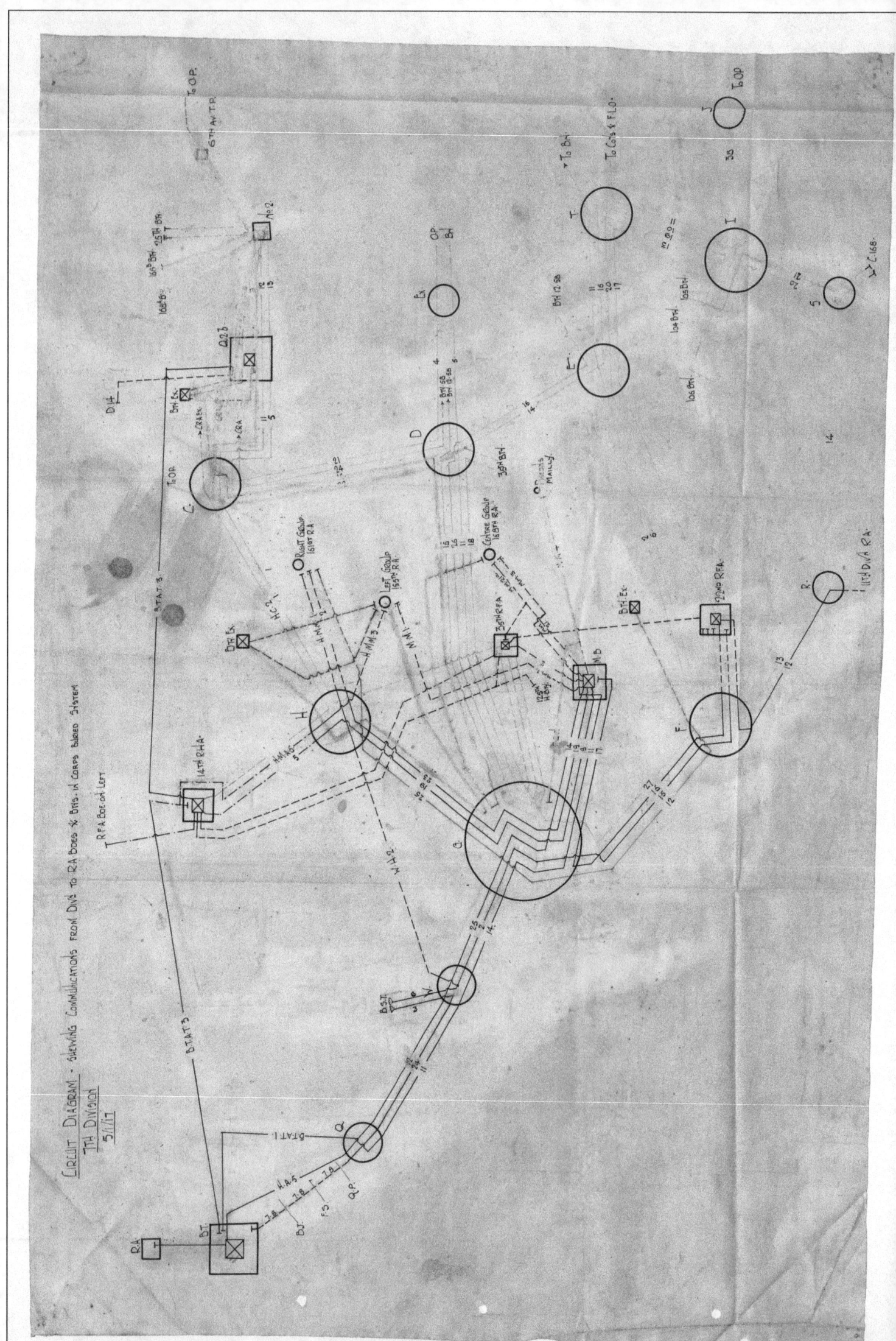

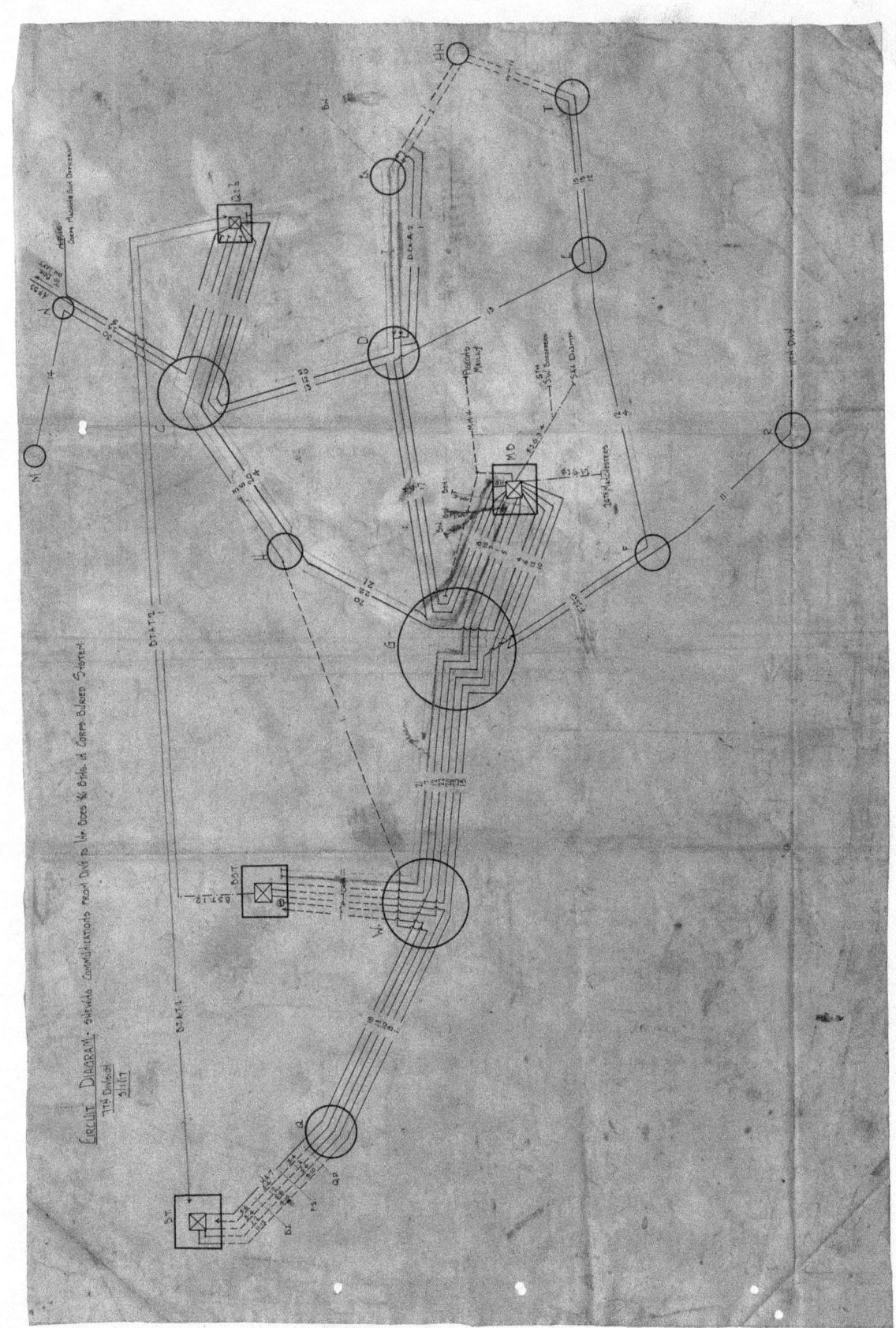

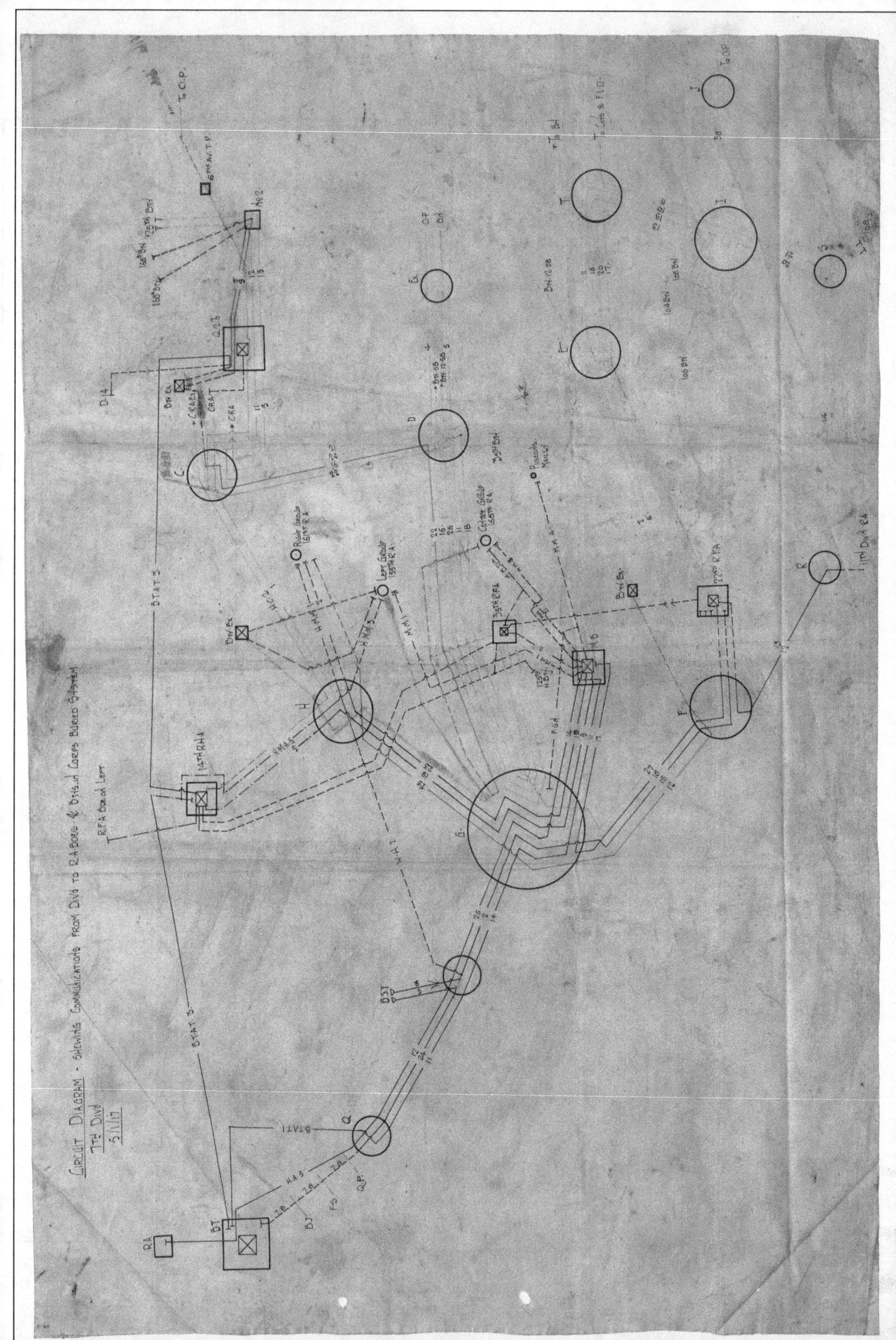

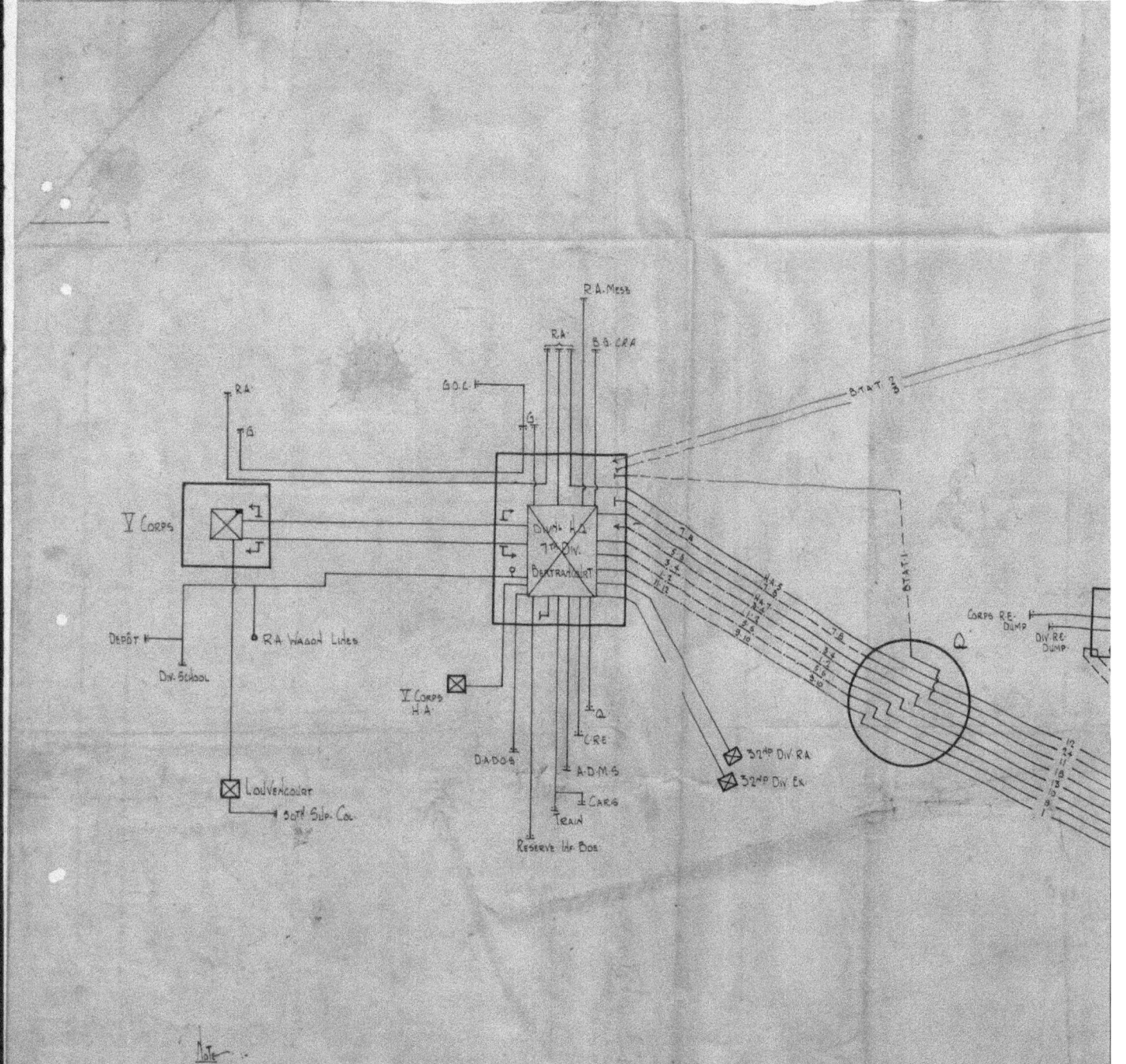

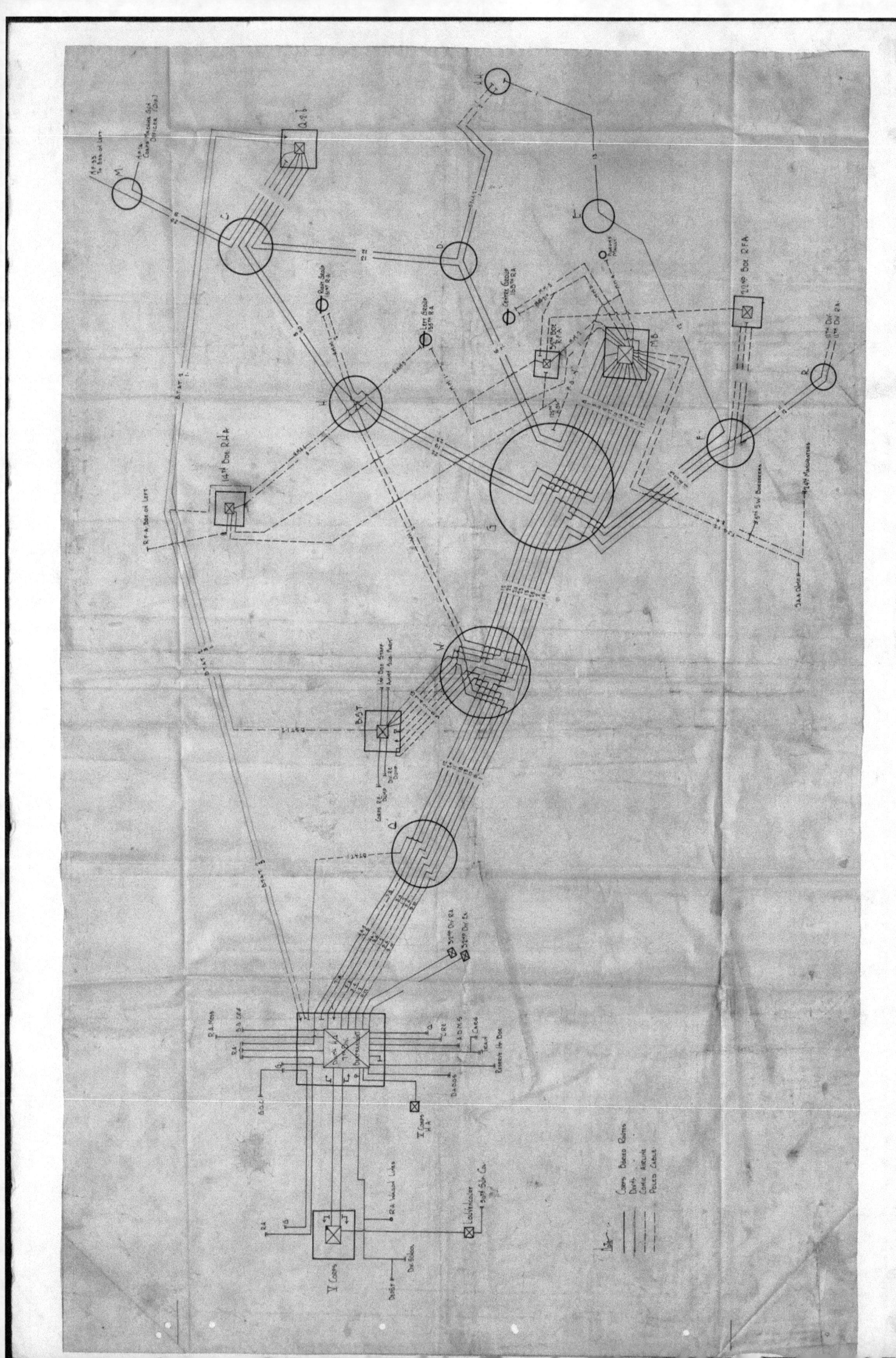

Communications - 7th Division
Shewing Lines from Divn to Infr Bdes, Arty Bdes, & Divnl Troops
Jan. 20th 1916

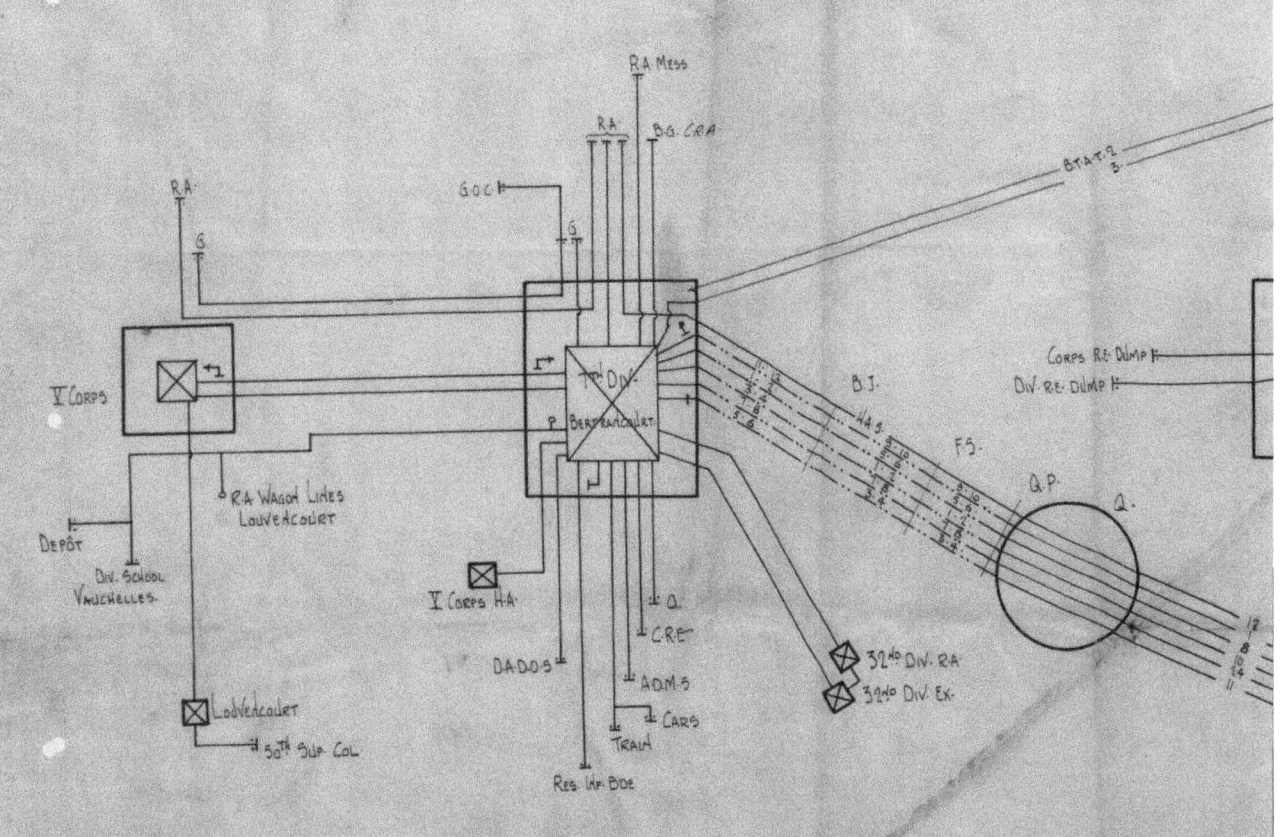

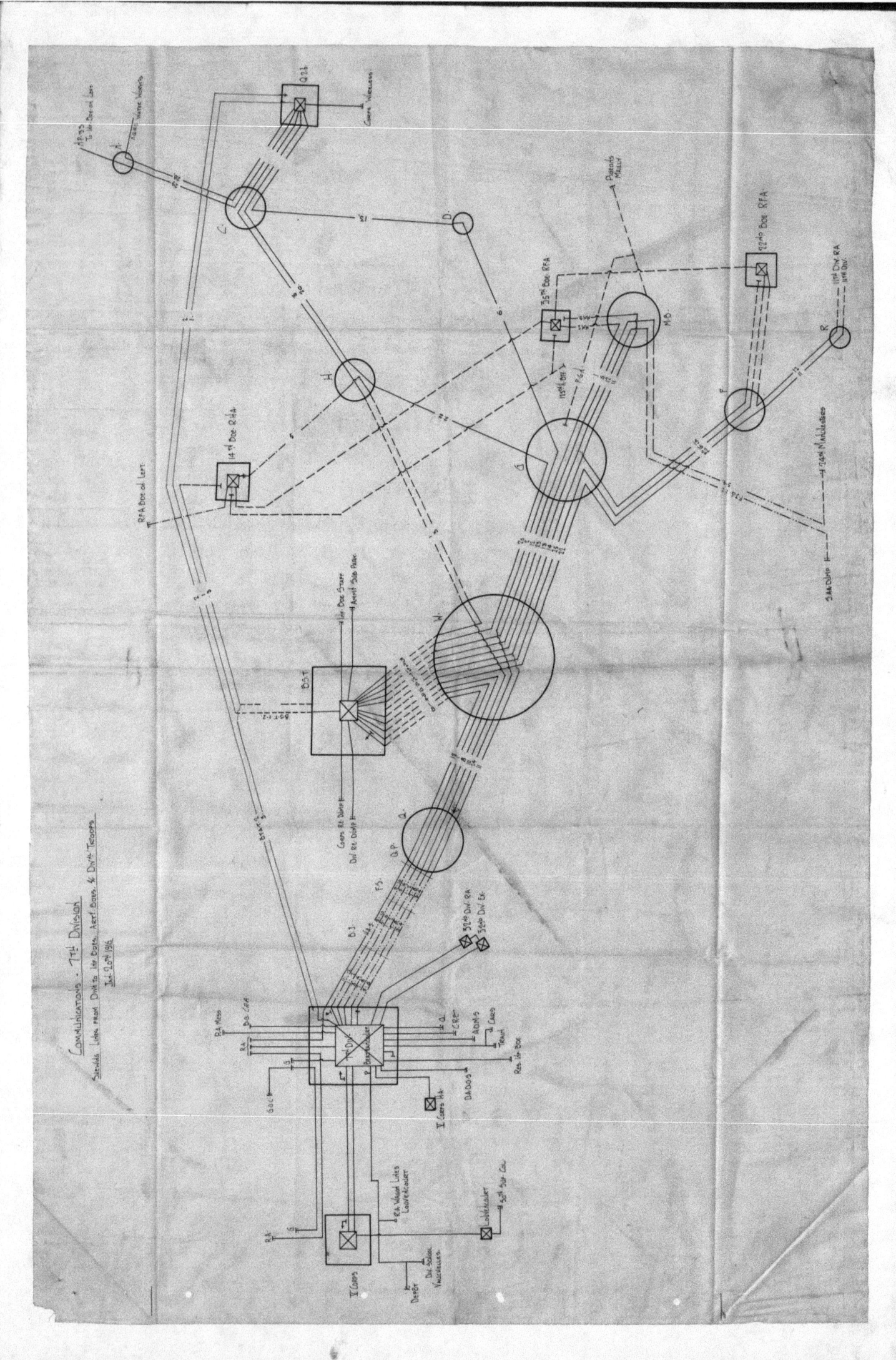

Army Form C. 2118.

WAR DIARY
or
INTELLIGENCE SUMMARY
(Erase heading not required.)

Instructions regarding War Diaries and Intelligence Summaries are contained in F. S. Regs., Part II. and the Staff Manual respectively. Title pages will be prepared in manuscript.

Place	Date	Hour	Summary of Events and Information	Remarks and references to Appendices
Zillibeke (Huns)	1/4/17 to 16/4/17		During this period the majority of the Signal company were devoted to training. The training may be divided under two heading (a) Signal School (b) Company training. Signal School. There was organised with a view to train Instructors for the Signal sections. Each Bn. in the Bde. provided two students apiece for training. The men had a certain idea of signalling before they joined the class. There was also a class for Signalling officers. The course included (i) Visual signalling with flag, lamp and shutter, (ii) Buzzing (iii) Semaphore (iv) Lectures on Elementary Electricity (v) Instruments (vi) Pigeons (vii) Power Buzzers and 1.T.S. (viii) Earth circuits (ix) D.MK III Telephone and Magnetos Telephones (x) Line Net and overhead work and (xi) Practical schemes. The majority of these under

instruction and give him the title of Gas Clean Operator, and further that a working knowledge of the more modern apparatus —

An during the period when the Company Trench School has been in operation, the majority of the Company instructors have been employed at that School. This training has not so thorough as might have been desired. The fully qualified also have hundred the buzzer & two officers and two NCOs. However much than some in Buzzing etc., however much than some in Buzzing etc., though electrical men planting listening in telephone expert from 5th Army given and a telephone expert from 5th Army Signal School also lectured to the Company. Further training consisted of Infantry drill, wagon drill and Physical Training

Army Form C. 2118.

WAR DIARY
or
INTELLIGENCE SUMMARY.
(Erase heading not required.)

Instructions regarding War Diaries and Intelligence Summaries are contained in F.S. Regs., Part II. and the Staff Manual respectively. Title pages will be prepared in manuscript.

Place	Date	Hour	Summary of Events and Information	Remarks and references to Appendices
In field	17/2/17		Inspection of Division near VAL DE MAISON (BEAUQUESNE area) by General Sir Douglas Haig.	
	18/2/17		Capt Whitham left for winter course GHQ.	
	19/2/17		Began to take over in BERTRANCOURT Section from 32nd Div -	
	20/2/17		however went 32nd Div with a view to taking lines etc.	
	21/2/17		Continues work of previous day.	
	22/2/17		Take over from 32nd Divn. Divn. Reports. 11th DLI in the line, communications behind Brigades being Simple.	
	23.2/17		The capture of SERRE. An hp. Idea at Waters Quarry. Visual communication established between Bde Hqrs at Apple trees and Bns in SERRE.	
	24/2/17		Written establd MOUSE POST and WALTER QUARRY Group signals to OZB directing stations - Sig Iggants Oakhollow lays line through BEAUMONT HAMEL to extend Capt Cherry.	
			11th DA signals joins the company Capt Whitham 1st returns from winter course -	

2353 Wt. W2544/1454 700,000 5/15 D.D. & L. A.D.S.S. Forms/C. 2118.

Army Form C. 2118.

WAR DIARY
or
INTELLIGENCE SUMMARY.
(Erase heading not required.)

Instructions regarding War Diaries and Intelligence Summaries are contained in F. S. Regs., Part II. and the Staff Manual respectively. Title pages will be prepared in manuscript.

Place	Date	Hour	Summary of Events and Information	Remarks and references to Appendices
In the field	25/2/17 26th 27th		Put lines through to 58th & 59th Brigades RFA in my alley. Put his through to 22nd RFA near Sutton Dumps, hy Bde Sections during this period lines of Twisted cable and D Two cable over the Lahoun entailed was very convenient, and the circuits could only be laid on the ground owing to difficulty of maintaining a supply of poles. Opl Allentino Loy. between hy Bde and white city as an infantry drug between these points is necessary to prove satisfactory results —	
	28th			

W M Strahan Capt
to OC 7th Inv.dn R.E.

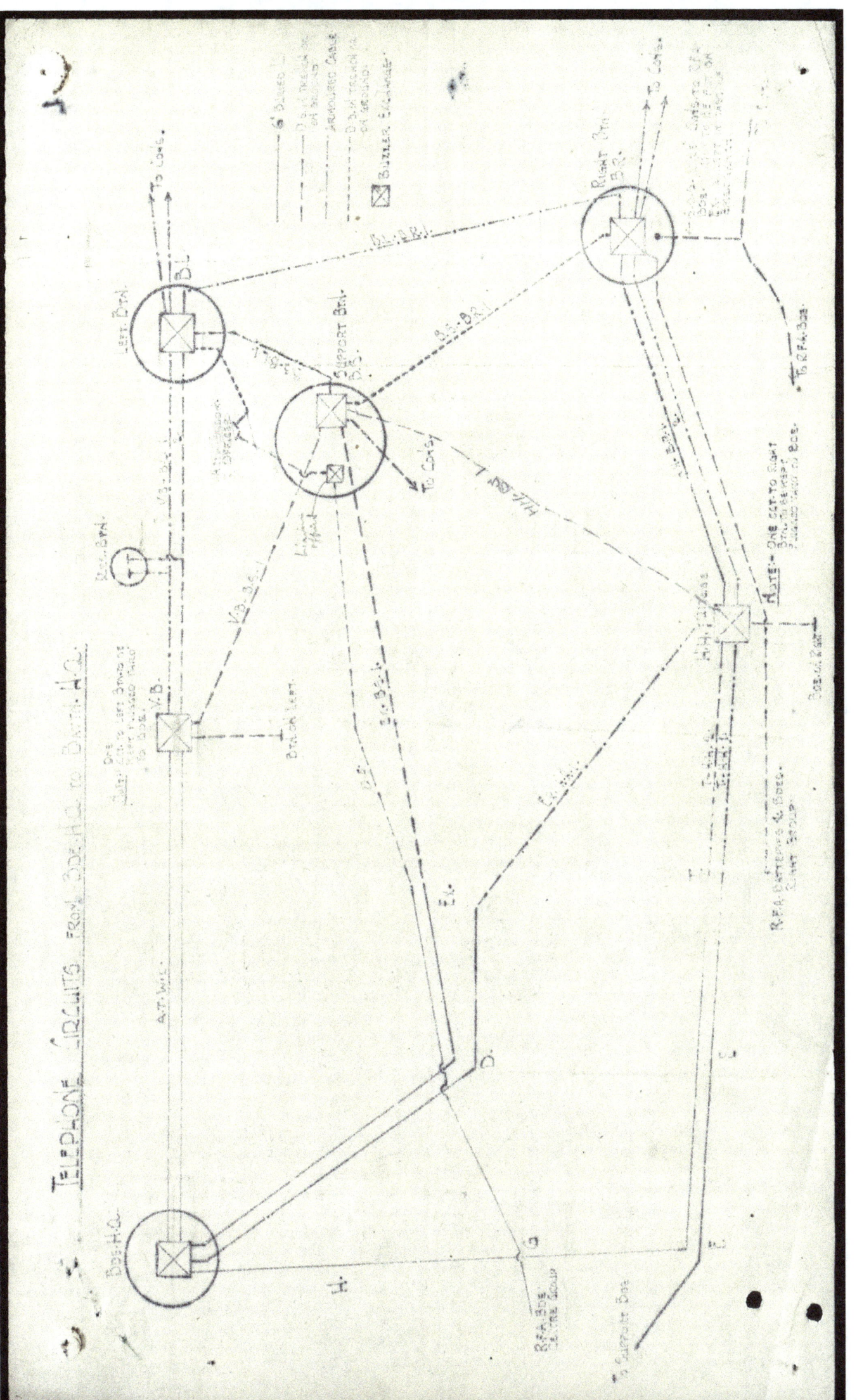

Communications - 7th Division.
31st Jan. 1917 -

7th Division Marieux.
- "G" Branch
- "Q" Branch
- Train
- O.C. Signals
- Signal School
- 5th Corps for R.A. Bde.

Beauquesne Ex. (Adv. G.H.Q.)
- C.R.A.
- C.R.E.
- Ordnance
- Musketry Officer

15th Corps Doullens.

91st Inf. Bde. Puchevillers

22nd Inf. Bde. Rubempré.

20th Inf. Bde. Canaples

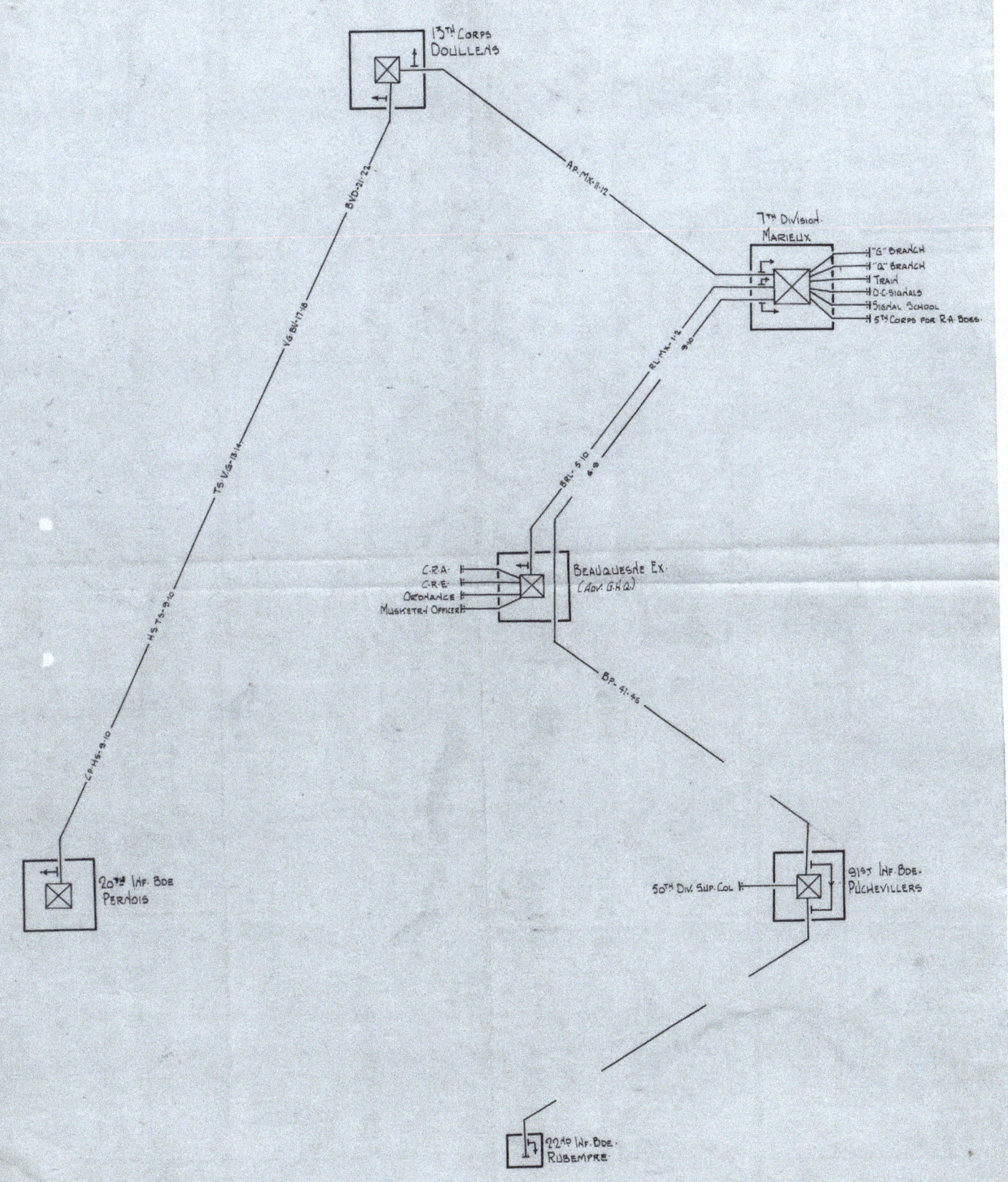

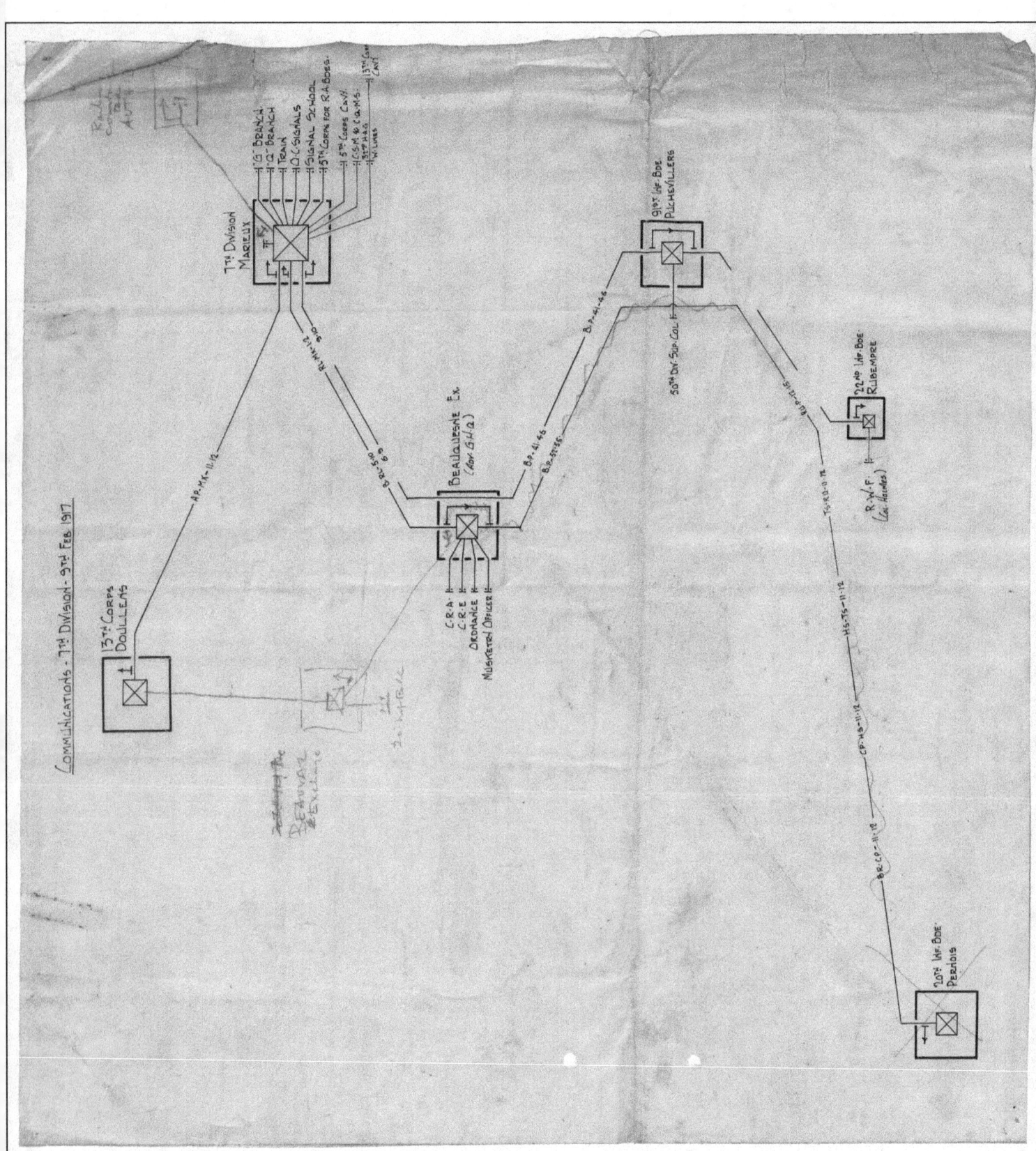

WAR DIARY
INTELLIGENCE SUMMARY

Army Form C. 2118.

7th DIVISIONAL SIGNAL COMPANY, R.E.

Place	Date	Hour	Summary of Events and Information	Remarks and references to Appendices
2nd fwd	1/3/17	1.	Mailly офис prepared for occupation by Divn. – Phone calls not laid to extend cups. Going to BAILEY QUARRY.	
		2.	35th RFA in Mailly connected to Mailly exchange – 2umm work in MB офис and on local lines in MAILLY-MAILLET village.	
		3.	White City route closed – Iron pond frame got through – (N: 2 first look to WHITECITY офис until an hour later – Cpl. COOK was went to MAILLY at Infantry Dets connects? afstructively – order for the RFA in MAILLY connected to exchange –	
		4.	BUCQUOY attack. Orders for relief of 7th Divn by 31st Divn – 2 Pairs laid WHITE CITY to WALKER QUARRY. Plan route known over Thirty cut up ground – with heavy casualties very heavy labour. BEAUCOURT-PUISIEUX road connected –	
		5.	35th RFA in BEAUCOURT-PUISIEUX road connected.	
		6.	Capt. Brown hit by shell of unkt. – he was hit by Alft explosive shell between SERRE and PUISIEUX while reconnoitring. Counted and died about 7 hours later –	
		7.	22 RFA adv. connected. 3 pairs 1 wire cable laid from WALKER QUARRY to Advanced Inf/Bde. Hqrs in dug-out.	

Army Form C. 2118.

7th DIVISIONAL SIGNAL COMPANY, R.E.

No. .... Date ....

WAR DIARY
or
INTELLIGENCE SUMMARY.
(Erase heading not required.)

Instructions regarding War Diaries and Intelligence Summaries are contained in F. S. Regs., Part II. and the Staff Manual respectively. Title pages will be prepared in manuscript.

Place	Date	Hour	Summary of Events and Information	Remarks and references to Appendices
in TEN TREE ALLEY	8		Our line 6ts on ground laid by 81st Bde detachm from the batty pres to MOUSE POST on MAILLY - SERRE road - Advanced party withdrawn from OPs - BERTRANCOURT except for a small party of linesmen - line laid OPs to 7th Bde - line laid SR - SW - PLC	
	9		Cable Stairs MP - NT - 1st RFA connected to OPs by existing airline 22 - RFA advanced line - 19th DA. Lead over 2 pairs to SW. SW exchges opened - No'c'y'op's Benh'r. Ground cable laid SW - NT by party from dipots 11th DA.	
	10		81st Bde RFA connected to div exchge - Pair picked up 0915 - 62 Divn - MP - NT lines confirmed.	
	11		OC no. 135 reference attack on PUCQUOY. Preparations incomplete only 13m cable - line laid TT to NT and MP - SR -	
	12		Day employed on maintenance work and Cpl Stevens	

2353 Wt. W2544/1454 700,000 5/15 D.D.&L. A.D.S.S. Forms/C. 2118.

WAR DIARY
or
INTELLIGENCE SUMMARY

Army Form C. 2118.

7th DIVISIONAL SIGNAL COMPANY, R.E.

Place	Date	Hour	Summary of Events and Information	Remarks and references to Appendices
	13.		Connects 91 & 158 Bdes RFA RFA Exchange - Qrs/M route (2 pairs fitted OS cable) laid. - Rug'g line to 22 RFA installed.	
	14		1st Divn relieve 21 Divn 9:0am. - Divn Sigs ordered to move to APPLETREES in the evening for attack on BUCQUOY by 91st Inf Bde. -	
	15th		Attack on BUCQUOY failed - Communications was maintained to Bde throughout. - Divn HdQrs moved back to Authieuxcourt. Day employed on maintenance work and generally squaring up -	
	16th		Tent boards fitted at tent sites, otherwise general maintenance.	
	17th		One detachment (No 1) warned to move at ½ hours notice. - Capt. Keeling joins company. Divn HdQs move to APPLETREES again re BUCQUOY ex accepted by enemy and as No 1 detachment starts out to establish a corps signal station at DIERVILLE FARM. (This and from

Army Form C. 2118.

7th DIVISIONAL
SIGNAL COMPANY,
R.E.

No.
Date

WAR DIARY
or
INTELLIGENCE SUMMARY.
(Erase heading not required.)

Instructions regarding War Diaries and Intelligence
Summaries are contained in F. S. Regs., Part II.
and the Staff Manual respectively. Title pages
will be prepared in manuscript.

Place	Date	Hour	Summary of Events and Information	Remarks and references to Appendices
	18th		Move Company Camp from Berlencourt to Apple Trees (Q2b) get all staff local connections fixed - electric light etc.	
	19th		Strong Party commence building two-pair poled cable route to extend Corps route from PUISIEUX to ABLAINZEVILLE. Another party in camp building lines to connect Corps route into Div. Signal Office.	
	20th		Established forward camp at ABLAINZEVILLE with two detachments - finish poled cable route. 20th Brigade move to GOMIECOURT - connected to Div: by extending Puisieux-Ablainzeville route using to a large extent old enemy overhead open wire routes. Finish line to Corps route. More Salvage Party & one detachment to camp at PUISIEUX.	
	21st		Forward detachments improving & putting into good order the new lines from Puisieux to Gomiecourt local lines in Div Camp transferred to Air line to improve work & save cable.	
	22nd		Sent forward detachment from PUISIEUX to ABLAINZEVILLE. Put into working order one pair on old enemy route from ABLAINZEVILLE to ERVILLERS extend to MORY for use of 35th Bde R.F.A. One detachment lays cable line from GOMIECOURT (21st Bde R.F.A.) to 119th Heavy Battery (attached) at BÉHAGNIES.	
	23rd		Division HQ advances from APPLE TREES to COURCELLES reopening at 1.0 p.m. Temporary	

WAR DIARY
or
INTELLIGENCE SUMMARY.
(Erase heading not required.)

Army Form C. 2118.

7th DIVISIONAL SIGNAL COMPANY, R.E.

Place	Date	Hour	Summary of Events and Information	Remarks and references to Appendices
	24		Office established in village at 10.0 a.m. & Signal Office opened in DHQ camp at 2.0 p.m. Move all the Company from APPLE TREES and ABLAINZEVILLE to camp near DHQ leaving Salvage Party at PUISIEUX. 91st Inf Brigade moved to PUISIEUX and 22nd Inf Brigade to APPLE TREES, the latter making arrangements for traffic. Telephones to two parts of DHQ remaining behind. Make all lines to Staff telephones permanent on trestle route running through camp. Electric lighting established. Enemy buried cable found, test taken into use for traffic from DHQ to Brigade at ABLAINZEVILLE + etc. Visual station established from DHQ to 20th Bgde. Wireless control station moved to suitable camp close to Div'l Signal Office - according with work to Lucknow Cav: Brigade.	
	25		Build 5 pr open wire route from Div Sig Office to join ABLAINZEVILLE - ERVILLERS route using old enemy poles & insulators to replace temporary cables. Build line from DHQ to 231 Siege Battery at ERVILLERS.	
	26		Stores slowly putting into working order - one 4 pr enemy route from BAPAUME - ARRAS Road.	
	27		Build 4 pair open wire Route to meet 10 enemy route from COURCELLES to ST LEGER	

Army Form C. 2118.

Instructions regarding War Diaries and Intelligence Summaries are contained in F.S. Regs., Part II. and the Staff Manual respectively. Title pages will be prepared in manuscript.

7th DIVISIONAL SIGNAL COMPANY, R.E.

WAR DIARY
or
INTELLIGENCE SUMMARY.
(Erase heading not required.)

Place	Date	Hour	Summary of Events and Information	Remarks and references to Appendices
	27th		91st Brigade moved to Ervillers – the direct line to DHQ lateral to 20th Brigade & in both cases old enemy routes that had been put in order. Visual & WT Stations established from ST LEGER to Brigade Headquarters. Line to 35th Brigade RFA put into order & a new line (partly old enemy air-line – partly cable) built to Head Quarters of 16th RHA Brigade.	
	28th		Finish wiring CL-SLA line night back to camp. Extend poles cable line from end of CL-ERV line to 310 Brigade RFA in MORY.	
	29th		Regulate old enemy wires on CL-SLA line – clean off reel up cables around through the new air line & update the necessary pair of poles cables left on the poles. Commence to build 16 Bays of CL-GT Route (Cancelles – Fonsicourt) acting arm for 6 pairs to come in from Corps new position + 2 pairs for local circuits. Regulate CL-ERV Route. Only one bad line from DHQ now cable. Finish the 16 Bays CL-GT Route.	
	30th			
	31st		Orders for Operations morning of April 2nd require Air Report Centre & 2 Brigade advanced report centres to be established. All attachments out laying cable lines from Air R.C. to both Brigade R.C's & a lateral between them.	

2353 Wt W2544/1454 700,000 5/15 D.D.&L. A.D.S.S. Forms/C. 2118.

CAPT.
CMDG. 7th DIVL. SIGNAL COY R.E.

Army Form C. 2118.

7th DIVISIONAL SIGNAL COMPANY, R.E.

No. ....
Date ....

WAR DIARY
or
INTELLIGENCE SUMMARY
(Erase heading not required.)

Place	Date	Hour	Summary of Events and Information	Remarks and references to Appendices
	1917 April 1st		Build poled cable route from Div HQ to 21st Div HQ at COINIFER WOOD – also lateral from left brigade HQ 7th Div to right brigade HQ 21st Div. Arrange necessary lines personnel for two divisional OPs – also WT stations from Brigade report centres & Power Buzzer stations from forward positions to report centres. Visual station established from MORY to GOMIECOURT. Thence to Div HQ.	
	2nd		Send cable detachment to ERVILLERS to stand by in case Brigade Sections need help during operations. Communications very good throughout. Rest of men reeling up & repairing disused cables.	
	3rd		Severe blizzard about 5am causing a great deal of trouble on open wire routes – send out all men to clear clogged snow from between insulators – two or three lines fail but communication to all forward stations kept up. All lines to Corps down. Whole company repairing and regulating open wire routes after effects of snowfall.	
	4th		91st & 20th Brigades come back to rest areas at BUCQUOY and ABLAINTZEVILLE respectively. Whole company repairing and regulating open wire routes after effects of snowfall.	
	5th		62nd Division take over – this Div HQ remaining in the same place. 22nd Brigade	

Army Form C. 2118.

7th DIVISIONAL
SIGNAL COMPANY,
R.E.

No. ....
Date ....

WAR DIARY
or
INTELLIGENCE SUMMARY
(Erase heading not required.)

Instructions regarding War Diaries and Intelligence
Summaries are contained in F. S. Regs., Part II.
and the Staff Manual respectively. Title pages
will be prepared in manuscript.

Place	Date	Hour	Summary of Events and Information	Remarks and references to Appendices
	6th		Moved to COURCELLES. Three detachments altering lines to provide an RA Exchange at ERVILLERS – another detachment repairing old enemy route from A17 central to Ervillers.	
	7th		Two detachments repairing – running & adding two extra pairs to old enemy route running from Corps Route A12 to Ervillers Exchange thus replacing cables from CL-SLA Route to ERVILLERS. One detachment fixing poles ready to substitute open wire for cables on GOMIECOURT – ERVILLERS route. Artillery detachment lay two pairs of cables from Ervillers Exchange to new position of 22nd Brigade RFA at B10 b 5.5.	
	8th		All ranks in camp cleaning mud from horse lines, cleaning harness, wagons etc. Inspection of horses & re-arrangement made in accordance with new establishment.	
	9th		Easter Sunday – Rifle & Gas helmet inspection. Except for work on horse lines men given a free day.	
	10th		Stringing party re-staying regulating Corps Route as far as Gomiecourt. Poling down ready to join up CL-ERV Route to the ERV-MY (Ervillers-Mory) Route. Wire & Repairs CL-ERV and ERV-MY Routes.	
	11th		Final work started on 10th. More salvage party to COURCELLES. Inspection of	

2353 Wt. W2544/1454 700,000 5/15 D.D. & L. A.D.S.S. Forms/C. 2118.

WAR DIARY
or
INTELLIGENCE SUMMARY

(Erase heading not required.)

Army Form C. 2118.

7th DIVISIONAL SIGNAL COMPANY, R.E.

Place	Date	Hour	Summary of Events and Information	Remarks and references to Appendices
	11th		22nd Brigade Section. 22nd Brigade moves to ERVILLERS – 20th to COURCELLES and 91st to ABLAINZEVILLE.	
	12th		Brigades move back to positions occupied on Wednesday. ADS are now carrying two pairs from ERVILLERS to 500 yards short of MORY on ERV – MY Road.	
	13th		Lay lateral cable line between 412th & 35th RFA Brigades. Straighten up all cable lines running into Signal Office & run permanent poles.	
	14th		Lay cable from BAC's new position to Signal Office. 62nd Division. Reel up old one. Great improvement in weather during afternoon all ranks cleaning mud from stables & grooming horses. All ranks washing, repairing & re-packing wagons.	
	15th		Reel up double line from 7 Div H.Q. 6 – 21 Bde H.Q. as latter has moved forward. Employed up to 62nd Div Arty H.Q.	
	16th		Batten. General camp work. General work in Camp.	
	17th / 18th		Repair & Regulate one pair of CL – SLA Route. Maintenance parties on all open wire routes. Lines from 22nd Bgde RFA to 35th Bgde RFA realined to open wire route to D3 Central. Pole carrying cable.	
	19th		91st Brigade move to L'Homme Mort – come under orders of 62nd Div. Trench wiring party re-wiring telegraph poles along railway cut away CL – SLA + CL-ERV routes without any warning. Causing several poles to five way. Strong party repairing damage & burying armoured cable across the railway.	

A.5834 Wt. W4973/M687 750/1000 8/16 D.D. & L. Ltd. Forms/C.2118/13.

WAR DIARY or INTELLIGENCE SUMMARY

Army Form C. 2118.

7th DIVISIONAL SIGNAL COMPANY, R.E.

Instructions regarding War Diaries and Intelligence Summaries are contained in F.S. Regs., Part II. and the Staff Manual respectively. Title pages will be prepared in manuscript.

(Erase heading not required.)

Place	Date	Hour	Summary of Events and Information	Remarks and references to Appendices
	20th		Maintenance Parties repairing both routes to Ervillers. General work in Camp.	
	21st		Inspection of all routes by Divisional Gas Officer. Lay cable line to rest camp of 35th Brigade R.F.A. 20th Brigade relieve 91st Brigade - the latter moving to ABLAINZEVILLE	
	22nd		Church Parade - Rifle Inspection - Squad Drill - Exercise horses. Half-holiday.	
	23rd		Line Patrols. Harness cleaning - general camp work.	
	24th		CL-ERV 3rd Buried aero railway. Visual training scheme all day. NCO's given instruction in map reading.	
	25th		Special party detailed to put air-lines to ABLAINZEVILLE - BUCQUOY into good order partly to reel up cable, partly to leave area in good condition for Brigade rest camps party for instruction of men weak in Air-line work. Rest of Company cleaning harness.	
	26th		Same party on work at ABLAINZEVILLE. Patrol over all main routes. Commence course of instruction in visual signalling to Artillery signallers.	
	27th		ABLAINZEVILLE - BUCQUOY party as before. One detachment preparing leads for New Div H.Qrs. at MORY & running local staff lines. One detachment replacing some weak poles on CL-SLA route. Lieut G.S. RIDOUT joins Company from B. Corps signal. Having been posted for Air Artillery work.	
	28th		Strong salvage parties out retrieving & running through old cable. Reinforcements to R.F.A Sub Stations arrive.	
	29th		Rifle & Kit Inspection - General work in Camp. All ranks to Divisional Baths during afternoon.	
	30th		Section Attachment Commanders on special instructional work with parties reconnoitring improvement in certain trenches of work. 91st Brigade relieve 20th Brigade.	

[signature] Major
O/MDG. 7TH DIVL. SIGNAL COY. R.E.

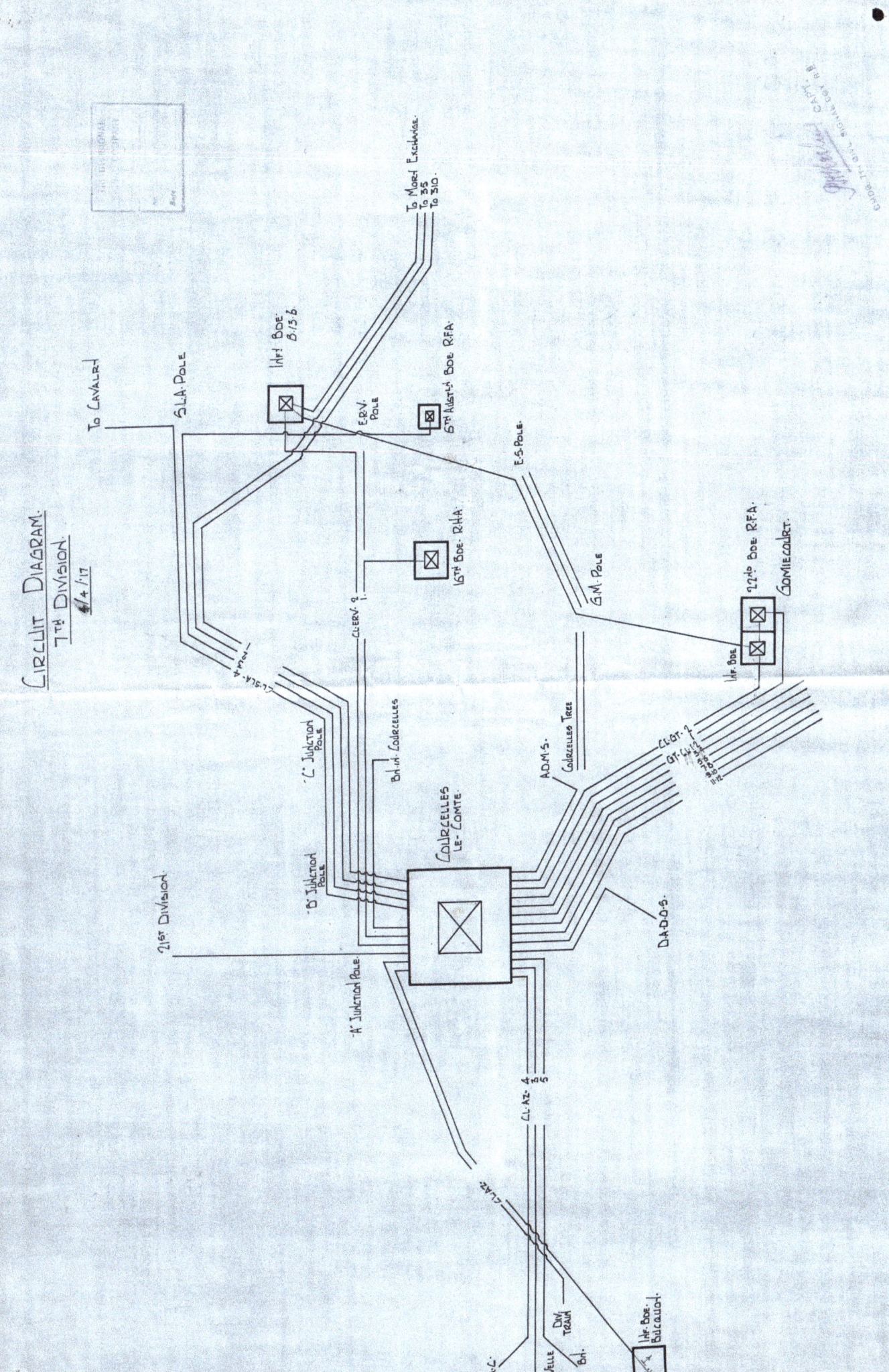

7th Division Communications
Working Circuits
15/4/17

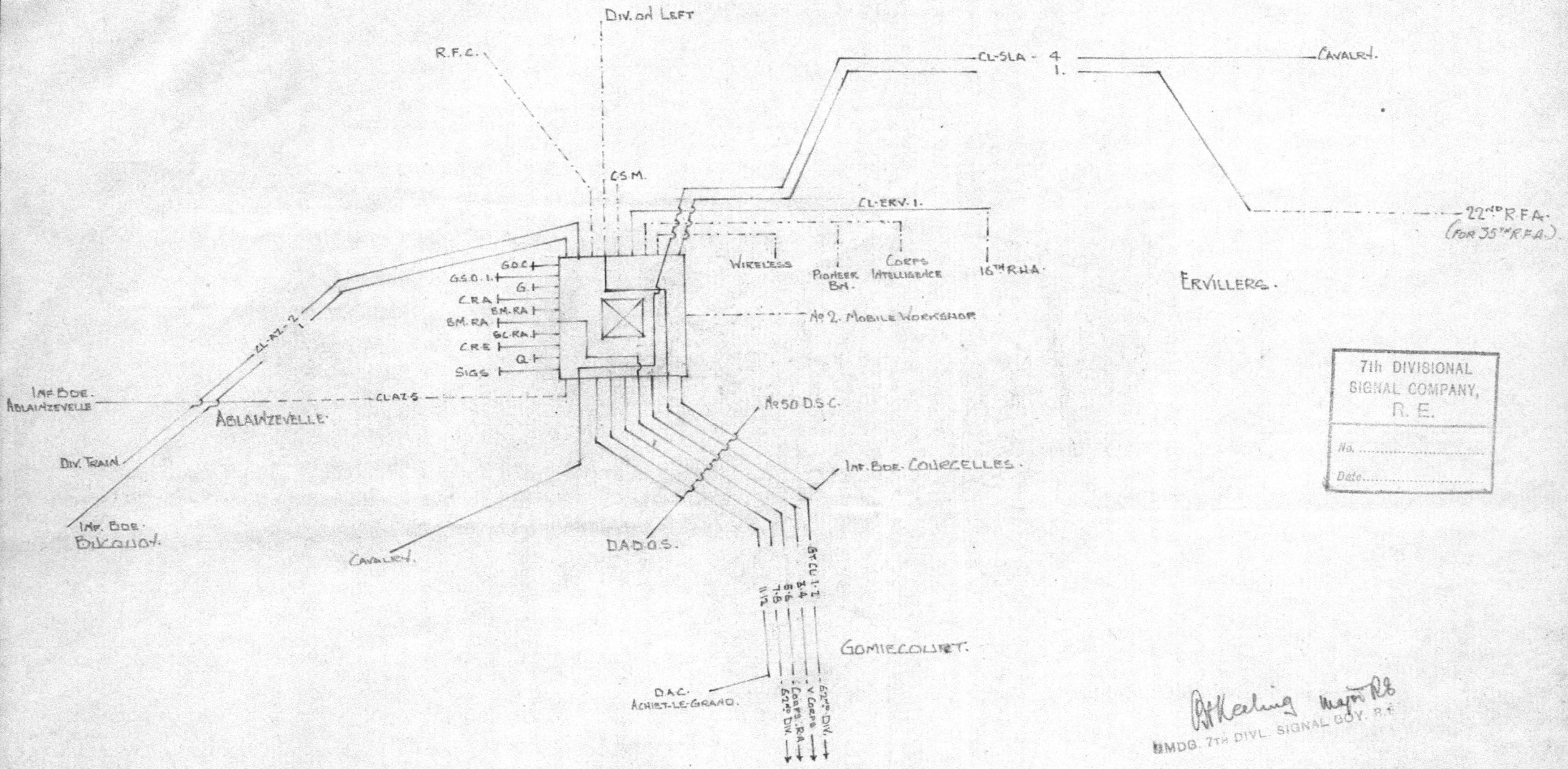

(Schematic diagram of 7th Divisional Signal Company communications circuits)

Labels on diagram:
- Inf. Bde. Ablainzeville
- Div. Train
- Ablainzeville
- Cl. Nz. 2
- Cl. Nz. 5
- Inf. Bde. Bihucourt
- Cavalry
- Sigs. Q.I
- C.R.E.
- B.M.R.A.
- C.R.A.
- G.S.O.I.I
- G.S.O.I
- G.I
- B.M.R.A.I
- S.C.R.A.I
- R.F.C.
- Div. on Left
- C.S.M.
- Cl. Erv. 1
- Wireless
- Pioneer. Intelligence. Bn.
- Corps Intelligence
- 16th R.H.A.
- D.A.D.O.S.
- No. 50 D.S.C.
- No. 2. Mobile Workshop
- Inf. Bde. Courcelles.
- D.A.C. Achiet-le-Grand
- Gomiecourt
- Bt/CL I.I. / 3.4 / 5.6 / 7.8 / 9.10 / 11.12
- V Corps
- Corps. R.A.
- 62nd Div.
- 63rd Div.
- Ervillers
- Cl. Sla. 4
- Cavalry
- 22nd R.F.A. (also 35th R.F.A.)

7th Divisional Signal Company, R.E.
No. _____
Date. _____

BMDG. 7th Divl. Signal Coy. R.E.

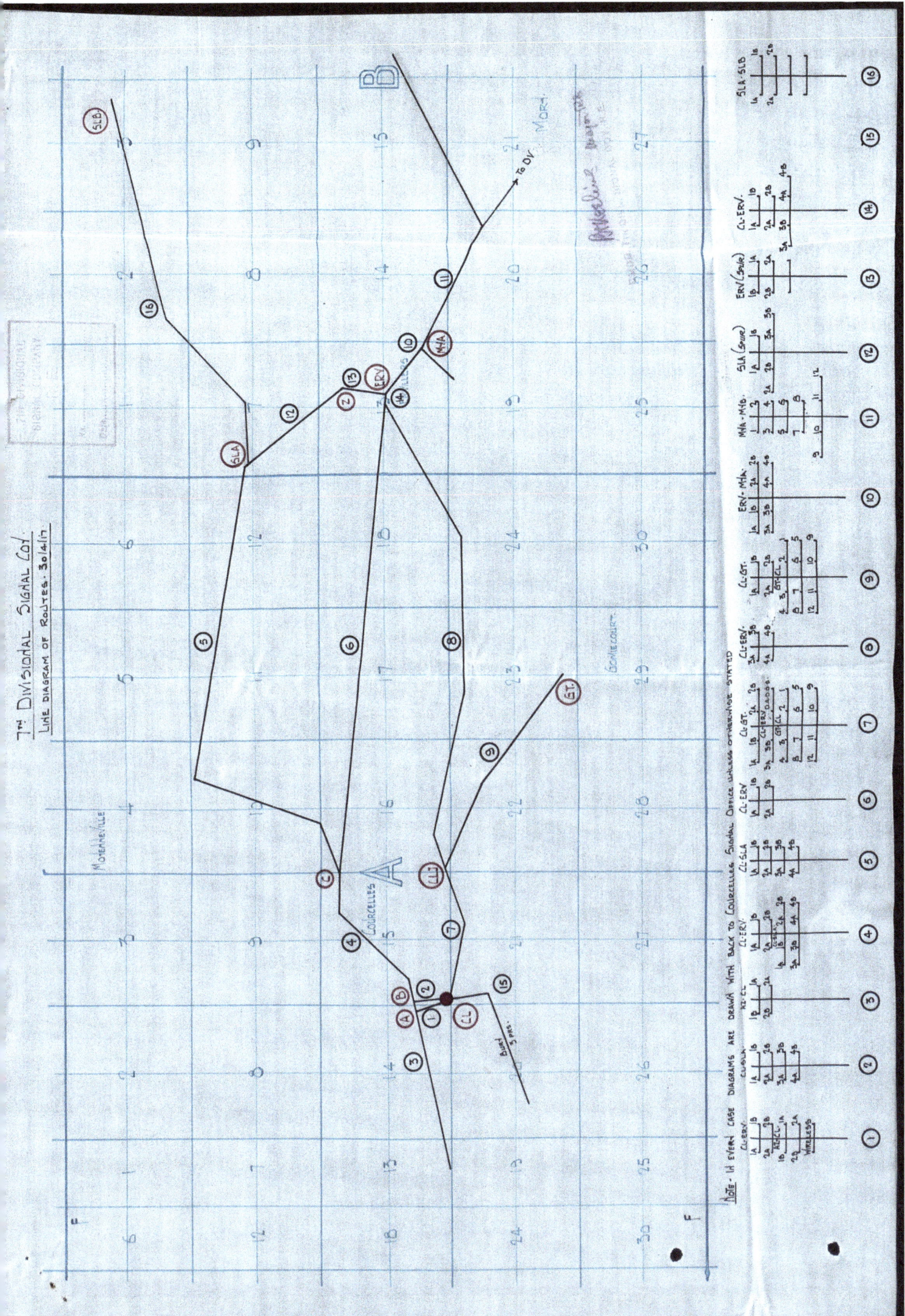

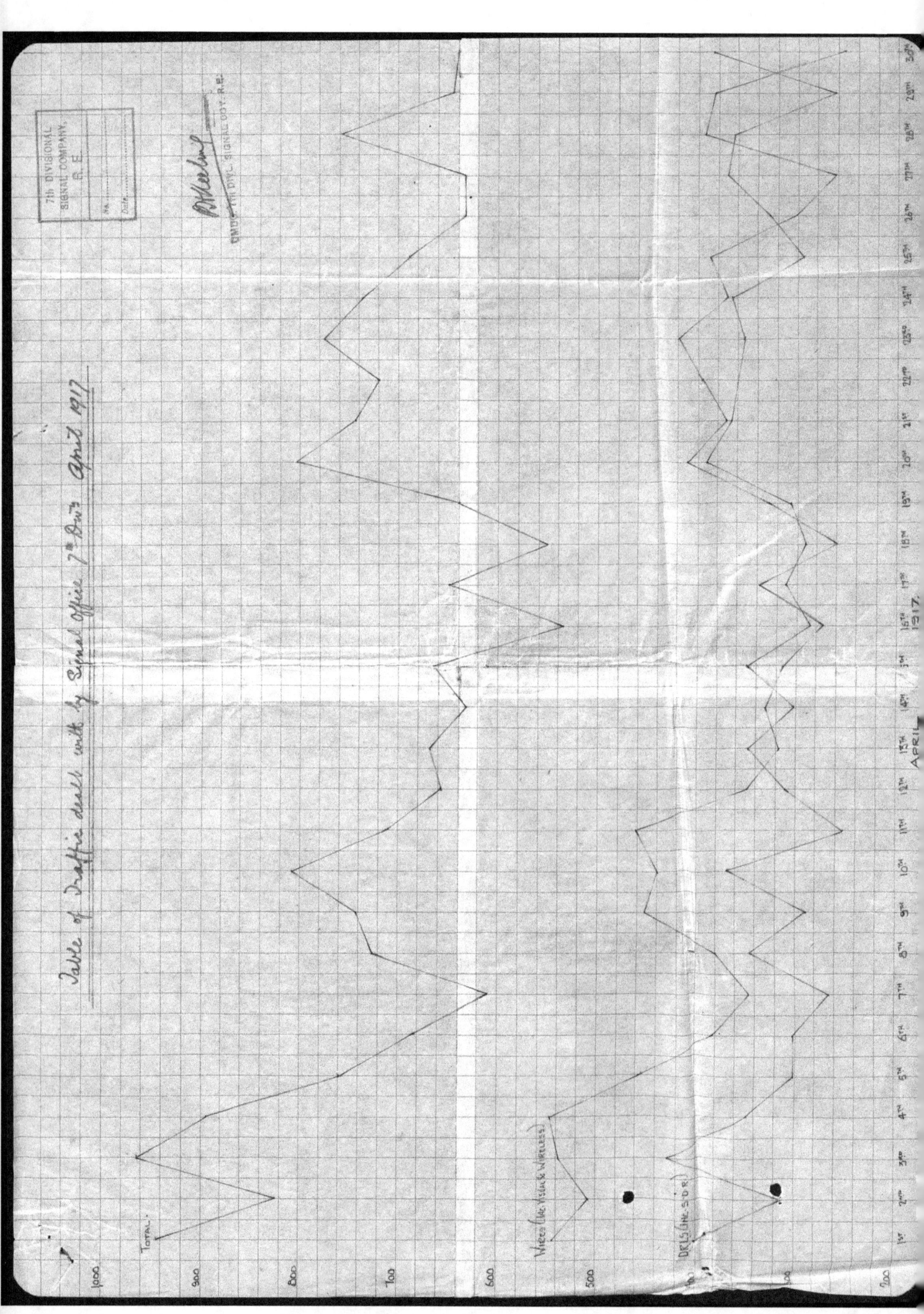

7th DIVISION.

7th DIVISIONAL SIGNAL COMPANY.

MAY 1917.

WAR DIARY
INTELLIGENCE SUMMARY
(Erase heading not required.)

Army Form C. 2118.

7 D Signal Coy
Sept 17

Place	Date 1917	Hour	Summary of Events and Information	Remarks and references to Appendices
	May 1st		Regulate put in order two pairs in German Route running from MORY to SAPIGNIES to connect Divisional Advanced HQ with 2nd Australian Division main found route (OU-NZ).	
	2nd		Patrol & instructional work except one detachment which is building some air line to join to route put in order the day before - making up Bri-NZ Route.	
	3rd		During the attack Division prepared to carry into action from Advanced HQ MORY - when Signal office there a more Signal office Staff - & detachments & visual Signallers to camp close to MORY. Leave out office at COURCELLES & HQ transport.	
	4th		20th Bgde move to L'homme Mort + 20th Brigade to MORY. Commence poling cables from BCA junction B/c to L'HOMME MORT (6pm) Run cable lines for two battalion camps near to MORY. Buried	
	5th		Finish poling cable route started day before. Regulate & Put in order another pair in AU-NZ Route. 20th Bgte move to L'HOMME MORT (6pm). Commence poling cables from MYB junction B/c to L'homme mort to Branch Brigade HQs (One program	
	6th		cable detachments lay cable from L.F.A. Brigade to ECOUST, wireless installed ECOUST & B Bon 1st Australian F.A. Brigade during operations at ECOUST - L'HOMME MORT for work during attack. All communications through steady for attack. 20th Brigade move to ECOUST.	
	7th		Detachments standing by in case of need during attack. One split up to provide linemen at Test Points on on to Bayer. One collecting old enemy telegraph stores near camp. Buzzer installed at Company HQ - Buzzer + Amplifier at Battalion HQ and Buzzer + Amplifier at Ecoust, Wireless between Ecoust & L'homme mort in operation at latter place to save delay in Transmission to Bn HQ.	

WAR DIARY
or
INTELLIGENCE SUMMARY

(Erase heading not required.)

Army Form C. 2118.

Place	Date	Hour	Summary of Events and Information	Remarks and references to Appendices
	8/5		Line patrols and general repair work.	
	9/5		Build another pair on DV-NZ Route using ex German stores - prepare stores to add another two pairs later if necessary.	
			Lieut H. KING (Seaforth Highlanders) joins the Company vice Lieut E.M. SMITH appointed as interpreter to Portuguese Forces.	
	10/5		Reel up several disused poled cable routes. 91st Brigade relieve 20th Bgde.	
	11/5		Three detachments building two four-pair poled cable routes from C.8.b to new Brigade HQ in Ecoust. All times patrolled and made ready for an attack on 12th inst. (Diagram attached)	
	12/5		During to heavy enemy barrage all lines fail - messages sent back by power Buzzers & Pigeons. During afternoon get line laid in communication trench but is less satisfactory than those in open as it gets broken by traffic as well as shell fire.	
			Capt. WHISHAW goes forward to Brigade HQ (adv) to assist Brigade Section.	
			Two detachments Nos 2 & 4, relay Brigade to Battalion lines during the night.	
			Send up another Power Buzzer & an Amplifier for forward station, thus making three complete stations. WDD at Embankment & WDO at Ecoust.	
			Also in touch with Australian Stations Q and QA. Wireless Station in Bullecourt only able to work at night - impossible to maintain aerial during daylight.	
	13/5		173rd Brigade (58th Div.) relieve 15th Australian Brigade & come under command of 7th Div. MORY shelled during the morning as result of which one driver wounded, 2 horses killed, 1 mule wounded. Lines to Brigade & Battalions only kept through with difficulty as	

Date	Hour	Summary of Events and Information	Remarks and references to Appendices
14th		Advance Brigade HQ now in use in very bad position from Signals point of view. 173rd Bgde HQ Signal office destroyed by shell fire causing following casualties; Dvr 7th Dvr DR killed near Noreuil. Two detachments leave at midnight to re-lay necessary Brigade lines in forward, broken but full recognition. During morning built alternative route from L'Homme Mort to Ecoust using spare pair in 62nd Div Buried System part of the way. During afternoon build fo6rd cable spurs from Mory-Ecoust Rent to 310th, 312th RFA Brigades new positions. Power Buzzer stations working satisfactorily.	
15th		Shelling much quieter, lines therefore working better. Power Buzzers Pigeons both work well. 173rd Brigade establish new office in Morteuil. 58th Division Signal Company arrive + commence preparations for taking over.	
16th		174th Brigade relieve 91st Brigade during the night. All men lent to Brigade Section return. 58th Division take over at 10 a.m. YG opens at Courcelles same hour. Capt Ridout with RA HQrs Section + No 2 Detachment remain with 58th Div for RA work. No 1 Detachment lay cable to 91st Brigade Rest Camp at Achiet-le-Petit.	
17th 18th		General Duties in Camp. Clear the ground + move horse lines to new Bumping Ground - old camp getting very foul.	

WAR DIARY
INTELLIGENCE SUMMARY

Army Form C. 2118.

Place	Date	Hour	Summary of Events and Information	Remarks and references to Appendices
	19th		Move Camp to new position close up to old ground.	
	20th		Rifle & Gas Helmet Inspection - General work in Camp. Draw from each battalion two Signallers as permanent Divisional Power Buzzer Section. These men commence their duties & are put under command of Cpl Jones for special course of instruction & practice.	
	21st		All ranks at collecting old enemy poles simulators for future war. Divisional Signal Schools for Infantry Officers & NCOs commences.	
	22nd		Collecting old enemy poles simulators.	
	23rd		Receive orders that Div HQ are to move to Achiet-le-Petit. Send forward No 4 Detachment to prepare new Camp. Special Detachment of men in need of training commence building & repair permanent route (old enemy stores) from Ablainzevelle to Achiet-le-Petit for new Div HQ. (AP-AZ Route)	
	24th		Special Detachment continue work on AP-AZ Route. No 4 Detachment build necessary cable huts in Ablainzevelle village. Power Buzzer Squad practicing with 22nd Brigade.	
	25th		Receive news that HQ is not to move to Achiet-le-Petit. Send all available transport to bring stores back. No 4 Detachment returns. No 3 Washing wagons cleaning harness. No 1 Detachment painting wagons & cleaning harness - preparing to go into action. Power Buzzer Squad practicing with 22nd Brigade.	

Army Form C. 2118.

WAR DIARY
or
INTELLIGENCE SUMMARY.
(Erase heading not required.)

Place	Date	Hour	Summary of Events and Information	Remarks and references to Appendices
	26th		No 3 Detachment returns. No 2 Detachment for Artillery wh. now 58th Division. No 4 Detachment lays cable line from Div HQ to 33rd Div Arty at Hamelincourt using a pair of Ch-SLA Route as far as A11 a 7.7. No 1 Detachment cleaning and painting wagons.	
	27th 28th		Rifle & Gas Helmet Inspection. Necessary stable fatigues only. No 1 & 2 Detachments fixing poles for the re-wiring of Div HQ with open wire & preparing poles to replace the existing cables. No 4 collecting poles & stores not used for the ATP-AZ Route. No 1 Detachment wiring new open wire system for Div HQ board. – No 2 painting wagons. No 4 Camp Fatigues & preparing stores to replace cable lent on Saturday to Corps Air Line.	
	29th		No 1 Detachment finish wiring Div HQ system & run cable to Offices from Terminal Poles. No 4 building Annie Air line & leading up the cable lines replaced by 33rd DA.	
	30th		No 2 painting wagons. No 3 Detachment training with 20th Brigade. Power Buzzer Signed Power Buzzer Signaled with 20th Brigade. Baths & Camp Fatigues.	
	31st		No 3 Detachment returns to Camp – to be used by 58th Div of Reserve – but not sufficient work on hand to warrant them staying at MoRY.	

Signed/ Major R.E.
CMDG. 7TH DIVL. SIGNAL COY. R.E.

B.C.I.

7TH DIV.
Special Battle Communications
5/5/17

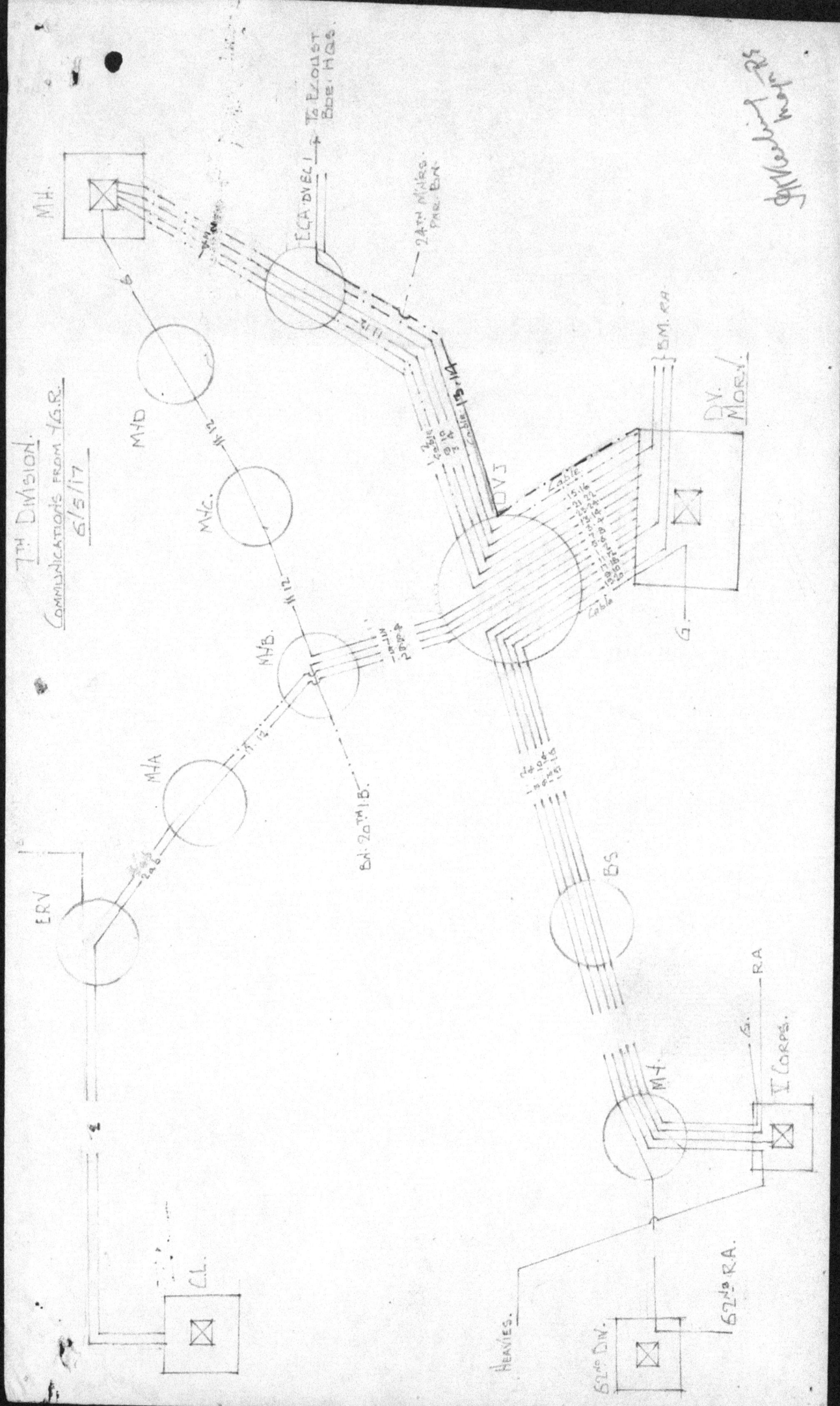

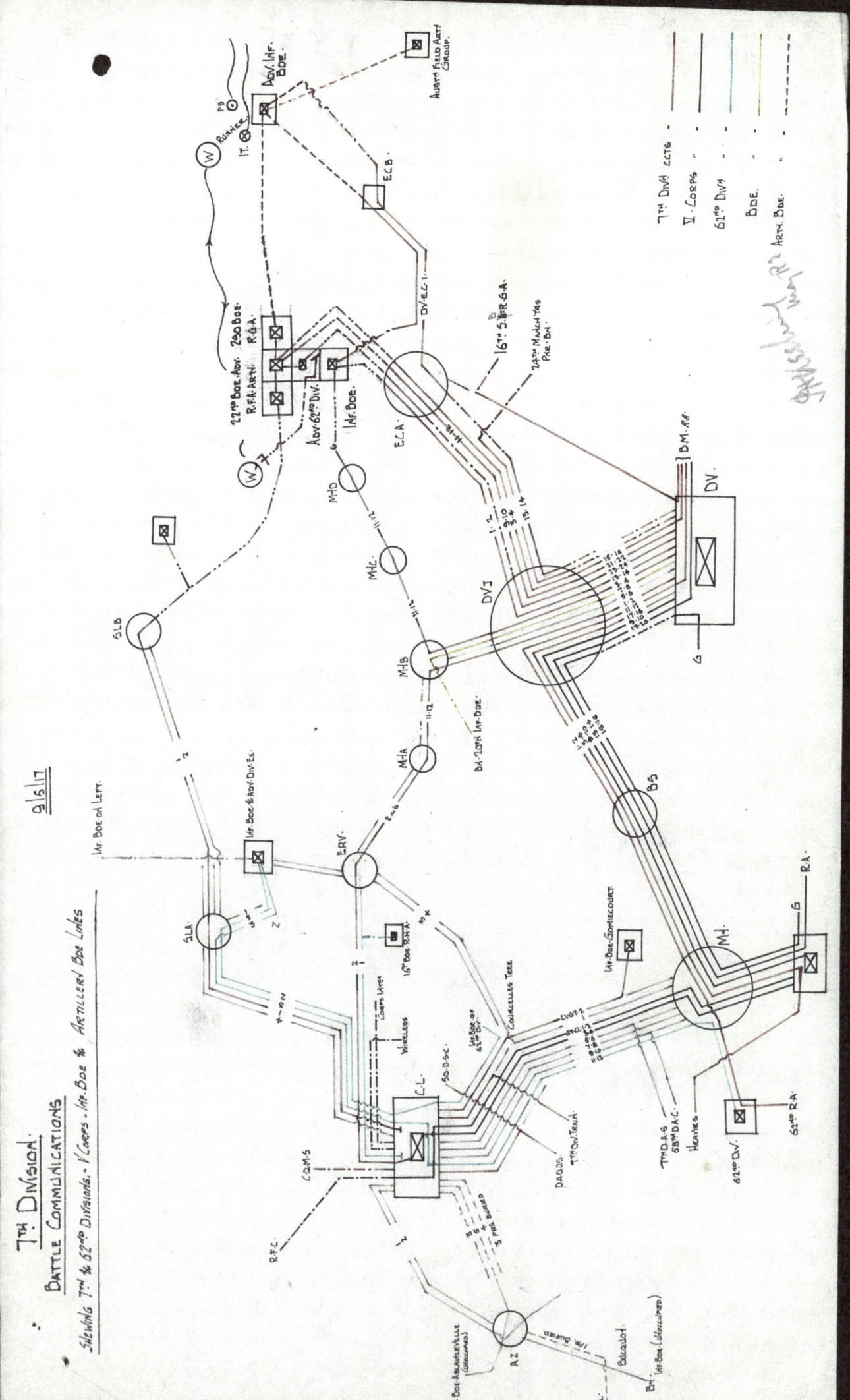

7TH DIVISION
BATTLE COMMUNICATIONS FOR 12.5.17
SHOWING INFANTRY AND LIAISON LINES ONLY

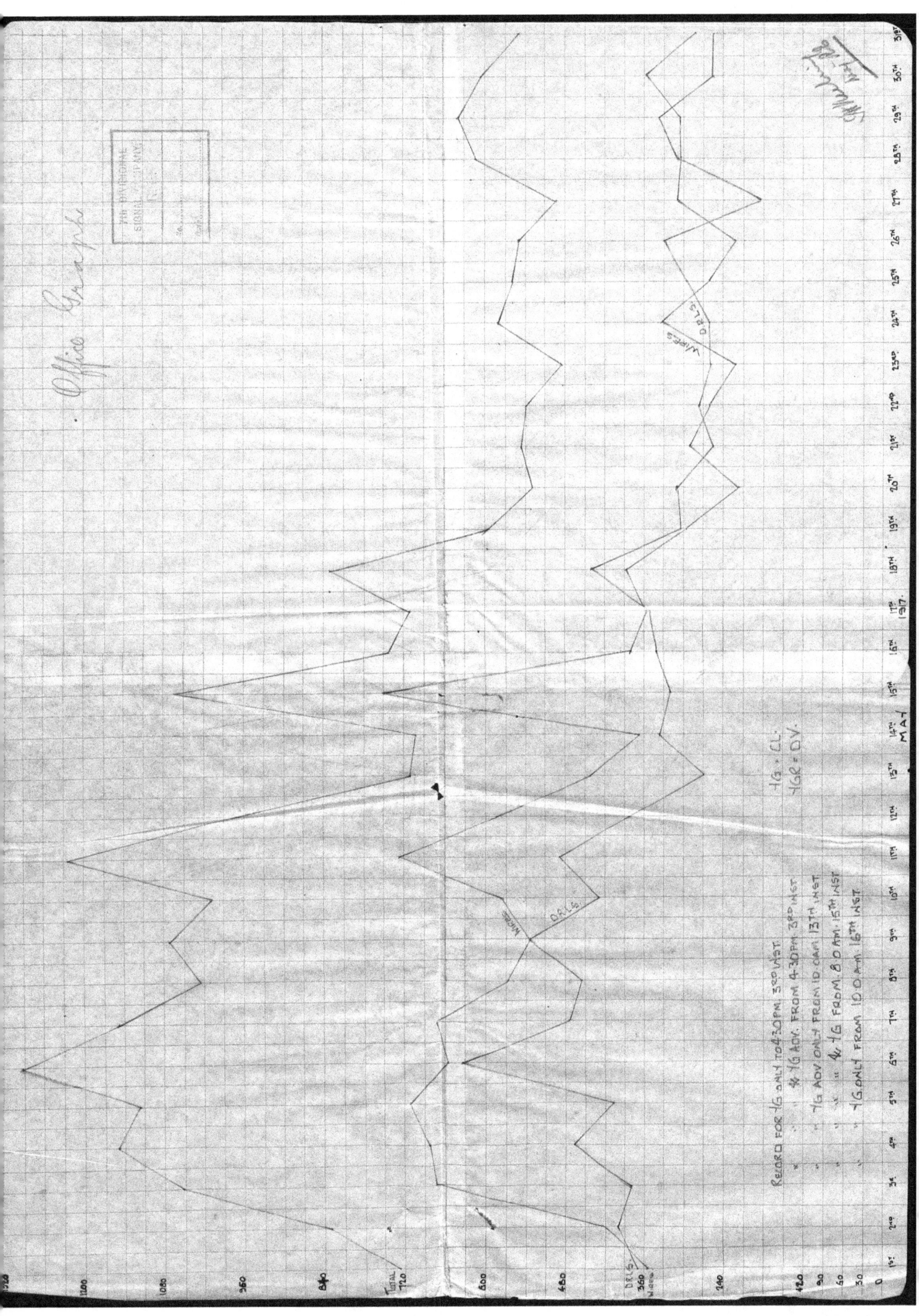

7th DIVISION.

7th DIVISIONAL SIGNAL COMPANY.

JUNE 1917.

Army Form C. 2118.

7th DIVISIONAL SIGNAL COMPANY, R.E.
No. .... Date ....

WAR DIARY
or
INTELLIGENCE SUMMARY.
(Erase heading not required.)

Instructions regarding War Diaries and Intelligence Summaries are contained in F.S. Regs., Part II. and the Staff Manual respectively. Title pages will be prepared in manuscript.

Place	Date	Hour	Summary of Events and Information	Remarks and references to Appendices
	1917 June 1st		Change over all circuits at Div HQ. from old cable system to new open wire system. All new men commence a course of cable wagon drill and riding school. Lineman instruction for Artillery Signallers.	
	2nd		Clean up all old cable lines at Div HQ. – Instructional work as before.	
	3rd		Church Parade. Rifle & Gas helmet inspection. Personal Baths.	
	4th		Erect new terminal pole for CI-AZ Route to give sufficient clearance for Motor Omnibuses. Maintenance patrols over all routes. Instruction for new men as before.	
	5th		General work in camp & instruction.	
	6th		Commence to build Air line to 22nd Brigade Scheme. Power Buzzer squads doing practice work with 20th Brigade.	
	7th		Complete Air line route to 22nd Brigade. Power Buzzer squads with 20th Brigade.	
	8th		Add another 6 pair arm to Div HQ. local route to connect up to 3T-CL Route. Cable instruction.	
	9th		General Scheme for Divisional Signal School. Air line instruction.	
	10th		Church Parade, Rifle & Gas helmet inspection.	
	11th		Collect old encamp'd pole & insulators for use in new Div HQ. camp at Béthysies. General fatigues in Camp.	

Army Form C. 2118.

7th DIVISIONAL SIGNAL COMPANY, R.E.

No. ....
Date ....

WAR DIARY or INTELLIGENCE SUMMARY.

(Erase heading not required.)

Instructions regarding War Diaries and Intelligence Summaries are contained in F. S. Regs., Part II. and the Staff Manual respectively. Title pages will be prepared in manuscript.

Place	Date	Hour	Summary of Events and Information	Remarks and references to Appendices
	12th		Builds comeon airline to replace local cable lines to A.P.M. - No 2 Mobile Sorwe Workshops. General Scheme for Signal School. Instruction in incomenwork to new men.	
	13th		General repairs maintenance to 33rd DA line & 22nd Brigade RFA line. Maintenance patrols on all permanent routes.	
			20th Brigade return 113th Brigade (38th Div?) = Lt KING out to 20th Bde vice Lt BRIGGS in Camp. Inspection of harness, how Rations, Weekly Rans, Field dressings. General work in Camp.	
	14th			
	15th		Signal School Examinations.	
	16th		General work & instruction in Camp. Signal School Examinations.	
	17th		General work & instruction in Camp. Recreation.	
	18th		Rifle & Gas helmet inspection. Maintenance parties doing repairs to Permanent Routes. Send Salvage Party to collect cable water stores in Beaucourt.	
	19th		Hoisting insulators, preparing cables, poles &c to new Div HQ. Running through Cable. Salvage Party at Beaucourt vicinity.	
	20th		Move No 3 & 4 Detachments to new Camp at Meaulte - also No Section transport taking poles and stores. Also Power Buzzer Signals set up in Rd line.	
			No 1 & 2 Detachments running through Cable & general work in Camp. Salvage Party reeling up old permanent stores from Q.2.13 Camp; No 3 & 4 Detachments get all poles erected in new Div HQ Camp. HQ Section began moving stores to Behagnies. No 1 Det. patrols repair work. No 2 Det. & Salvage Party collecting stores.	
	21st			

WAR DIARY
INTELLIGENCE SUMMARY

Army Form C. 2118.

7th DIVISIONAL SIGNAL COMPANY, R.E.

Place	Date	Hour	Summary of Events and Information	Remarks and references to Appendices
	22nd		All poles in on new Bn HQ wired. Joinings for Signal Office made and most of the indoor wiring done. Salvage Party sorting stores. Running through cables.	
	23rd		Signal School breaks up and Officers + NCOs return to their units. Salvage Party return to their units. Nos 3rd Detachments finish wiring Signal Office. Clearing up of local circuits. Nos 1 + 2 Detachments make all preparations at all junction poles for changing over. All Stores moved to Camp	
	24th		Divisional move to Behagnies completed by 10 a.m. — all circuits working. Build by 4 p.m.	
	25th		Small parts repairing + repairing ERV - MY Route. Linemen posted at MORY (Reserve Brigade). L'Homme Mort (2 to cut Right + left Brigades and Artillery Brigade). Rest of Company cleaning up refuse, manure etc. Left by but occupants of Signal Camp. Sorting + stacking poles etc.	
	26th		22nd Brigade relieve 20th Brigade at L'Homme Mort, latter moving to MORY. Take over Divisional Wireless Detachment + such stores as are available from 5th Army Wireless Company. Build local lines to DAC - DADOS - APM. Survey + lay out new route from Bruslures to L'Homme Mort to replace ERV - MY Route which has got into very bad repair running through chaussée and shelled country. {Staff instructional School for W/T operation + Dismantle Comic Air line route from 33rd DA to A10 & 9.9. Dulliphone operators for Artillery Commences 16 diamonds Cl - S1A Route from A15 B.6.8 to 107 = 5.6. the poles + stores being used for the new route (EV1 - JTM Route)	
	28th		Dismantling CL - S1A Route - digging holes for EV1 - JTM Route	
	29th		Digging holes for EV1 - JTM Route, carrying + erecting poles. Runs line to 220th M.G. Coy from BnTHQ	

Army Form C. 2118.

7th DIVISIONAL
SIGNAL COMPANY,
R. E.
No..............
Date.............

WAR DIARY
or
INTELLIGENCE SUMMARY.
(Erase heading not required.)

Instructions regarding War Diaries and Intelligence
Summaries are contained in F. S. Regs., Part II.
and the Staff Manual respectively. Title pages
will be prepared in manuscript.

Place	Date	Hour	Summary of Events and Information	Remarks and references to Appendices
	30th		Continue erecting poles E.N.J - WM Roads - Very heavy rain all day do bring men into camp at 4 p.m. Nos. 1 Detachment commences dismantling old German over pair circuits from Busigny to Bohain not in use.	Diagram of lines & offices traffic sheet attached

J.M. Keeling Major R.E.
O.C. 7TH DIVL. SIGNAL COY. R.E.

7th DIVISION.

7th DIVISIONAL SIGNAL COMPANY.

JULY 1917.

WAR DIARY
or
INTELLIGENCE SUMMARY
(Erase heading not required)

7th DIVISIONAL SIGNAL COMPANY, R.E.
Army Form C. 2118.

Vol 21

Place	Date	Hour	Summary of Events and Information	Remarks and references to Appendices
	1917 July 1st		Three detachments working on EVJ – MM Route. No.1 Detachment preparing poles etc. for re-building poled cable line from L'Homme Mort to MM Rat Box, 1000 yards West of Bronol. Commenced the work at nightfall. 58th Divisional Artillery go away – Artillery Exchange at L'Homme Mort shut down – Lines to Brigades put through direct to Brigade Major.	
	2nd		All Detachments on same work as yesterday	
	3rd		No.s 1, 2, & 3 Detachments wiring EVJ – MM Route. No.4 completes poled cable route from L'Homme Mort	
	4th		No.s 1, 2, & 3 Detachments wiring EVJ – MM Route. No.4 building cable lines from DHQ to 35th Bgde	
			Wagon lines & Divisional Gas Officer.	
	5th		All Detachments working on EVJ – MM Route – all open wire work completed.	
	6th		Arrested a Salvage party – one man from each Infantry Battalion & each Battery to collect old cable. 3rd Detachment building poled cable to connect Infantry circuits to the Brigade HQs. 1 – 2 Detachments general work in camp.	
	7th		3rd Detachments building poled cable to connect Artillery circuits of EVJ MM Route to the Bdy Bgde HQs No.2 Detachment putting through line on an V pole laying cable from V pole to Q T Rat–HQ to give direct communication from DHQ to Brigade Commander during raid.	
	8th		No.1 Detachment general work in camp. NCOs, batmen & linesmen transferring circuits from ERV – MY Route to EVJ – MM Route. Rest of Company fatigues general work in camp.	
	9th 10th		All hands dismantling ERV – MY Route.	

WAR DIARY
or
INTELLIGENCE SUMMARY.
(Erase heading not required.)

Army Form C. 2118.

7th DIVISIONAL SIGNAL COMPANY
R.E.

Instructions regarding War Diaries and Intelligence Summaries are contained in F. S. Regs., Part II. and the Staff Manual respectively. Title pages will be prepared in manuscript.

Place	Date	Hour	Summary of Events and Information	Remarks and references to Appendices
	11th 12th		1 & 2 Detachments building new permanent route ½ way to BADOS - 10min route to 38th & 20th Bdes RFA Wagon Lines, to replace old cable lines hurriedly taken into use & not satisfactory	
			3rd Detachment building BH - BSA Route (spare) to supplement relief BH - BS Route, also Coy to Coy Arcs cut on b BH - BSA Route	
	13th		1 & 2 Detachments dismantling old wires to Camp, BADOS, wagon lines etc	
			3 & 4 Detachment washing wagons, cleaning battery etc	
	14th		3 & 4 Detachments existing poles for new permanent Route from MYA Pole to L'Homme Mort (JTM) to replace existing Comic Air line built by ½ Coys divn Hqrs but state of repair	
	15th		1 & 2 Detachments washing wagons, cleaning battery etc	
			3 & 4 Detachments on fatigues	
			Rest of Company Rifle & Gas Helmet inspection - Church Parade - Recreation	
	16th		3 & 4 Detachment running MYA - JTM Route	
			1 & 2 Detachments building Comic Air lines to battalions in reserve area	
	17th		3 & 4 Detachments dismantling old comic route MYA - JTM	
			1 & 2 Detachments laying out & digging holes for new Permanent Route (spare) from L'Homme Mort to St Leger (JTM - LR) to replace existing cable lines	
	18th 19th 20th		1 & 2 Detachments building JTM - LR Route	
			3 & 4 Detachments building poled cables - generally straightening up the leading in cables from the Permanent Routes terminating at L'Homme Mort to the four Brigade Head Quarters	

7th DIVISIONAL
SIGNAL COMPANY.
R.E.

Army Form C. 2118.

WAR DIARY
or
INTELLIGENCE SUMMARY.
(Erase heading not required.)

Instructions regarding War Diaries and Intelligence
Summaries are contained in F. S. Regs., Part II.
and the Staff Manual respectively. Title pages
will be prepared in manuscript.

Place	Date	Hour	Summary of Events and Information	Remarks and references to Appendices
	21st		1 & 2 Detachments held line from Bgde HQ at MORY to Bgde School. ERVILLERS	
	22nd		3rd Building fencing for grazing paddock. Rifle, Gas Helmet inspection - Recreation	
	23rd		1 & 2 Detachments rebuilding first 1000 yards of M-E Poles Cable Route which was in very bad state of repair. 3rd Detachment arming poles & preparing stores for new 6pr permanent route from L'Homme Mort to join MORY Bernal main route at V Pole (HM-V Rte Cr) Salvage Power men making & second grazing paddock	
	24th		3rd Detachments building HM-V Route 1 & 2 Building 2 pair poled cable route from 35th Bgde RFA HdQrs to B12 & central to replace existing worn out cables on the ground.	
	25th		3rd Detachments building HM-V Route 1 & 2 Detachments - Salvage Party clearing up the remains of the new divisional CL-St A Route.	
	26th		3rd Detachments finish HM-V Route. No 2 Building Field cable from MORY Exchange to new position of 230th M.G. Company. No 1 clearing up old wires in St Leger Valley.	
	27th		No 3 rd Detachments general work in camp. No 1 & 2 Detachments poling two pairs of ground cables from 22nd Bgde RFA HdQrs to B6 & central.	
	28th		3rd Detachment erecting terminal poles at 22nd Bgde RFA and regulating ledging in cables. No 2 & 3 rd Detachments general work in camp.	
	29th		Church Parade, Rifle, Gas Helmet inspection, Recreation.	

WAR DIARY
or
INTELLIGENCE SUMMARY

7th DIVISIONAL SIGNAL COMPANY, Army Form C. 2118.
R.E.

Place	Date	Hour	Summary of Events and Information	Remarks and references to Appendices
	30		No 1 Detachment regulating Poles & Cable Route from ECB Pole to Beauval. No 2 Detachment regulating M-E Poles Cable Route. No 3 1-T in conjunction with VI Corps Air line Section, working on re-arrangement of M Y A Air Pole which includes slight diversion of route, building Test-Hut etc.	
	31		Nos 1 . 3. 1-T Detachments as yesterday. No 2 Detachment commence improvements necessary at V pole as visibility beyond to work with safety on M E Poles Cable Route	

S.H. Keeley Major R.E.
CMDG. 7TH DIVL. SIGNAL COY. R.E.

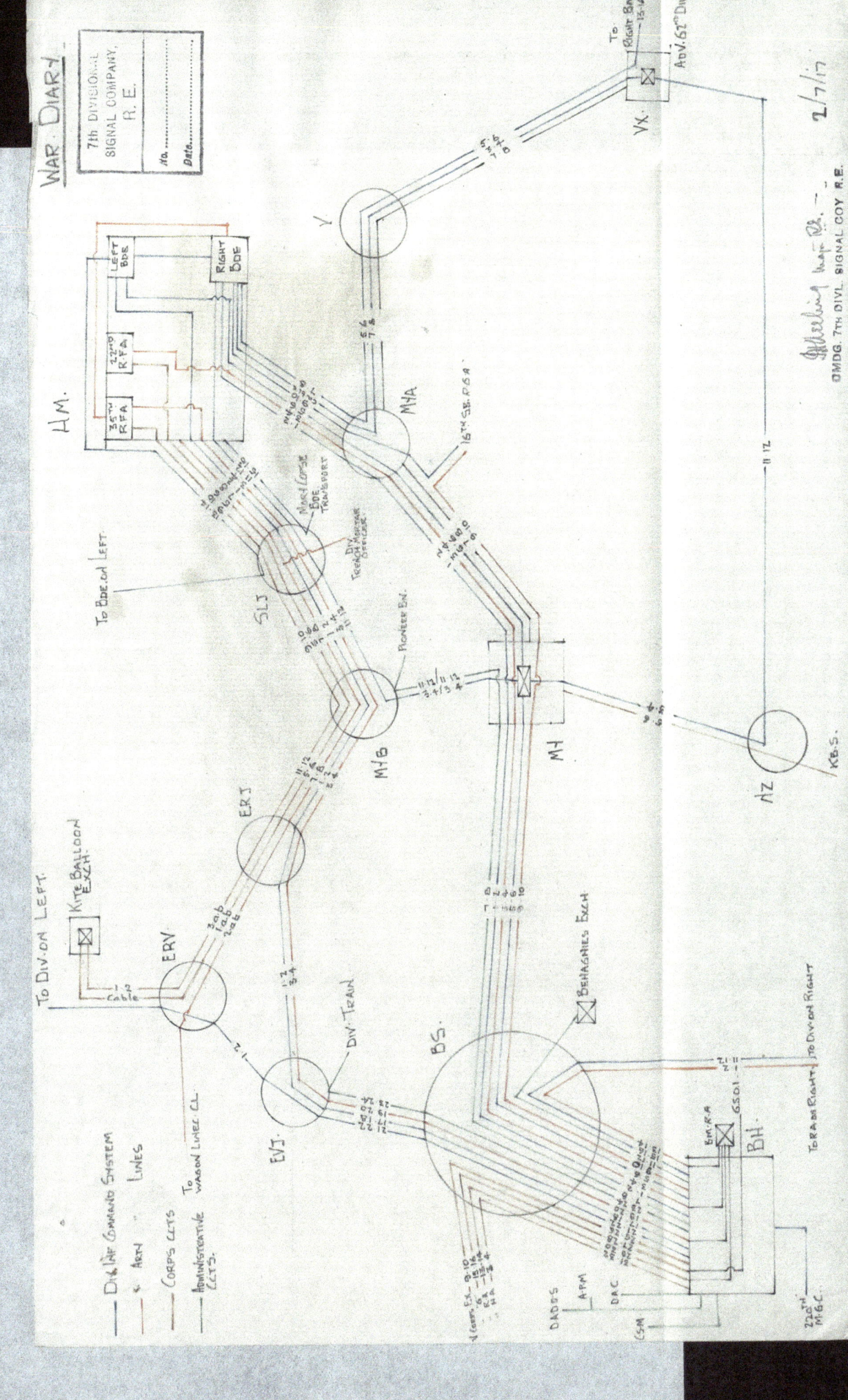

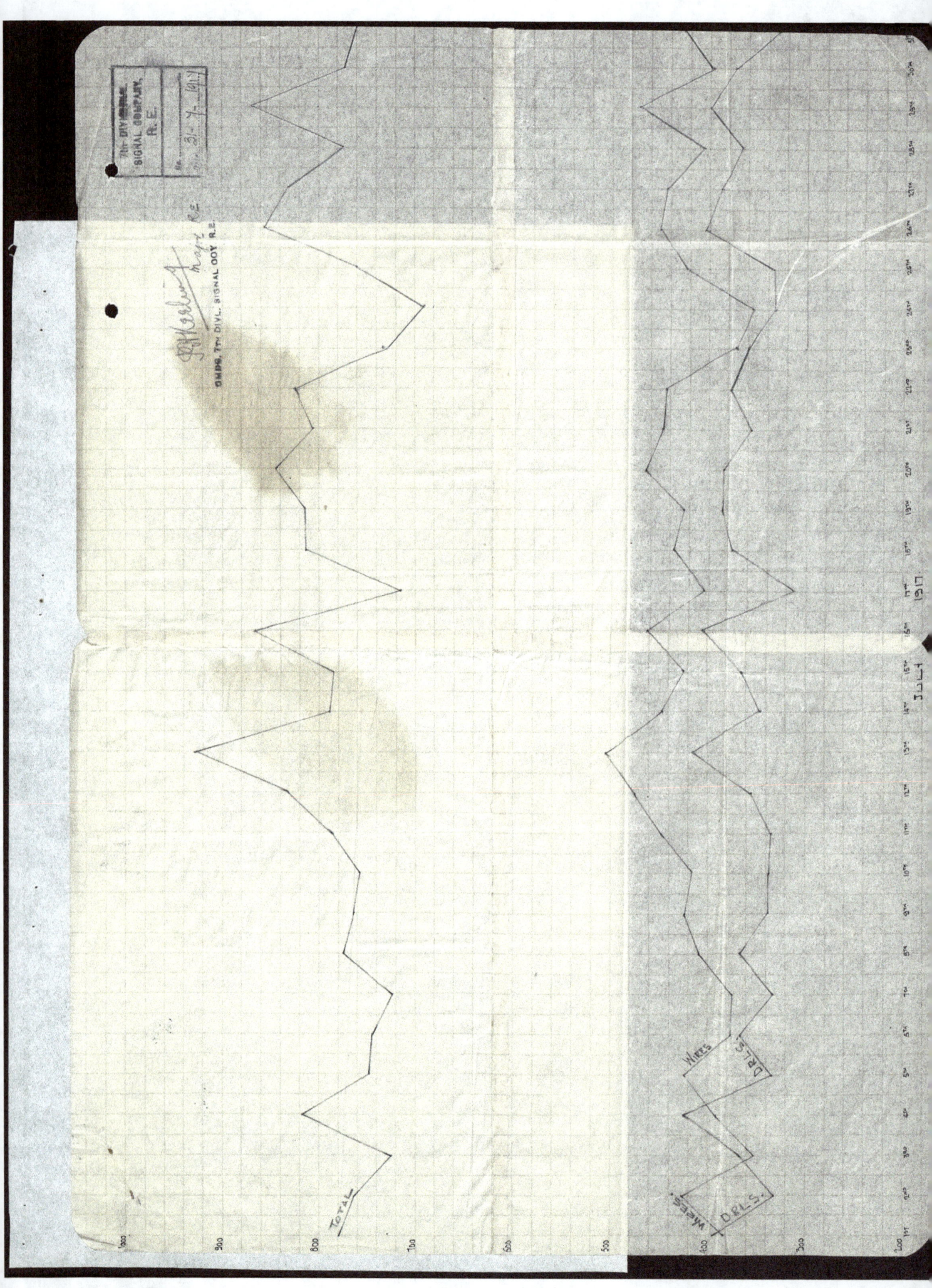

7th DIVISION.

7th DIVISIONAL SIGNAL COMPANY.

AUGUST 1917.

WAR DIARY
or
INTELLIGENCE SUMMARY.
(Erase heading not required.)

Army Form C. 2118.

7 Div Signals
Vol Z.2

Place	Date	Hour	Summary of Events and Information	Remarks and references to Appendices
	1917 August			
	1st		No 2. Detachment re-building field cable route from l'Homme Mort to E test-box – M.E Posts	
	2nd 3rd 4th		Nos 1, 2, 3 Detachments general work in camp, sorting stores etc	
			Nos 1 & 2 Detachments building four permanent routes from LR Pole to meet 21st Division route near Judas Farm. No 3rd Detachments general work in camp.	
	5th		Nos 1 & 2 Detachments adding aims running another two pairs to JAM – LR Posts	
	6th		No 3rd Detachment Dismantling MY13 – MY7 four pair come on line route now diverted	
	7th		All routes general work in camp. Divisional eliminating contacts to Fi Corps Horse Shoot. All four Detachments repairing making necessary connections on routes to be taken into use when Division moves to BRETENCOURT area.	
	8th		No 3rd Detachment making necessary alterations to poled cables at l'Homme Mort for handing over lines to 62nd & 21st Divisions. Nos 1 & 2 Detachments general work in camp.	
	9th		All hands packing wagons, dismantling temporary buildings, cleaning camp.	
	10th		Division moves from BETHAGNIES to BRETENCOURT – Signal Offices close at former place at 10 am. Reopens at latter at same hour. Company marching became at 10.30 am arrives at 2 pm	Diagram of this it attached overleaf
	11th		All hands building brush huts etc in camp, cleaning billets, unpacking stores	Diagram of line in use is not now attached
	12th		Church Parade – Rifle and gas helmet inspection – Recreation	
	13th		Commence general course of Training :- NCO's party at refresher cable drill practice under CSM. – Signalling School for Infantry Officers 9 other ranks under Serjt Mysko – Wireless School – School for Lineman Corpl Hepper – Power Buzzer Operators under Corpl Harper	

Army Form C. 2118.

WAR DIARY
or
INTELLIGENCE SUMMARY.
(Erase heading not required.)

Instructions regarding War Diaries and Intelligence Summaries are contained in F. S. Regs., Part II. and the Staff Manual respectively. Title pages will be prepared in manuscript.

Place	Date	Hour	Summary of Events and Information	Remarks and references to Appendices
	13th Cont'd		Power Buzzer Operators under Cpl Bird. - Practice work for Power Buzzer & Amplifier Squad under Cpl Bourne. - Detachments slow cable drill under Section Officers	
	14th		Schools as usual - All detachments cable wagon drill under Detachment Commanders.	
	15th			
	16th			
	17th			
	18th		Except necessary men for stable & Signal Office duties all ranks given day's holiday to attend Cpl's Horse Show	
	19th		Rifle & Gas Helmet Inspection. Church Parade. Recreation.	
	20th		Signal School as usual under Serjt Hughes & QSM Greed	
	21st		Wireless School under Cpl Bourne - Power Buzzer Practice under Cpl Hogg.	
	22nd		Cable Wagon drill for Detachments under Section Officers & Detachment Commanders.	
	23rd			
	24th			
	25th		Divisional Fair - all men possible given day's holiday.	
	26th		Inspection of Anti-Gas appliances by Divisional Gas Officer. Recreation	
	27th		Schools as usual	
	28th		Warning Orders for move received. Signal School temporarily broken up. All Wagons, Stores cleaned & greased	

WAR DIARY
or
INTELLIGENCE SUMMARY.

Army Form C. 2118.

Place	Date	Hour	Summary of Events and Information	Remarks and references to Appendices
	29th		All hands packing wagons & preparing to move. Capt. Whitehead goes forward by car to take over lines & arrange billets.	
	30th		Whole Company - except mechanical transport - entrain at 7.20 a.m. for RHENINGHELST, arriving in camp at 6.30 p.m. Temporary quarters arranged for the night & all local subscribers put on to telephone exchange.	
	31st		As temporary camp is very bad - move to another camp at other end of village, following day to, and make arrangements for training to commence following day.	& chart showing amount of traffic attached

signature
Major R.E.
C.M.D.G. 7th DIVL. SIGNAL COY. R.E.

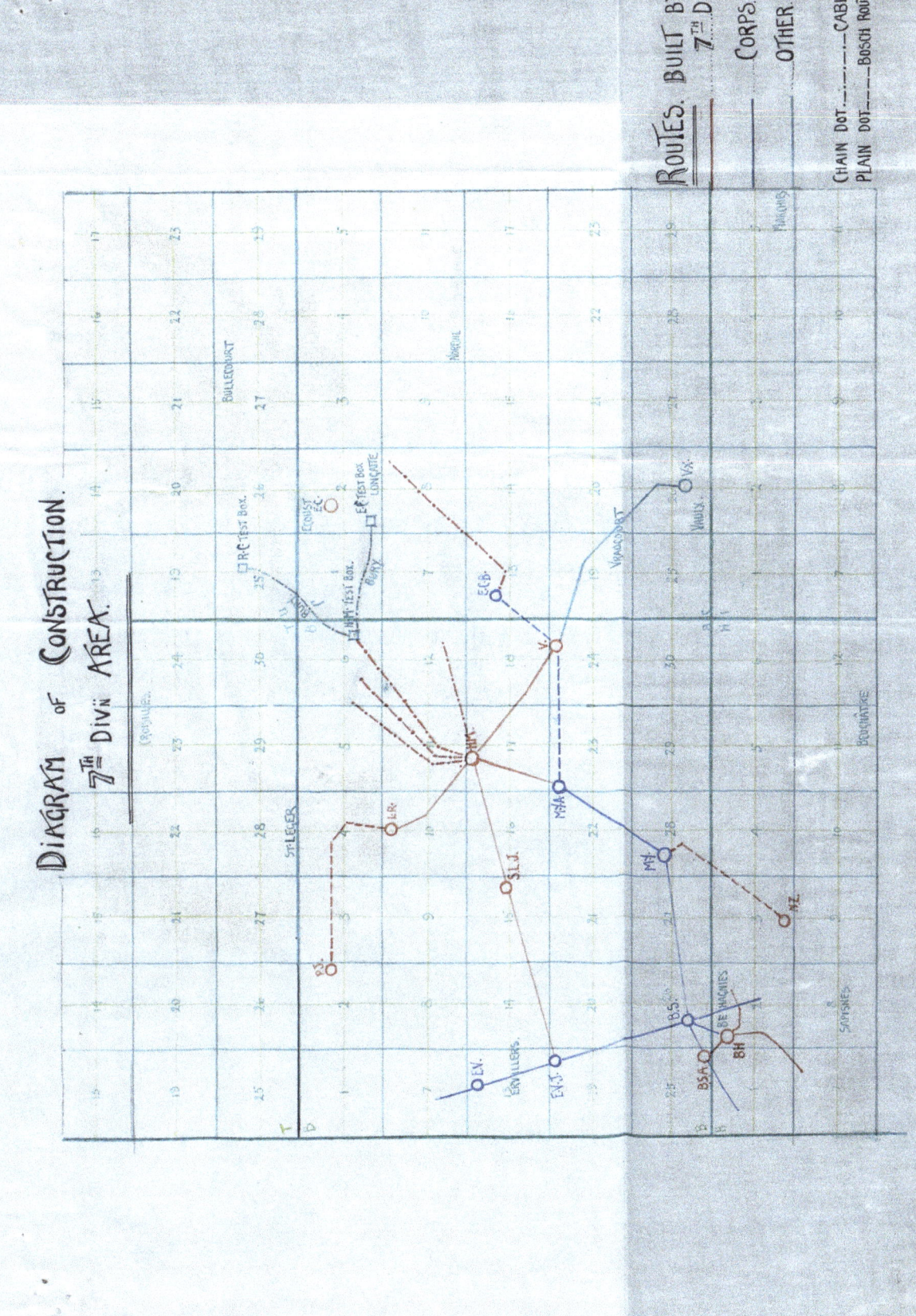

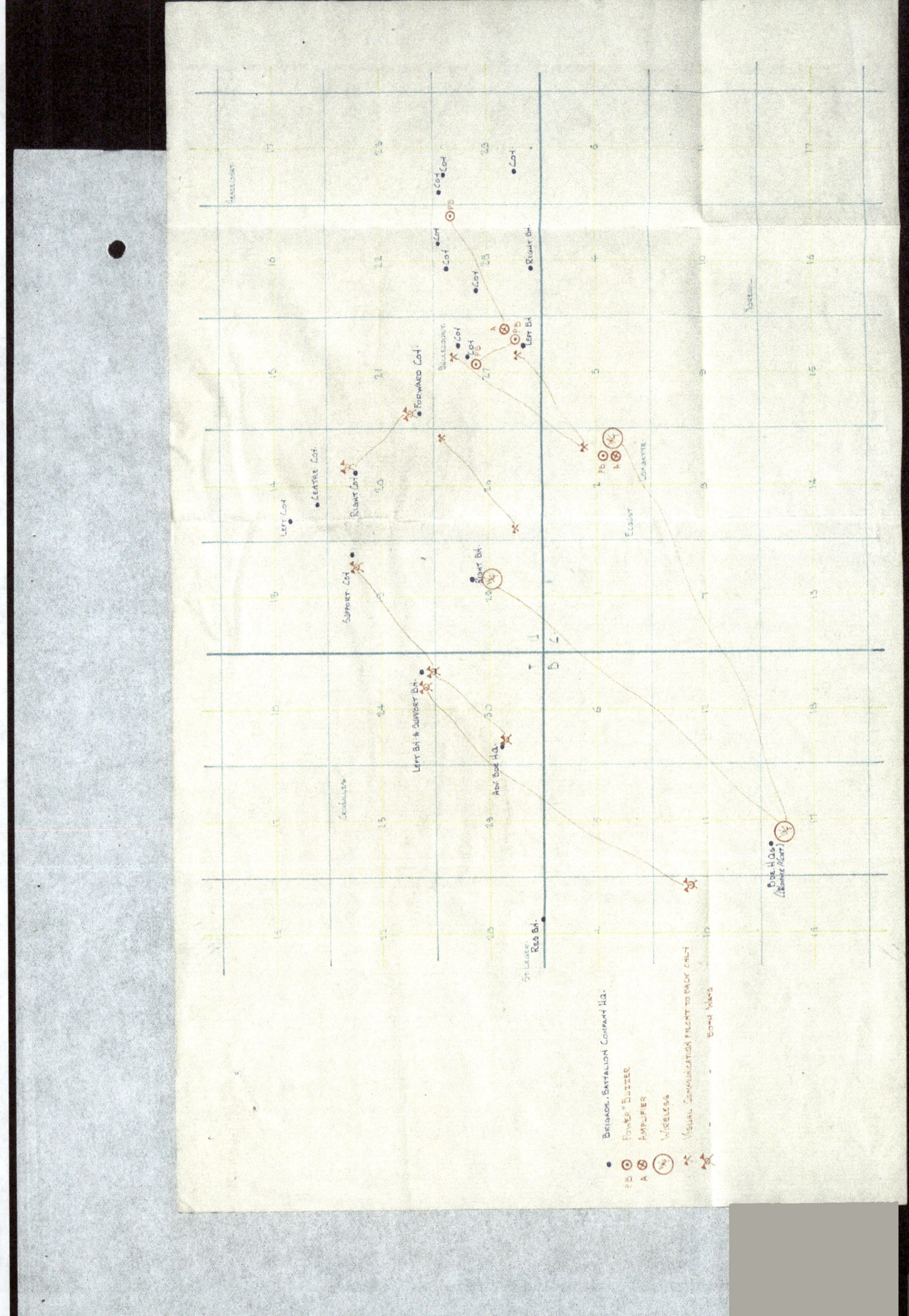

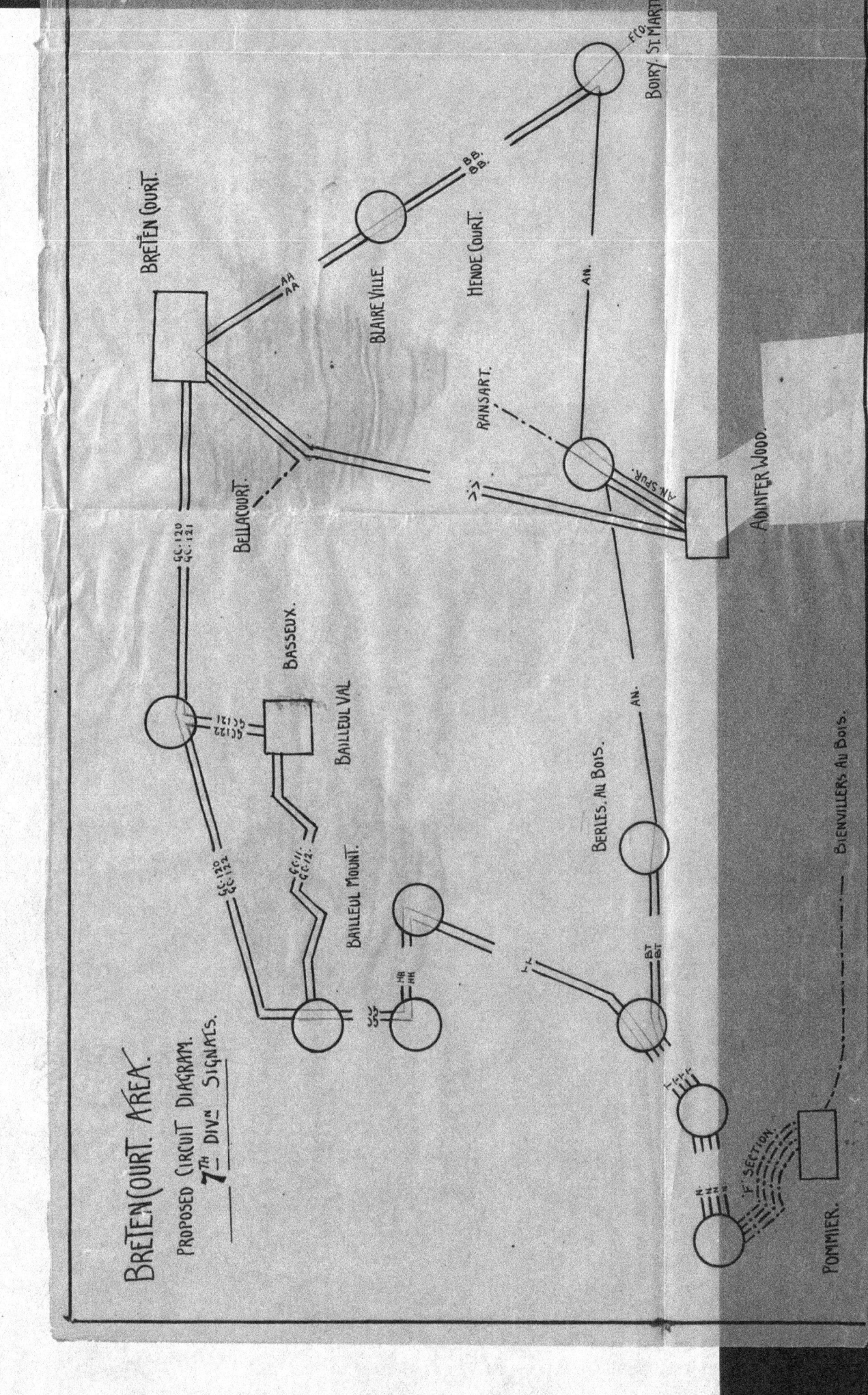

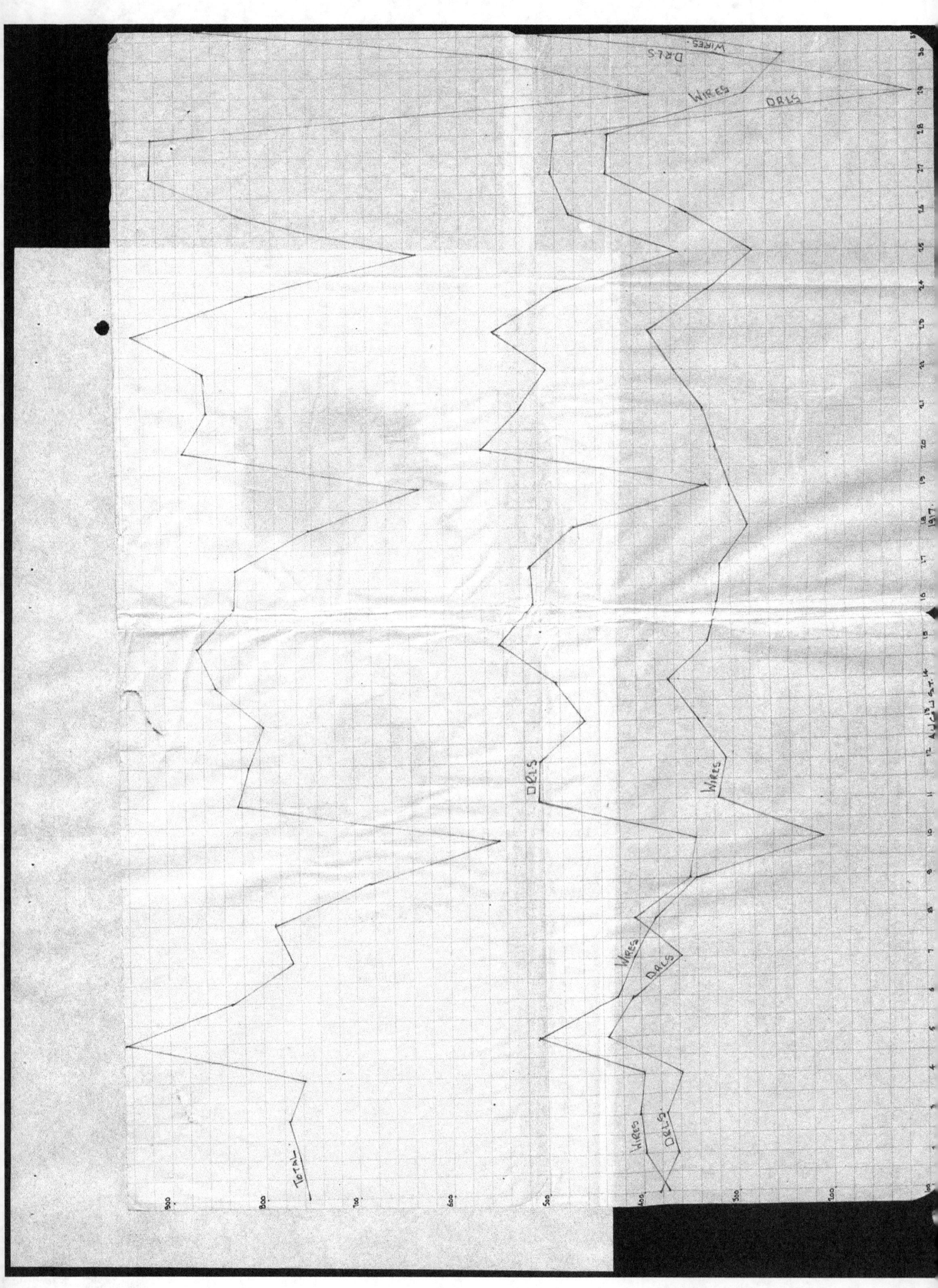

7th DIVISION.

7th DIVISIONAL SIGNAL COMPANY.

SEPTEMBER 1917.

Army Form C. 2118.

70 Signal.
Vol 2 3

WAR DIARY
or
INTELLIGENCE SUMMARY.
(Erase heading not required.)

Place	Date	Hour	Summary of Events and Information	Remarks and references to Appendices
	1917 Sept 1st		General work in Camp - cleaning harness wagons etc	
	2nd		Camp fatigues, levelling ground for horse lines etc. About 9.30 pm village bombed by enemy aeroplane setting fire to ammunition dump alongside company camp. All ranks turned out & removed horses to clear of village towards Westoutre. About 10 pm dump exploded wrecked officers mess cook house - horses picketed on Westoutre Road for the night. One man severely wounded	
	3rd		Receive warning to move to narrower altered at 11.30 am to 2 pm that day. Leave Reninghelst 3.15 pm - close office 3 pm - re-open Hagebrouck same hour. Billet Signal Office Staff in Hagebrouck and make camp for the rest at Cinq Rues. All traffic dealt with by one telephone line from HZ office who also took all telegraph work. Fix up Signal Office run lines to local subscribers & different lines to HZ & Fish, up 2nd Army lines to Brigade. RA HQ Detachment & No 1 Cable Detachment leave for Merris	
	4th		Fixing up horse lines, forage harness shelters - cleaning wagons and harness.	
	5th		Divisional Signal School re-assembles	
	6th		Three Detachments practice cable wagon drill. No 3 Detachment build cable line from camp to Signal Office	
	7th		During afternoon all ranks cleaning harness wagons. RA Section move to Locre	
	8th		Training course commences consisting of gas helmet practice - work in gas helmets - cable drill riding school for new cable hands - Buzzing practice & small schemes for lower buzzer signal. Visual practice for signallers - elementary instruction for new Power Buzzer men. Driving drill.	

WAR DIARY or INTELLIGENCE SUMMARY

Army Form C. 2118.

(Erase heading not required.)

Instructions regarding War Diaries and Intelligence Summaries are contained in F. S. Regs., Part II. and the Staff Manual respectively. Title pages will be prepared in manuscript.

Place	Date	Hour	Summary of Events and Information	Remarks and references to Appendices
	9th		Rifle Inspection - Church Parade - Recreation. Cpl Hodgson & five linesmen leave for 1st Corps on loan to assist with cable jointing on new buried route. Sens Sergt.	
	10th		Jowers & 20 men on lorry to Locre to build 12/pr poled cable route from Confusion Corner to "P" Dug out.	
	11th			
	12th		Training for all ranks as commenced last week.	
	13th		Artillery Section at Confusion Corner working under orders of 19th Divisional Artillery	
	14th			
	15th			
	16th		Move from Mayobruch to Wigonnes. Office closes & re-opens 10 a.m. No.s 3 & 4 Detachments reel up cables to local subscribers & come on later. 10 NCOs & men leave for Corps to attend a cable jointing school - 10 NCOs men for Power Buzzer School, 3 men for Wireless School & 10 men for elementary linesmen's course. Firing camp & wiring local subscribers	
	17th		General work in camp	
	18th			
	19th		Cleaning wagons & harness	
	20th			
	21st		Composite detachment reeling up cables to Bujanes - replaced by open wire pairs on existing Corps Army routes.	
	22nd			
	23rd		Make necessary preparations for Divisional practice attack. Artillery section returns to Merris	

A5834 Wt. W4973 M687. 750,000 8/16 D. D. & L. Ltd. Forms/C2118/13.

Army Form C. 2118.

WAR DIARY
or
INTELLIGENCE SUMMARY.
(Erase heading not required.)

Place	Date	Hour	Summary of Events and Information	Remarks and references to Appendices
	24th		Divisional Practice attack - 1st Day	
	25th		Divisional Practice attack - 2nd Day. Parties return from Cable jointing and Power Buzzer Wireless Courses	
	26th		Divisional Practice attack - 3rd Day	
	27th		Pack wagons etc ready for move - Signal School disperses	
	28th		Move from Wizernes to Westoutre - Office opens noon. Dismounted men move by train - Wagons & mounted men by road	
	29th		Commence moving stores to Chateau Segard - also fit up Signal Office & run lines for DHQ subsections. Artillery Section rejoins company.	
	30th		Move from Westoutre to Chateau Segard. Opening office at 7pm. Horses, wagons & wireless under CSM left in camp at Westoutre. Much bombing by enemy aeroplanes.	

R.M. Maxwell
Major RE
CMDG. 7TH DIVL. SIGNAL COY. R.E.

7th Divisional Signal Coy. R.E.

September 1917

Chart axes: 100–900 (vertical), days 1–30 (horizontal)

Lines labelled: WIRES, DRLS, TOTAL

Annotations:
- Coy. moved from Reninghelst to Hazebrouck.
- Coy. moved from Hazebrouck to Wizernes.
- Coy. moved from Wizernes to Westoutre.
- Coy. moved from Westoutre to Chy. Segard.

7th DIVISION.

7th DIVISIONAL SIGNAL COMPANY.

OCTOBER 1917.

WAR DIARY
~~INTELLIGENCE SUMMARY~~
(Erase heading not required.)

Army Form C. 2118

7 D Signal Co Vol 24

Place	Date	Hour	Summary of Events and Information	Remarks and references to Appendices
	1917 Oct 1st		Launch building lines to DHQ Subscribers. Lay cables from Artillery Brigade Headquarters at Halfway House to the Batteries.	
	2nd		Sent 6 linemen to join Corps Area Party. Sgt Holroyd and five other ranks killed by shell fire on Menin Road - various loss to Company. As most circuits on Corps buried system allotted to us not in working order - lay two ground cables from Belfort House (end of poled cable route) to Reserve Bge HQ at Zillebeke Halte, one from Reserve Bge HQ to Div HQ at Hooge, one from Reserve Bge HQ to Arty Bgde Exchange to Batteries.	
	3rd		Send forward rest of Power Buzzer Squad to Hooge Tunnels with spare Gen & Charging Set. Send two PB squads with instruments to join two attacking battalions. Build line to Prisoners Cage & Brigade Pack Train Camps. Build from extra pairs on route from Div HQ to XT Test Box (central test-box of Buried System). Gradually got out some working lines on buried system. Send spare Wireless Set forward for use of 91st Bgde.	
	4th		Battle commences 6 am. Lines hold fairly well on the whole. Linemen & Office Staff work well, keep things going. Strong party out assisting to open 60/20 poles cable communication to Bedford House. Route from XT to Bedford House. Casualties 1 OR killed, 2 missing, 3 wounded.	Diagram of communications attached
	5th		Strong party re-building XT - G.L. Route - 3 bays forward had been smashed by shell fire. Commence to build sand-bag protection to Signal Office.	

Army Form C. 2

WAR DIARY
or
INTELLIGENCE SUMMARY.
(Erase heading not required.)

Instructions regarding War Diaries and Intelligence Summaries are contained in F. S. Regs., Part II. and the Staff Manual respectively. Title pages will be prepared in manuscript.

Place	Date	Hour	Summary of Events and Information	Remarks and references to Appendices
	6th		All hands poling the four pairs of cables laid to Reserve Infantry & Artillery B'dqrs. Capt. Risont in charge of special party of linemen have camp 3 am Ray	
	7th		Laddered cable from WK (Westlock) to Jubilee Bde for Artillery Registration. Line kept through all day. Power Buzzer Amplifier stations got in to good working order by O.C. wireless & Capt. continues to ring cable to the Tuilleries - also poles the cable line from Div H.Q. to Wagon line. Much trouble on buried lines experienced about 6 pm but mostly put in order again by about 2 am.	
	8th		Attack commenced 5.20 am. Found lines to ward of cable there broken by enemy barrages but Sigems & Power Buzzers work splendidly all day. XT - G.L. Route down in two places one caused by enemy shellfire one by premature from 6" How's - All trunks put through by 8 am. Not many faults on Brigade lines. Donnents work for stretcher & attempt made to repair ladder cable lines ervmi of Cattle Kraal.	
	10th		Busy day repairing broken lines both on buried & overhead routes. Healths Shelling of area around Brigade Head Quarters very heavy all day.	

Army Form C. 2118.

WAR DIARY
or
INTELLIGENCE SUMMARY.
(Erase heading not required.)

Instructions regarding War Diaries and Intelligence Summaries are contained in F. S. Regs. Part II. and the Staff Manual respectively. Title pages will be prepared in manuscript.

Place	Date	Hour	Summary of Events and Information	Remarks and references to Appendices
	11th		Hand over to 232 Division - move to Bertham - opening at 12 noon Bapot Redout with R.A. and No 3 Detachments Remain at Chateau Segard with C.R.A.	
	12th		Fix up camp - Baths for all men out of the line - Sol Stores etc	
	13th		General work in camp.	
	14th		Rifle & gas helmet inspection. Church Parade. Recreation.	
	15th 16th 17th 18th		Cable Wagon drill to search detachment of new drafts. Power Buzzer Squad drawing horse lines & following road drains. All cable run through and repaired.	
	19th 20th		Stripping horses, cleaning harness etc	
	21st		Recreation. Power Buzzer Squad taking instruments representing with General Antennas. Wireless Set.	
	22nd		General Work in Camp - sorting Stores ready to move into line.	
	23rd		Nos 1 & 3 Detachments move to Scottish Wood to prepare Div A.S.	
	24th		Personnel for two Power Buzzer Stations, two Visual Stations & Divisional Ordnance Exchange move into the line & take over. Complete Signal Office relief move to Scottish Wood.	
			Div: Hd Qrs moves to Scottish Wood - Horse lines at Westoutre.	
	25th		Send out linesmen to join area parties - also man & test horses on buried cable route to left Brigade Sections. Lay lines to Reserve Brigade Hd Qrs, Pigeon loft, Prisoners of War Cage - Transport lines & Brigades in line.	

A5834 Wt. W4973/M687. 750,000 8/16 D. D. & L. Ltd. Forms/C.2118/13.

WAR DIARY
or
INTELLIGENCE SUMMARY.
(Erase heading not required.)

Army Form C. 2118.

Instructions regarding War Diaries and Intelligence Summaries are contained in F. S. Regs., Part II. and the Staff Manual respectively. Title pages will be prepared in manuscript.

Place	Date	Hour	Summary of Events and Information	Remarks and references to Appendices
	26th		Attack on GHELUVELT commence 5.40 am - All communication good until 6.45 when arrival of the Wireless Station hit by shell destroyed - Buried cable kept in touch until 10.30 am, repaired by Lt King - HQ Bde under heavy shell fire telephone Communication re-established at 12.30 pm. Visual Power Buzzer stations though not the whole time notwithstanding very heavy shell fire chiefly due to splendid work of Serjt Hughes, L/Cpl Oram, L/Cpl Newlands & Pte Milne. Buried pair buried south broken by direct shell at 12.50 pm. leaving only one line by another route to both brigades. Corps maintenance party located fault at 3 pm & commence repairing - Lt Bayre party endeavour to bridge fault with over-ground cables but unable to repair them as fast as they are broken. During day hundred pair route repaired and complete communication to Brigades established by 6.30 pm. JH - HO route broken - by ammunition cable from Dunn barn Road to HO box. 2nd CORYN forms company line to CAONY'S. Relief Reed up Reserve Brigade. Pigeon Left Newport lines and P.O.W Cage lines Relief of forward lines. Power Buzzer stations by 39th Divn personnel commence Relief completed - Divn HQ moves to Blauwepoort opening at 2 pm. Unpacking stores, fixing billets, building latrines, parrieus, shops etc	Diagram of communication attached. Sheet of Office traffic attached.
	27th			
	28th			
	29th 30th 31st			

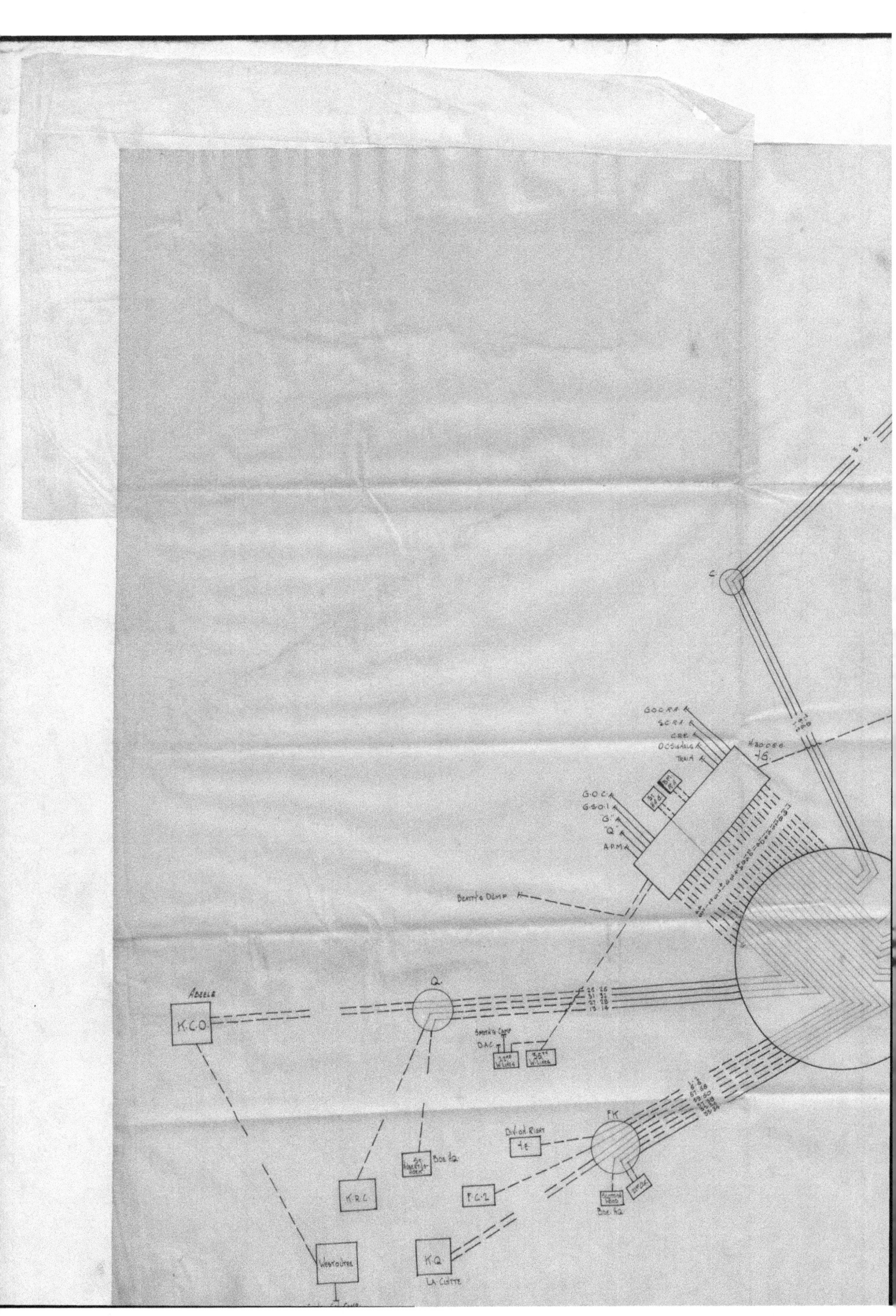

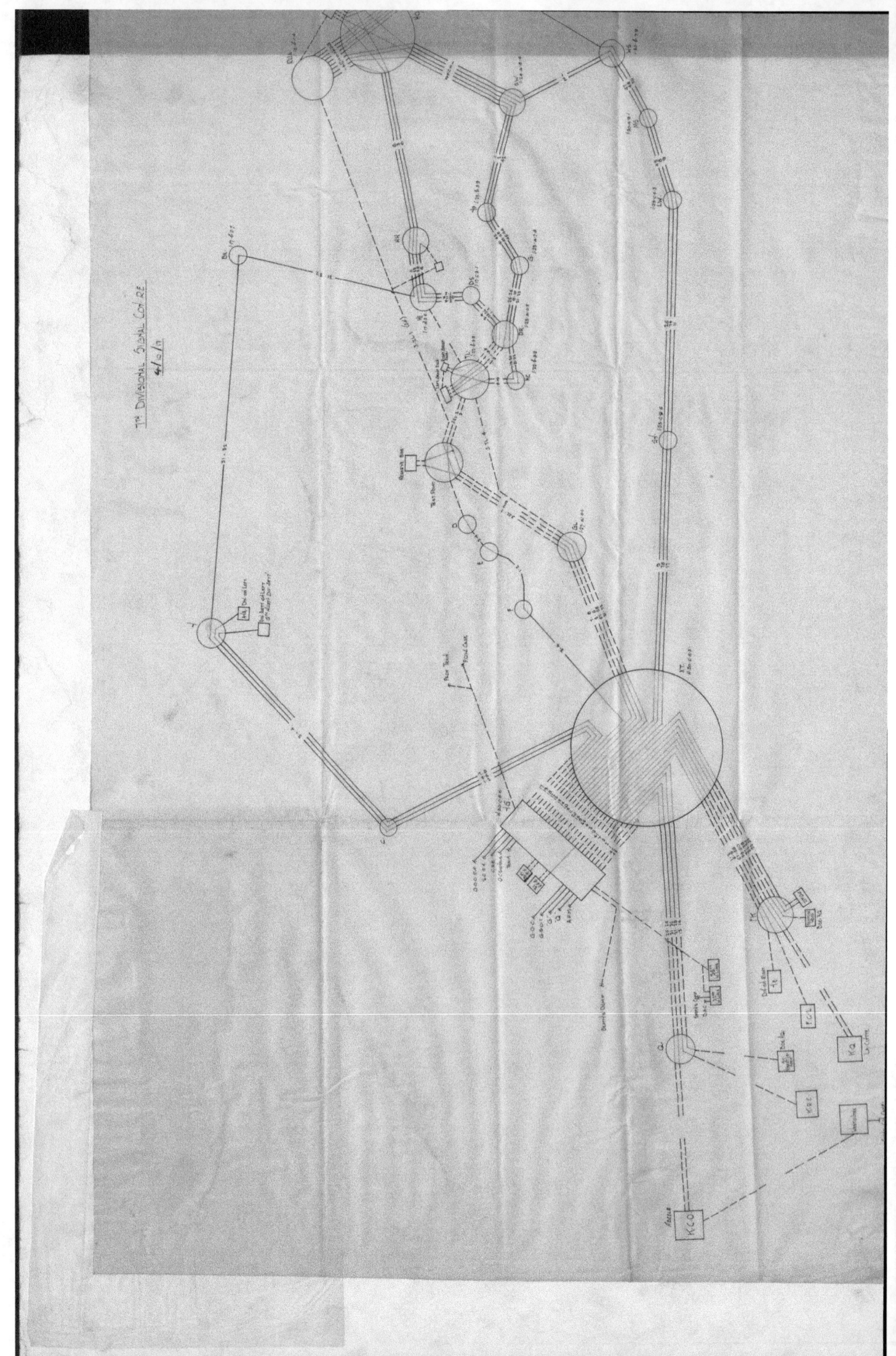

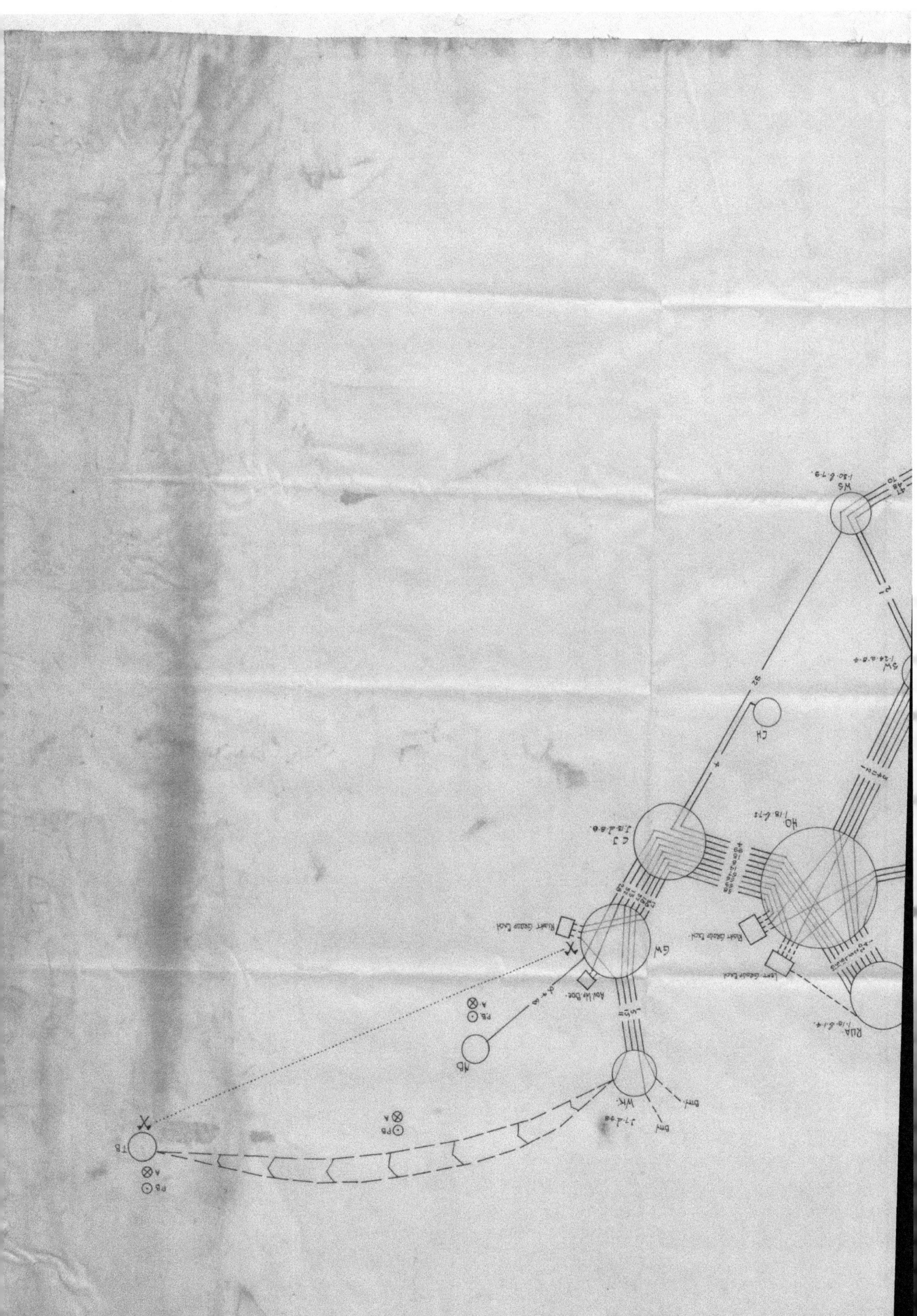

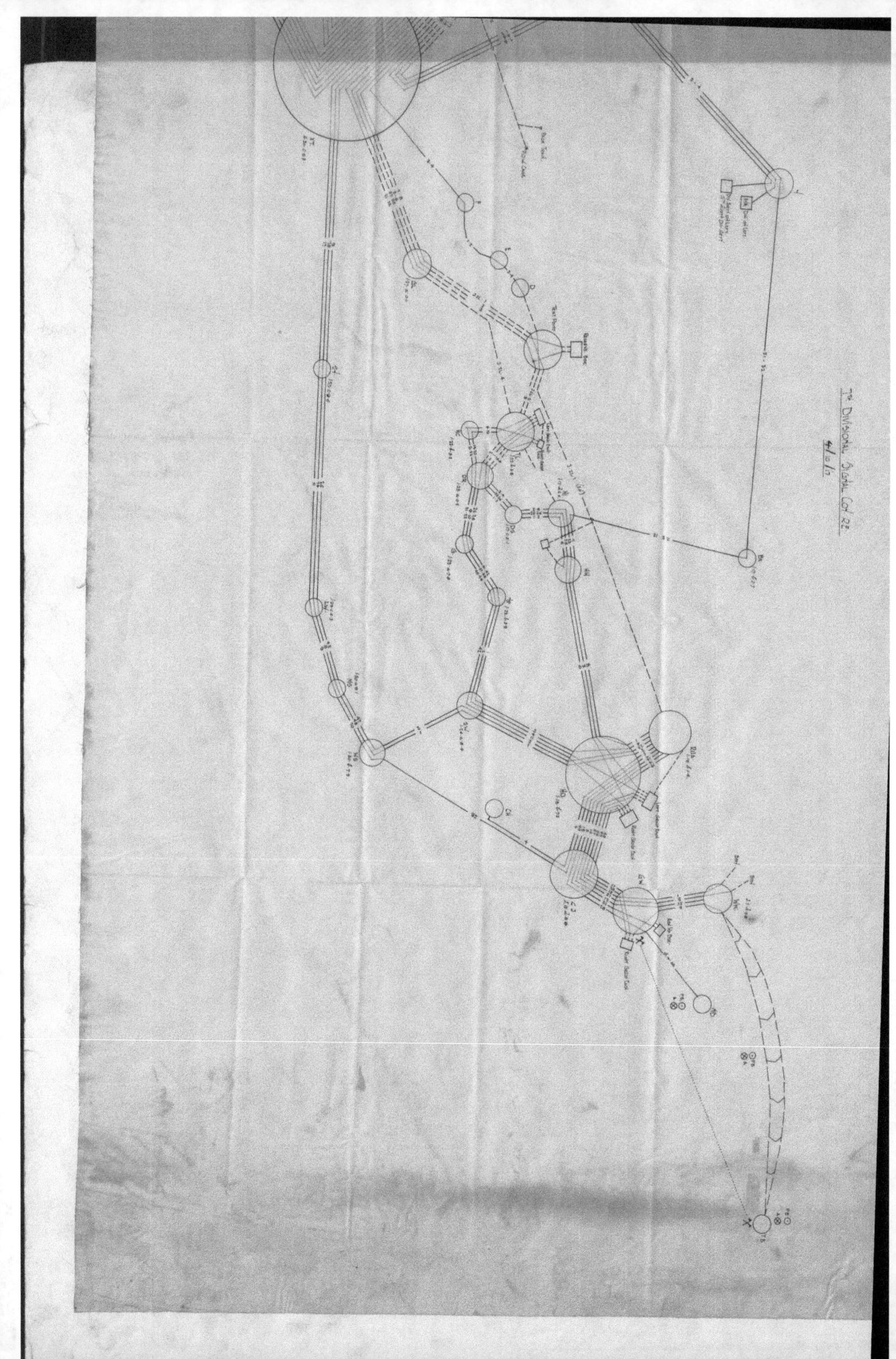

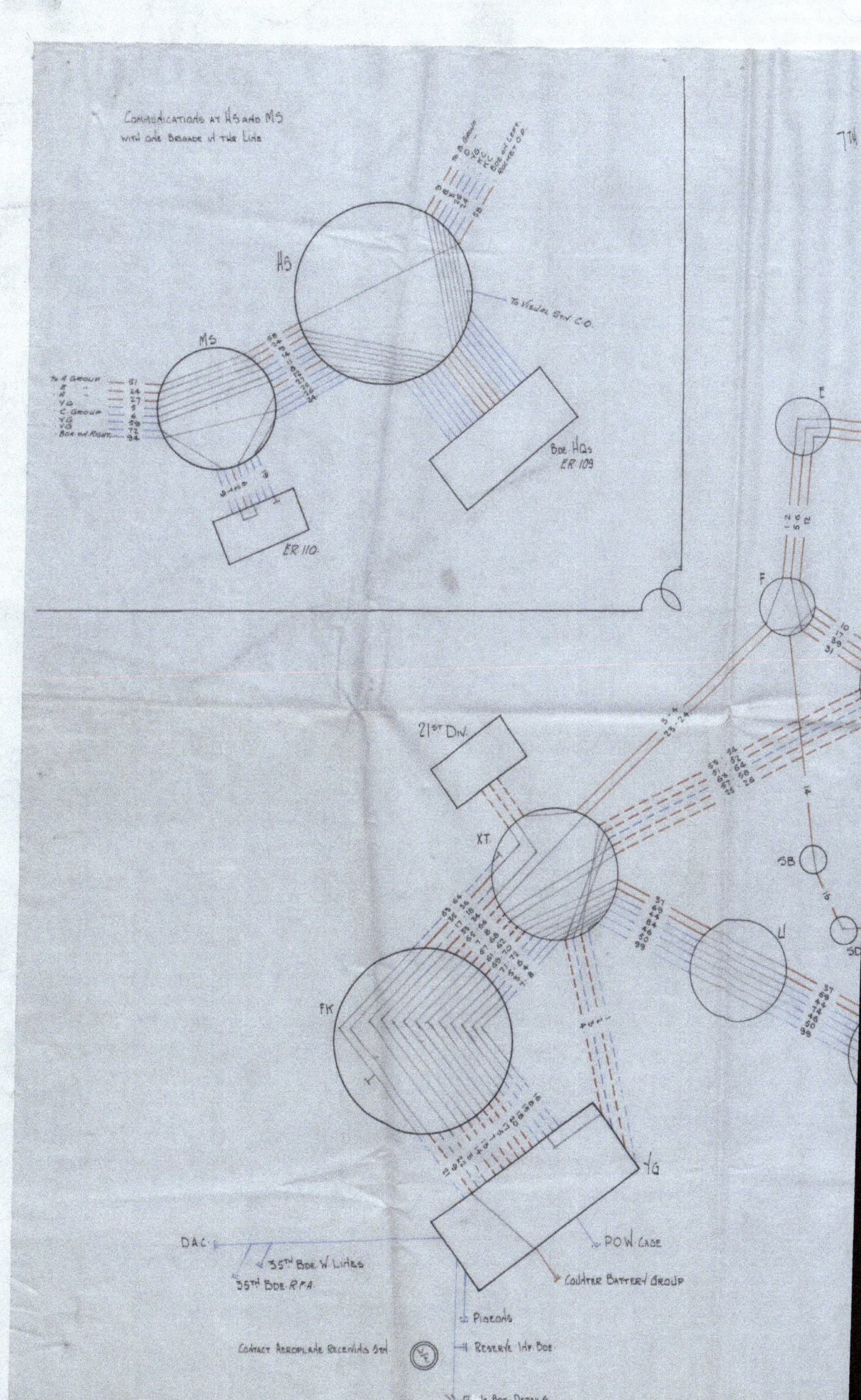

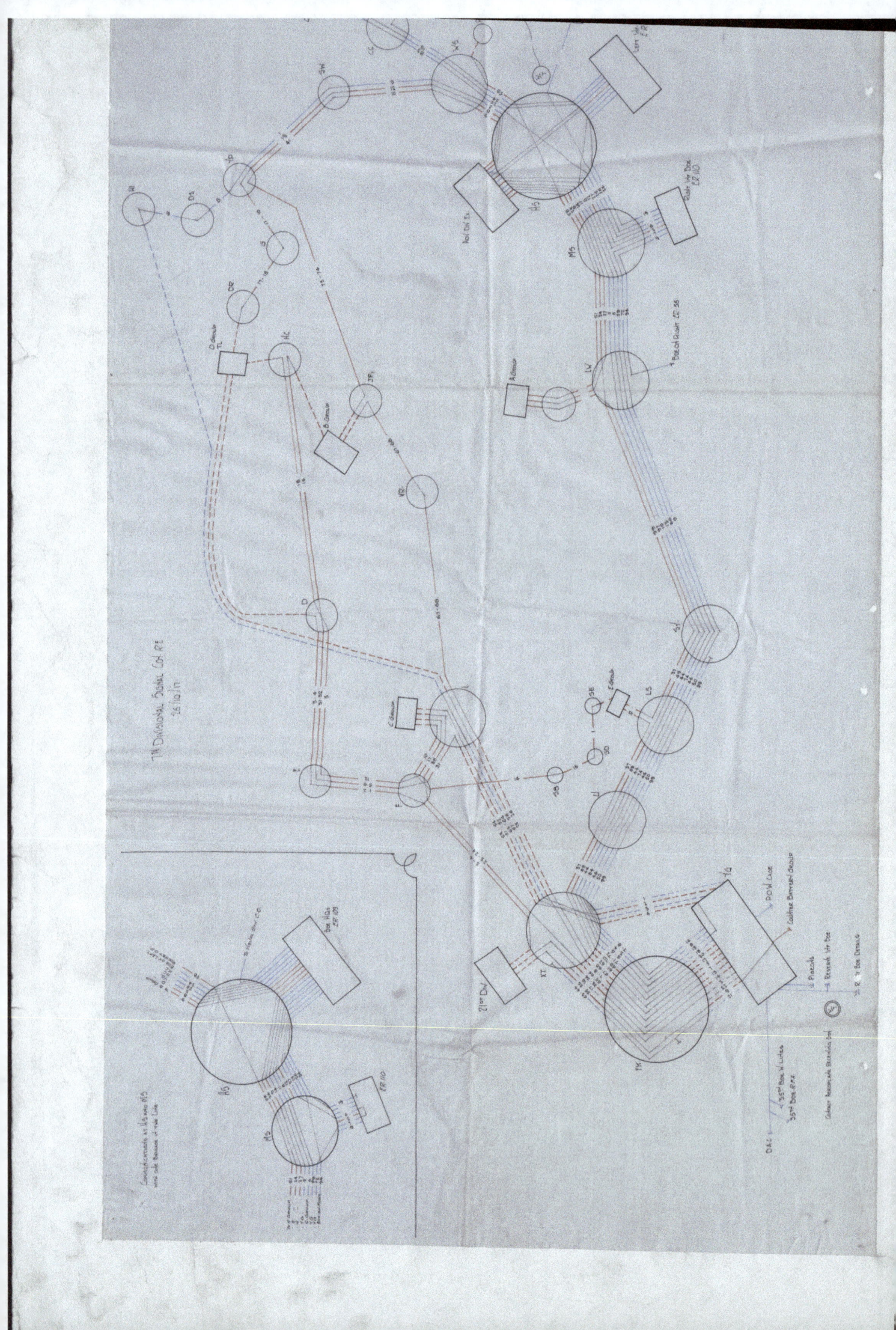

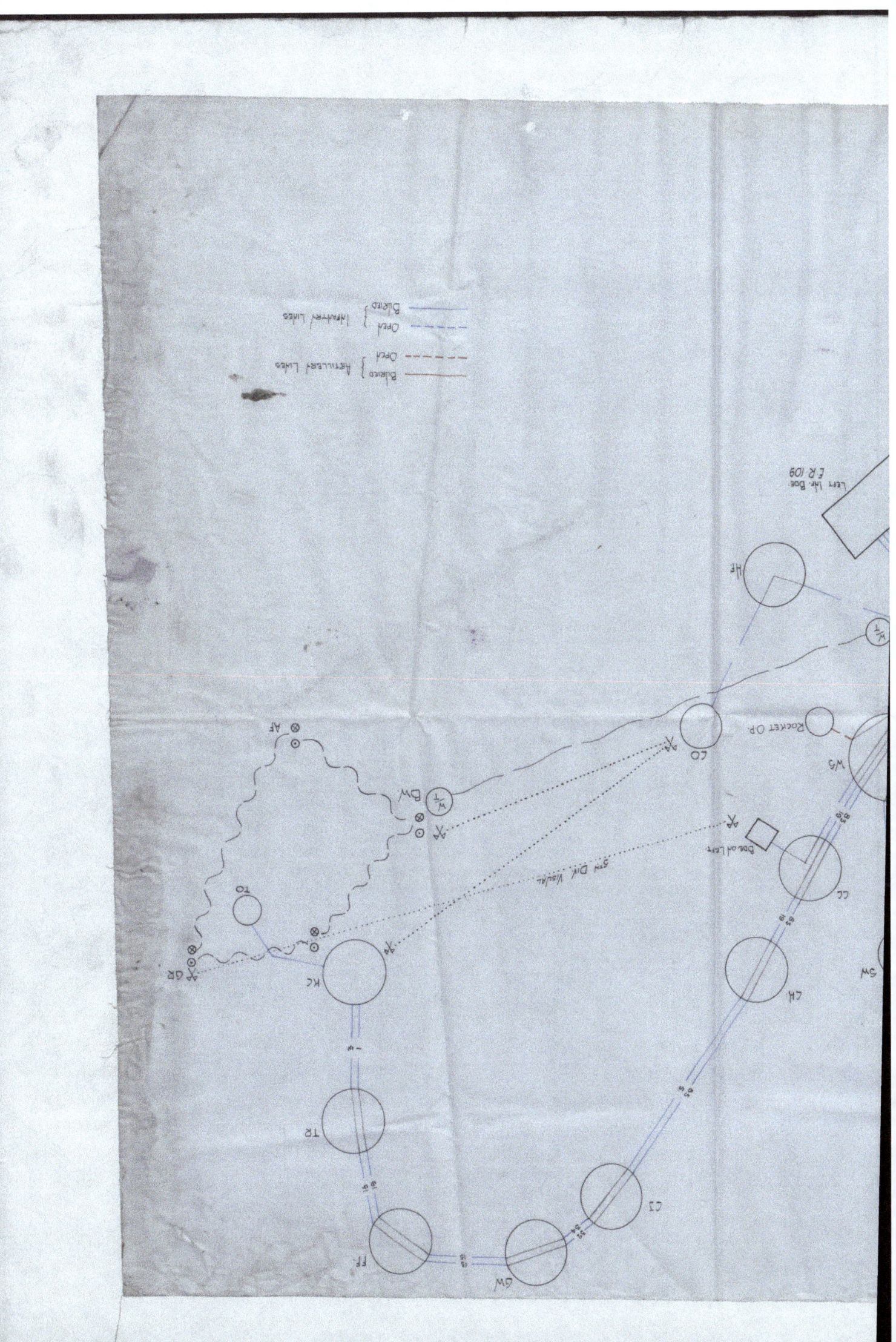

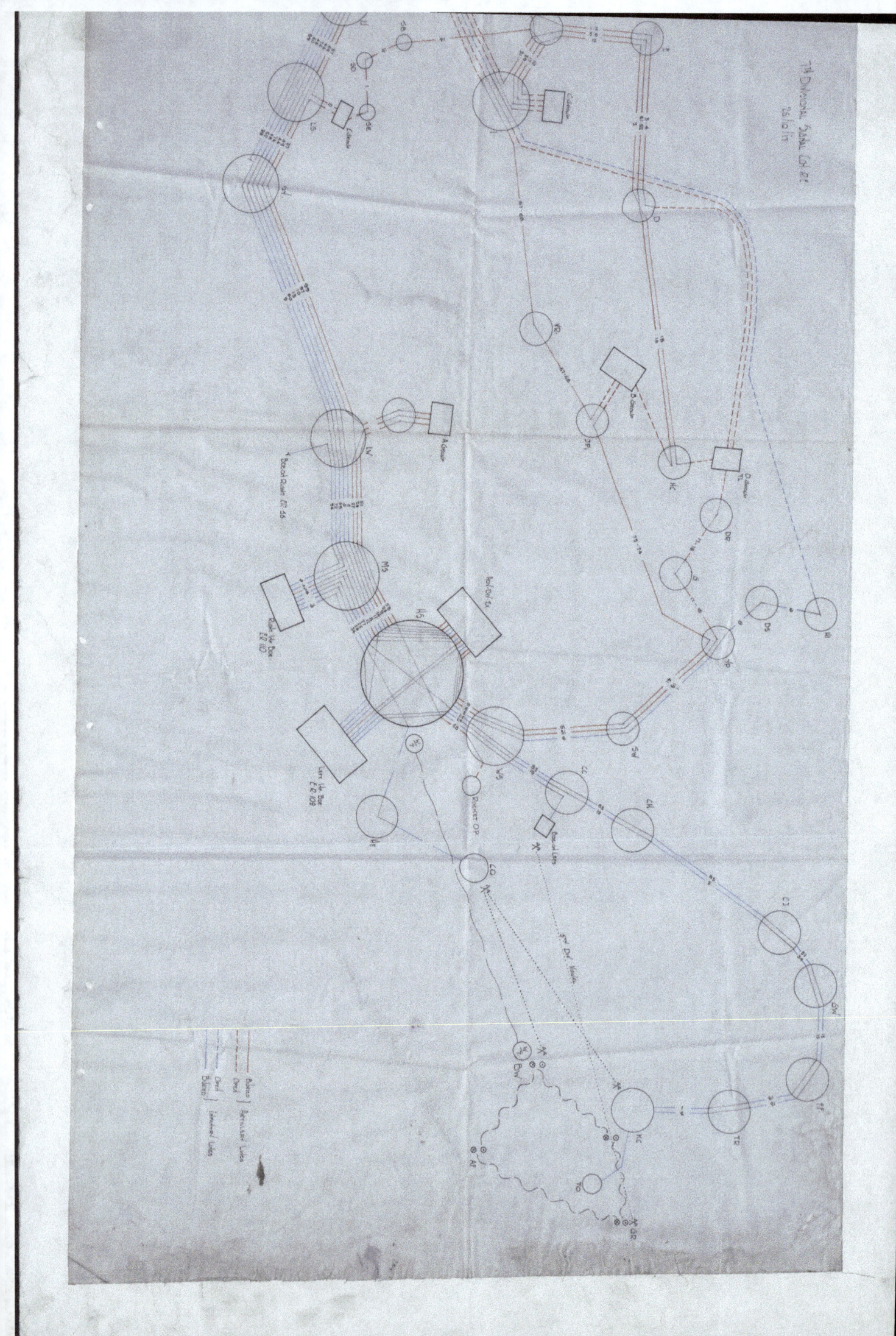

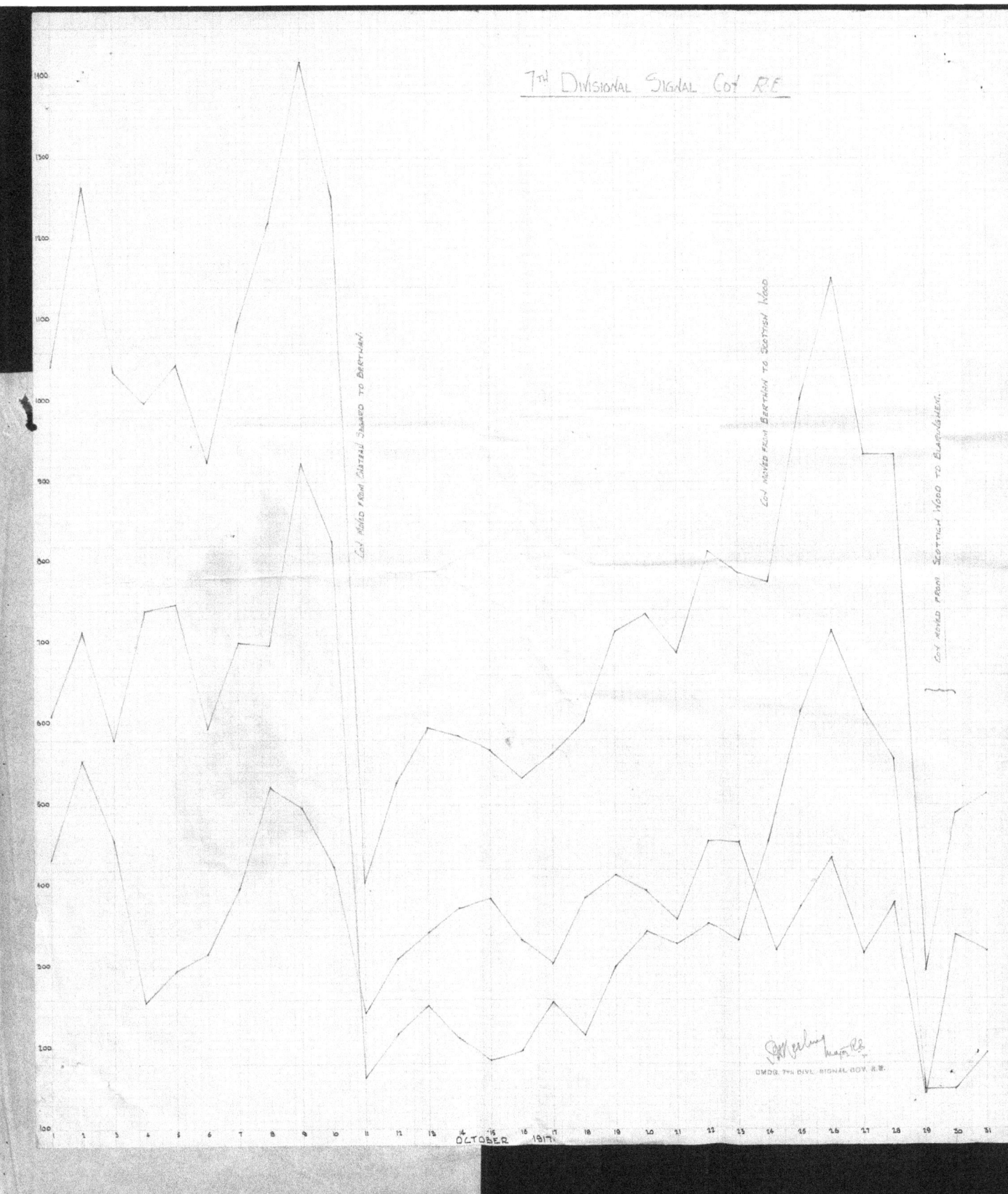

7th Division

7th Divisional Signal Company

November. 1917.

7th Div HQ

7th DIVISIONAL SIGNAL COMPANY, R.E.
No. CB 1127
Date 9/12/17

Reference your wire A 234. of yesterday.

The early portion of November was spent in Rest Areas and the circuits used were Army ones and not Divisional circuits.

Afterwards the whole of the work was done by D.R.

No circuit diagram is therefore necessary to accompany War Diary for November

O.H. Weeling
Major RE
O.C. 7th DIVL. SIGNAL COY. R.E.

Army Form C. 2118.

WAR DIARY
or
INTELLIGENCE SUMMARY.
(Erase heading not required.)

7TH DIVISIONAL
SIGNAL COMPANY.
R.E.

VA 2 5

Place	Date	Hour	Summary of Events and Information	Remarks and references to Appendices
	1917 Nov 1st		Washing Wagons, cleaning harness, checking stores.	
	2nd / 3rd		Wireless Squad leave for 110th Corps School. 2nd Lt A.H. CORYN takes over No 2 Section	
	4th		Cleaning harness, clipping horses off.	
	5th		Rifle and Gas helmet inspection — Church Parade	
	6th		Slow bolt drill for new draft.	
	7th		Signing practice for linesmen	
	8th			
	9th		Lectures on Serial Training	
	10th		Recreation during afternoon	
	11th		Pack up preparatory to moving to FAUQUEMBERGUES.	
	12th		Move to FAUQUEMBERGUES.	
	13th		Receive orders to proceed to stop Unit advanced column to MARESQUEL.	
	14th		Move to MARESQUEL	

WAR DIARY
or
INTELLIGENCE SUMMARY.
(Erase heading not required.)

Army Form C. 2118.

Instructions regarding War Diaries and Intelligence Summaries are contained in F. S. Regs., Part II. and the Staff Manual respectively. Title pages will be prepared in manuscript.

7TH DIVISIONAL
SIGNAL COMPANY
R.E.

Place	Date	Hour	Summary of Events and Information	Remarks and references to Appendices
	15th		Overhauling stores & ready for move	
	16th			
	17th			
	18th		Pack up ready for entraining. Entrain Histon evening at 11 p.m.	
	19th		In train proceeding to Italy	
	20th			
	21st			
	22nd		Detrain at LEGNAGO about midnight & bivouac for the night	
	23rd		Move to COLOGNA	
	24th		Send a column back to bring up all surplus stores	
	25th		Send detached column with stores to ALBETTONE	
	26th		Move to ALBETTONE	
	27th			
	28th		Cleaning harness, wagons etc	
	29th			
	30th		Move to BEVADORO	

J.H. Keeling
Major R.E.
O/C. 7th Div. Sig. Coy. R.E.